Hugh Dolan is the author of *36 D*
Australian Air Force intelligence offi
masters degree in history at Oxford University, he enlisted in
the British Army as a private. He served in Bosnia as a junior
NCO and witnessed the importance of military intelligence
in operation planning. He then commissioned and served
as a Squadron Leader (Intelligence) in headquarters roles
in Australia and overseas. He now lives in Melbourne and is
busy raising three small boys.

Also by Hugh Dolan

36 Days: The Untold Story Behind the Gallipoli Landings

GALLIPOLI AIR WAR

The unknown story of the fight for the skies over Gallipoli

HUGH DOLAN

MACMILLAN
Pan Macmillan Australia

First published 2013 in Macmillan by Pan Macmillan Australia Pty Limited
1 Market Street, Sydney

National Library of Australia
Cataloguing-in-Publication data:

Dolan, Hugh.

Gallipoli air war: the unknown story of the
fight for the skies over Gallipoli/Hugh Dolan.

9781742611099 (paperback)

World War, 1914–1918—Campaigns—Turkey—Gallipoli
Peninsula—Aerial operations.
World War, 1914–1918—Aerial operations.

940.44

Front cover image: Commander Charles Samson at the Dardanelles.
Maps by Laurie Whiddon, Map Illustrations
Index by Sue Jarvis
Typeset in 12.5/16 pt Janson Text by Post Pre-press
Printed by McPherson's Printing Group

*To the members of 36 Squadron and 37 Squadron,
Royal Australian Air Force, and all aircrew and ground staff
who have accepted the challenge of the war in the air.*

CONTENTS

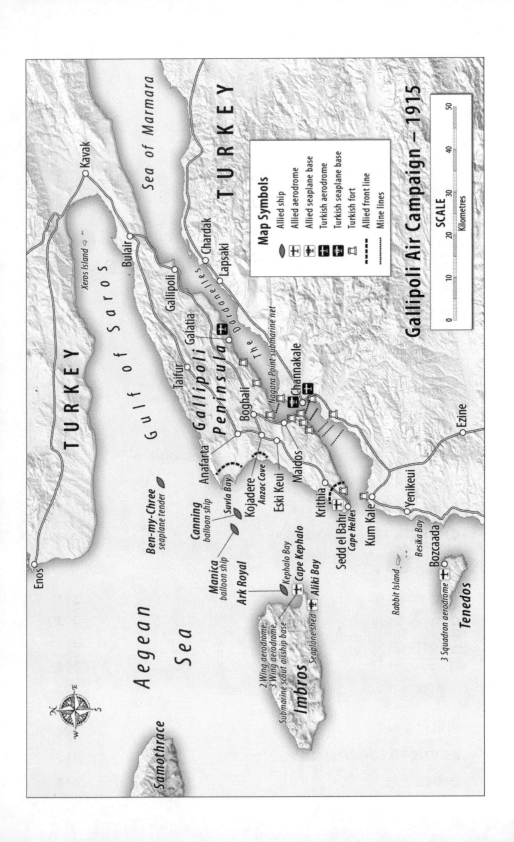

Gallipoli Air Campaign – 1915

Map Symbols

Allied ship
Allied aerodrome
Allied seaplane base
Turkish aerodrome
Turkish seaplane base
Turkish fort
Allied front line
Mine lines

SCALE

0   10   20   30   40   50
Kilometres

Sea of Marmara

Kavak

Bulair

Xeros Island

Gulf of Saros

TURKEY

Gallipoli

Galatia

Taifur

Gallipoli Peninsula

Boghali

Anafarta

Kojadere

Eski Keui

Maidos

Suvla Bay

Anzac Cove

Krithia

Chardak

Lapsaki

TURKEY

The Dardanelles

Ngaura Point submarine net

Channakale

Sedd el Bahr
Cape Helles

Kum Kale

Ezine

Yenikeui

Aegean Sea

Samothrace

Enos

Ben-my-Chree
seaplane tender

Canning
balloon ship

Manica
balloon ship

Ark Royal

Kephalo Bay

Cape Kephalo

Aliki Bay

2 Wing aerodrome;
3 Wing aerodrome;
Submarine scout airship base

Seaplane shed

Imbros

Besika Bay

Rabbit Island

Bozcaada

3 Squadron aerodrome

Tenedos

Black Sea

Constantinople
(Istanbul)

Bosporus

Muradh
(Corlu)

Tekirdag
(Rodosto)

Sea of Marmara

Gemlik

Panderma

Artaki

TURKEY

Bigha

Uzun Keupri

TURKEY

Kavak

Bulair

Gulf of Saros

Gallipoli

Dardanelles

Channakale

Eren Keui

Ezine

Yenikeui

Edremit

Gulf of Adramyti

Dikili

Aivali

Gulf of Smyrna

Smyrna

Keshan

Maidos

Anzac Cove

Sedd el Bahr

Besika Bay

Rabbit Island

Imbros

Tenedos

Mytelene

Mytelene

Yero Bay

Dede
Agach

Ferejik

Maritza River

Enos

Gulf of Enos

BULGARIA

GREECE

Thasos

Samothrace

Lemnos

Mudros

Hagios Strati

Patrol area of the
submarine scout airships

Skyros

Aegean

Sea

Psara

Chios

Gallipoli Air Targets – 1915

Map Symbols

Areas bombed by Allies

Areas bombed by Turks

Areas targeted but not bombed

SCALE

0   50   100   150

Kilometres

INTRODUCTION

When in future years the story of Helles and ANZAC and Suvla is weighed, it will, I think, appear that had the necessary air service been built up from the beginning and sustained, the Army and the Navy could have forced the Straits and taken Istanbul.

So wrote the Chief of Air Staff of the Royal Air Force in 1922. Air Vice Marshal Frederick Sykes was commander of all aircraft at Gallipoli from August until the withdrawal in December/January. It will undoubtedly come as a surprise to most that as many as 100 aircraft of all shapes and sizes flew over the ANZAC battlefields throughout the Gallipoli campaign. The world's first aircraft carrier operated off the coast from February 1915, supporting a menagerie of seaplanes, aeroplanes, balloons and blimps. Sykes was supported in his prescient opinion on the potential of air power by the official British air historian, H.A. Jones, who controversially concluded his examination of the Gallipoli air war by writing:

Had these two weapons [Allied submarines and aircraft] been on the spot, in sufficient numbers to attack decisively the precarious Turkish communications to the peninsula, the enemy could not have stood his ground. Inadequate as they were, they nearly did prove decisive.

1

The story of the Gallipoli air war has lain neglected for almost 100 years. Yet over 2000 missions were flown by the early aviators of both sides, engaging in bombing, reconnaissance, naval gunfire correction and torpedoing of enemy vessels. It was a dangerous occupation pursued by adventurous young men in flimsy craft often several thousand feet above enemy territory without the reassurance of a parachute. The diligence and passion of this small group of aviators also ensured the future of air intelligence, the information they both collected and conveyed challenging the excuse of 'failures in intelligence' proffered by British generals for their own disastrous failures of command. By contrast, ANZAC officers who saw these extraordinary craft grasped the opportunities they offered to learn what the enemy was doing on 'the other side of the hill'. Air intelligence was folded into the landing on 25 April and, more effectively, in the brilliant ANZAC withdrawal in December 1915. Among the intrepid aviators were dashing young Australians who flew over Anzac Cove as their compatriots landed in an amphibious assault that was to forever mark their nation's history. Indeed, the last Australian to die at Gallipoli was an Australian aviator. This is the story of those aviators who played a crucial, albeit largely unrecognised, role in the Gallipoli campaign as the eyes of those on the ground who could see no further than the next ridgeline.

I have used my (limited) experience as an Intelligence Officer in the Royal Australian Air Force to cast this story. Given my experience, my focus is naturally on both the story of pioneering aviation and its clever use, and the intelligence gained from the shrewd employment of what was then cutting-edge technology. *Gallipoli Air War* is the story of the triumph of this technology, and equally a tale of frustration and disappointment, of luddites and naysayers who refused to embrace this new weapon of war and stuck steadfastly to the ways of old, with the inevitable tragic consequences.

Like the campaign itself, this story is fast and pacey—indeed, almost breathless at times. Unlike the campaign, this story is easy to read. It is a deliberate departure from the traditional take on the Gallipoli narrative, which I have somewhat modernised to broaden its appeal and breathe new life into what has become, for some, a stale and hackneyed tale. For the most part, I have dispensed with cumbersome military titles and used first names so as to create a sense of identification with the people whose story this is. I have tried to erase the barrier of almost 100 years of intervening history to bring these men to life. The pages are populated by Harry, Charles, Herb and the like. Aviators, pilots and aircrew are an informal bunch. They rate people by their ability to perform under stress; they are (and were) largely unimpressed by titles or ranks. In this they had much in common with the Australian digger, that great disparager of military rank.

This is the story of real people who lived and breathed just as surely as you and me. Their lives were vastly different, but their passions, perceptions and frustrations often strikingly familiar. The story of the aviators and the Gallipoli air war they waged so long ago is now ripe for the telling.

CHAPTER 1

In the beginning: February 1915

Harry Strain was a regular chap. He fished on weekends and worked in an office in London before the war. How he became mates with a bunch of baggy-arsed Australians living atop the cliffs of Anzac Cove is a story worth telling. It's an unusual story that will also tell the tale of the air battle fought over the Gallipoli Peninsula. Harry, who flew seaplanes from the world's first aircraft carrier, had a decisive role in the survival of many hundreds of young men sheltering in the trenches of Steele's and Courtney's posts from April to December 1915.

Harry kept a detailed diary. After each mission he would describe the events he had witnessed 1000 feet below the canvas wings of his seaplane. He also visited the trenches and described the struggles he saw from the air. Harry was later joined by more than 100 pilots and observers who crewed all sorts of aircraft types: seaplanes, aeroplanes, several balloons and even a large blimp. Their voices are added to this account as they arrive at Gallipoli.

Harry was a capable airman but a terrible poet. He wrote some lines in his diary before he joined the British Royal Naval Air Service (RNAS) as an aircrew observer:

> There's a time when the silvery salmon
> is lost to the rod and the dish,
> when a trout can't be bought e'en by Mammon:
> There's an annual close time for fish.
>
> But in August the rod, gun and rifle
> are taken from the cupboard and case,
> and many a promising life'll
> end through the chance of the chase.
>
> Now a new sort of game is in season,
> the close time for Germans is o'er;
> from August the fifth for good reason
> we may bathe, if we please, in their gore.
>
> So let's shoot at their rocketing airmen,
> let us fish for their submarines sly,
> in the Game Book let's enter as 'Vermin'
> the total of Teutons who die.

Then Harry went off to war.

The 'shooting fest' in Europe in August 1914 prompted the Ottoman Empire (modern-day Turkey) to begin military mobilisation. Young men were called up for training across the country just in case war should reach their shores. While the 'Game Books' in Europe filled with the dead, Turkey remained teetering on the verge of neutrality for the next three months. Then dastardly 'Teutonic' diplomacy encouraged the Turks to sign a secret alliance.

Harry and I have something in common. We are both nuts about flying and we both worked in military intelligence. Harry fought at Gallipoli in 1915; I was in the Iraq War in 2003. Harry, and several pilots like him, had a profound effect on the battles that raged below on that broken promontory called the Gallipoli Peninsula. They told the generals what the enemy was doing on the other side of the hill. Descriptions of the role of intelligence will be added to the chattering of machine-guns and shriek of bombs that punctuate this story simply because intelligence was the most important element of that whole sordid campaign—as it was supposed to be in Iraq in 2003.

In 1914 the entry of two German warships through the Dardanelles, *Goeben* and *Breslau*, and their 'sale' to the Turkish navy further upset the balancing act in Istanbul. In London, the Admiralty and the Naval Intelligence Department were immediately concerned by the ships' lurking presence, as they had the potential to sortie into the Mediterranean, guns blazing, and sink Allied shipping. In the following weeks the Naval Intelligence Department in London received daily reports from spies on the movements of these two powerful warships.

Harry put away his fishing rod and said his goodbyes in his favourite London pub. By 14 August he was a commissioned officer in the RNAS. Harry was already a qualified civilian pilot, gaining his licence in May 1913:

> Flying in the early days had all the elements of sport. There are few thrills like doing one's first solo flight . . . in the air alone and that it depends entirely on oneself whether you get back onto the ground whole or as a haggis.

To avoid delay (training depots, periods of waiting and the usual boredom), Harry joined as an observer rather than retraining as a naval pilot, hoping to join the fast track to Hun-killing. But while he happily completed a quick course in semaphore, Morse, wireless, bomb-dropping and ship recognition at Eastchurch aerodrome, a new menace was developing.

The Admiralty informed British diplomats on 21 September by SECRET cipher in Istanbul that war was a breath away:

> For safety of our ships off Dardanelles would it not be well to inform Turkish Government that all Turkish ships of war and aircraft approaching them will be treated as hostile?

The Naval Intelligence Department wanted to deploy men like Harry to report on Turkish activity from the unique perspective that only an aircraft can provide. The concept of using aircraft for reconnaissance had been considered before war was declared, and was realised soon after the uneasy silence was broken by naval gunfire. Harry Strain was about to be swept up into something more horrible than the gutting board.

Then, in October 1914, the Turks closed the Dardanelles to sea traffic. Mines were sown and the 'Turkish Governor Dardanelles informed officially Foreign Consuls, Dardanelles, that straits have been closed for shipping'. The British Consul at Channakale, a port astride the Narrows, was already aware. He was a spy, and he was sending coded cipher to the British warships lurking outside the mouth of the Dardanelles. He recorded the placement of each row of sea mines, giving the location and bearing of each of the 198 deadly 'pineapples'.

The uneasy silence ended on 28 October 1914 with the

smashing of Turkish naval shells into Russian shipping in the Black Sea. A FLASH signal from the British Ambassador in Istanbul told London the news: 'Turkish Fleet bombarded Russian unfortified town of Theodosia and sank a gunboat in Odessa harbour yesterday morning.' The Allied declaration of war was immediate. There was a flurry of diplomatic activity, a withdrawal of foreign missions and a formal declaration of war by the Entente powers on 31 October 1914. But the dapper, bowtie-wearing Winston Churchill was ready. He sent a FLASH signal to the British warships lurking off Gallipoli:

> Commence hostilities at once against Turkey. Acknowledge.

> W.S.C. 31-10

As confirmation of this state of belligerence, Vice Admiral Sackville Carden's Eastern Mediterranean Squadron bombarded the outer forts guarding the mouth of the Dardanelles. Carden sent a quick report, but suspected that not all was well. They could not actually *see* the destruction of Turkish forts at long range:

> INDEFATIGABLE fired 46 rounds 12 inch at Helles Fort. Forts replied. Some projectiles fell in the neighbourhood of the Squadron but only one alongside. No ships were hit. Material damage impossible to estimate but large explosion with dense volumes of black smoke at Helles Fort. Range 13,000 yards.

Britain's response to Turkish attacks on Russia's Black Sea shipping took the form of a bombardment on 3 November of the outer forts that barred passage through the Dardanelles. The Admiralty in London built false hope on the ability of naval gunfire to destroy the 35 Turkish forts that were known to protect the straits.

But Vice Admiral Sackville Carden was no fool. Digging deeper on 12 November, he sent further updates, thus bringing Harry to Gallipoli:

> With 12 inch guns there is not much that can be done . . . endeavouring to locate guns . . . which could be dealt with [by] reduced charges or smaller guns. Also it may be possible to attack No.1 Fort and the new guns on Cape Helles from a position to the north west. The service of a seaplane would be valuable.

A plan evolved in London to end the 'foolhardy' Turkish venture into modern warfare. The plan involved deployment of a naval squadron to subdue the forts along the Narrows with the assistance of an aircraft carrier. The squadron would then proceed up the straits towards Istanbul. While Harry Strain visited a tailor and ordered a blue naval jacket with two gold stripes (he had been appointed a lieutenant in the Naval Reserve), unnamed naval staff officers were typing his fate in triplicate.

The use of aircraft in the looming fight over the Gallipoli Peninsula had been under consideration for quite some time. Rear Admiral Arthur Limpus, the head of the British naval delegation to the Sublime Porte, had considered using aircraft as early as August 1914 during the search for *Goeben* and *Breslau*. In a letter sent to the Admiralty, Limpus noted that, while aircraft could have been used for observation, they could have done little else lest they provide the

'Teutons' an excuse to complain during the three months of Turkish neutrality.

But now war had come to Turkey. So British naval intelligence began to submit formal requests for aeroplanes to undertake surveillance flights over the Dardanelles to assist Sackville Carden's 'blind' naval squadron. There was also a need for high grade intelligence, as key members of the diplomatic staff including Arthur Limpus and the Vice Consul at Channakale, Mr Charles Palmer, had ceased reporting. The Director of Naval Intelligence pursued the deployment of aeroplanes, sending a request to the Secretary of Foreign Affairs seeking permission to build aerodromes on the Aegean islands just off the Gallipoli Peninsula.

This proposal was endorsed by the First Lord of the Admiralty, Winston Churchill. On the SECRET pink file, Churchill wrote a question in green crayon: 'Can Tenedos be used?' The Secretary of State for Foreign Affairs, Sir Edward Grey, replied that Tenedos was in Greek hands and offered to approach its government via diplomatic means. Greece had seized Tenedos (now Bozcaada) from Turkey in 1912. The island was ideally situated, lying some 30 kilometres off the coast of the Gallipoli Peninsula. Having secured permission for the use of Tenedos, Sir Edward Grey also gained approval from the Greeks for the use of the islands of Lemnos and Imbros for the blockade of the Dardanelles. Vice Admiral Sir Rosslyn Wemyss was appointed Governor of the port of Mudros on the island of Lemnos.

On the other side of the peninsula, *Hauptmann* Erich Serno was the face of the enemy. A 29-year-old Prussian, Serno had been appointed to head the fledgling Turkish Air Service in January 1915. He had joined the German Army as a cadet in 1906 before commissioning in the 171st Infantry Regiment. He had much in common with pioneering British aviators such as the RNAS' Charles Samson and Richard Davies—like them, he too had left the mainstream of the military. Serno had gained his pilot's licence on a grass airstrip outside Berlin on 9 October 1912 before pursuing a career as a *feldfleiger*. At the outbreak of war he served over France in Abteilung 2 before being recalled for 'other duties'. In October, following the alliance with Turkey, Serno joined General Otto Liman von Sanders' Military Mission in Istanbul, arriving for duty at the training school at Yesilkoy Air Station outside Istanbul to greet his staff of 32 mechanics and 12 pilots. In November 1914, Serno was promoted to the rank of major in the Turkish Army. His war on this new front was about to begin.

While Turkey was proud of the calibre of its own pilots, they desperately needed the technical expertise of the Germans to continue flight operations now that the war had severed all trade with France. Turkey had bought a French Deperdussin aeroplane and two Bleriots. The Bleriot was an early attempt at sustained flight, a monoplane with a tiny 50hp Anzani engine. Approximately the size of a modern suburban ride-on mower, the Anzani engine pulled a wire-caged monoplane through the air. The wings suggested the shape of a bird's with gently rounded edges. The Turkish Army had bought the Bleriot after an impressive aviation demonstration in December 1909. It had then been overused as a trainer. The army's next purchase was the two-seater military version, with both pilot and observer sitting up high in the boxed forward section. The tail was attached to the forward section by bracing wires.

Germany had committed to equipping the Turkish Army with 24 modern aeroplanes. However, some difficulty was encountered in despatching these, along with their maintenance personnel and aircrew, across neutral Bulgaria.

In short, the rules of Bulgarian neutrality prohibited this. Undeterred, the Germans packed the aeroplanes in rail freight wagons and sent them to Turkey under the 'protection' of the Red Cross. This was both ingenious and illegal. Most shipments passed successfully, labelled innocuously as medical equipment.

Meanwhile, the Turkish Air Service had achieved some small victories. In January 1915, following the shelling and blockade, Turkey's two older aeroplanes were shipped across the Sea of Marmara to the Dardanelles port of Channakale on the open deck of a freighter. Channakale Fortress Command was crying out for reconnaissance.

On 3 January the Admiralty signalled Sackville Carden and his blind Eastern Mediterranean Squadron asking whether it would be feasible to attempt to break through the Dardanelles, steam into the Marmara and threaten Istanbul. Carden, however, did not fancy his squadron's chances of surviving a pounding by 35 Turkish forts along the Narrows (or the underwater hazards of five layers of sea mines). He was well aware of the risks, drawing on the latest intelligence in his wood-panelled office aboard HMS *Indefatigable*.

The first aeroplane flight in theatre was launched on 20 January 1915. The Turkish Air Service flew a reconnaissance mission from Channakale to Tenedos to report on enemy warships. A Turkish pilot, Captain Cemal, flew this first mission in the ageing Bleriot. A further two cross-ocean flights were conducted, the third flight because of reports of a submarine in the Aegean. Cemal looked down from his Bleriot on the newly arrived Australian submarine *AE2* before the Anzani engine considered it had achieved what had been expected of it and Cemal was forced to dash for home.

During Carden's first phase of attack on 17 February, Cemal desperately attempted to get his machine into the air. He ran the machine at full throttle along the grass strip outside Channakale, but the Anzani engine would not catch properly. Had it fired as required, Cemal may have met Harry in the air, each armed only with politeness.

By February 1915 the derelict training school outside Istanbul was operational. Six aviation tents were erected with a functioning workshop to repair the two elderly school machines. Misfortunes occurred. German bombs, hidden in drained beer kegs (to fool Bulgarian customs) were discovered when railway workers sought a quiet drink after work. The beer kegs had been included as medical supplies as beer was considered a 'restorative'. The bombs were confiscated. Three airframes had been smuggled into Turkey in direct contravention of the Articles of War. A British intelligence coup caught wind of the second attempt to hide aeroplanes under Red Cross banners and the machines were confiscated. It was now a matter of urgency that the growing naval threat outside the Dardanelles be met, and German pilot Frank Siedler responded, flying his Rumpler B1 over Bulgaria, direct to Turkey.

Carden, the Admiralty and the Naval Intelligence Department had corroborative intelligence of high quality from the former British Vice Consul concerning the Turkish defences blocking the Narrows. When Vice Consul Charles Palmer fled his post at Channakale he was carefully debriefed by Carden and his naval staff. A report which clearly described the threat was sent in triplicate to London. It was highly detailed, providing descriptions of the 35 forts, concealed gun batteries and troop locations while also supplying compass bearings showing the placement of the deadly sea mines. These were anchored to the muddy bottom of the straits and hung in underwater curtains. Palmer wrote:

Line A has 29 mines

Line B has 22 mines

Line C has 26 mines

Line D and E have 50 mines

Line F has 27 mines
An additional 45 mines were laid in various places to close channels making a total of 199. Four exploded, leaving a total of, as far [as] is known, 195. These are all contact mines.

Carden's reply to the Admiralty signal concerning an attempt to break through the Dardanelles and threaten Istanbul was sanguine. He told London that the Narrows could not be rushed but *might* be forced by extended operations using minesweepers and large numbers of ships. Despite his cautious response, Carden was directed by Churchill to develop a plan: 'The Admiralty should prepare for a naval expedition in February to bombard and take the Gallipoli Peninsula with Constantinople [Istanbul] as its objective.'

Carden's solution to Churchill's insistence on a plan was a seven-phase attack involving the methodical destruction of the outer forts, followed by domination of the inner forts and minesweeping of the Narrows. The attack would be launched by the naval squadron, assisted by aircraft reconnaissance. Harry was now committed to the coming battle.

The plan represented a purely naval attempt to force the Narrows without the aid of the army. In a telegram to Churchill on 11 January, Carden reiterated his key point, that he considered 'frequent reconnaissances by seaplanes indispensible'. In a response received two days later, the War Council in Whitehall committed Carden's Eastern Mediterranean Squadron to the Dardanelles. Also despatched was the RNAS' secret weapon, the aircraft carrier HMS *Ark Royal* and her flight of four seaplanes and four (wheeled) aeroplanes. Harry was hooked:

> On the 26th January a coded wire came to Dundee that I had to report forthwith on the *Ark Royal* at Chatham. I only had a couple of hours to pack and get away . . . I found pandemonium onboard when I got there, as she was being fitted with 12 pounders and other arms, taking in stores and I spent a very disturbed night with Dockyard Maties hammering over our head. The *Ark Royal* looked very curious among all the Destroyers, Cruisers and Battleships at Chatham. Two large cranes forward on a long sloping deck, which goes down especially at the bow, like an elongated flat iron, and aft a large testing house with an enormous bridge above it and engines right aft, while her stern sits up rather like a Victorian woman with a bustle.

Commander Robert Clarke Hall, captain of *Ark Royal*, had been warned to be ready to put to sea on 17 January.

Meanwhile Carden received a warning that the forts he had bombarded on 3 November may have been supplemented by new concealed gun batteries and howitzers. Carden's own warnings were returned—a sign of rampant bureaucracy. It seems nothing changes in the heady, secretive world of military intelligence. Information and warnings are recycled and embellished. In Iraq we called this circular reporting—for obvious reasons. The Eastern Mediterranean Squadron was told, 'You must conduct thorough aerial reconnaissances before commencing operations.'

Lieutenant Harry Strain was posted aboard *Ark Royal* as senior observer and Intelligence Officer for the seaplane squadron. The air war was about to begin. Final sailing orders arrived on 1 February 1915 ordering *Ark Royal* to proceed to the Mediterranean. The next day Harry was on his way: 'We are now sneaking down the Channel with all lights obscured, as there are German submarines in the neighbourhood.'

Carden now gave his orders knowing that he would have eyes in the sky—air reconnaissance. His fleet was no longer blind. His orders for the attack included a single foolscap page headed 'Instructions for Aircraft' which contained directions for *Ark Royal* and outlined reconnaissance tasks and spotting duties for her seaplanes. The orders listed the wireless/telephone or radio procedures to be followed, including signal styles. The principal duty of *Ark Royal*'s aircraft was to report on enemy defences. Her aircraft were not to attack the forts unless specifically ordered to do so.

The 180 sailors and aviators aboard *Ark Royal* were in for a fright. The ship was recently commissioned and had not seen active service. Not one practice flight had taken place before her hasty departure. The recently decanted civilian-cum-naval aviators did not take immediately to shipboard life:

> Nearly all the air mechanics [are] sea sick, not to mention seven of the officers. Our fresh provisions are out—first the bread was finished, then potatoes and now meat!

The RNAS supported the Royal Navy. It comprised naval personnel flying seaplanes, aeroplanes and conducting balloon operations, was characterised by inventiveness and keenly embraced new technologies. RNAS aviator Charles Samson had flown an aeroplane from the deck of a ship as early as 1912, giving rise to the design of *Ark Royal* as an aircraft carrier prior to the outbreak of war. A ship frame under construction had been purchased and totally redesigned with a flush front deck to allow aeroplanes to take off. *Ark Royal* was a marriage of vision and emerging technology.

Ark Royal was commissioned into the Royal Navy on 9 December 1914. Her captain, Robert Clarke Hall, was a gunnery specialist. She was built around the keel of a 7400-ton trader under production in the shipbuilding port town of Blyth, Northumberland, from the summer of 1913. Her speed was limited to eight knots as the frame held only a single screw propeller. The new design saw her three boilers placed aft, allowing a capacious forward hold for the storage and maintenance of aircraft. The ship's company totalled 180 including 80 RNAS personnel, comprising both officers and ratings. The ship's log contains a mysterious note stating that she also carried 'ten 4 inch diameter Torpedoes Mark X for Special Purposes' in a specially designed torpedo room supplied by the submarine depot at Chatham. *Ark Royal* and her seaplane flight were tasked with the sinking of *Goeben* and *Breslau* once the British squadron smashed all the forts, dodged the mines and steamed into the Sea of Marmara.

Ark Royal was a happy ship. And this was very important. The flight log is most unusual. It begins with a crew list, describing in some detail the crew members' pet names and previous professions. Commander Robert Clarke Hall was

'Clarkee' (although never referred to by this name in his presence), the Senior Flying Officer, 'Joe' Kilner, DSO, 'a most loveable messmate', Geoffrey 'Bromo' Bromet, the second most senior pilot, and 'Buster' Brown, a former yacht captain. Also seen in the happy wardroom was Viscount Torrington, who raced horses, sharing a pitcher of pink gin with a former apprentice watchmaker named 'Pussy' Garnett.

Harry Strain began to familiarise himself with his new domain. *Ark Royal* resembled a modern aircraft carrier with a flat flight deck, a cavernous, purpose-designed hangar and an engine workshop. All aeroplanes were stowed below and, in the case of the larger seaplanes, their wings were folded back. The seaplanes resembled giant moths pullulating inside a cave.

Prior to flight, the seaplanes were lifted out by steam cranes, placed on the forecastle, and their wings opened and locked into place—a procedure that had not yet been practised. The engine was then tested before the seaplane was lowered onto the surface of the sea. The four wheeled aeroplanes had a small enough wingspan to be stowed complete and could potentially be flown off the deck of the ship but could not land, owing to the aft-placed superstructure. Clearly this was a critical design fault. If no aerodrome was in range, the pilot was forced to ditch in the sea.

A note in Churchill's handwriting is testament to the ongoing debate concerning the relative usefulness of both seaplanes and aeroplanes: 'You will remember Carden saying that aeroplanes were not so useful as seaplanes.' Beneath this is a comment, signed by the Director of the Air Department, who adds, optimistically, 'not till you land'. The wheeled aeroplanes were intended for use in support of a military garrison once the Dardanelles had been penetrated.

Ark Royal was ordered to the Dardanelles with little careful thought concerning her various seaplane types. As a general rule, seaplanes had a reduced flying capability compared with wheeled aeroplanes owing to the weight (300 kilograms) and drag of the twin floats. They flew at 60mph and carried fuel for about three hours of flight. All seaplane types aboard *Ark Royal* had seating for an observer. Two of the seaplanes, however, could only fly when the sea state was moderately calm—an uncommon condition during the winter months in the eastern Mediterranean. On the eve of his departure, Clarkee recognised that the seaplanes held in *Ark Royal* were inadequate for the task ahead. Harry was sent off on a shopping trip:

> Clarke Hall immediately sent me back to London to interview the Director of the Air Department to get something more out of him—here we were going on a long cruise which may make history—and they were spoiling the ship for a half penny worth of tar. In other words we hadn't our proper complement of seaplanes or pilots.

Harry's trip proved successful, as two newer seaplanes alighted alongside *Ark Royal* two hours prior to her departure. The two latecomers proved the only reliable machines in the first months of the campaign.

Ark Royal's seaplanes could be fitted with one of two available 250-watt experimental Renzel wireless sets working on 830-feet wavelength with a range of 30 miles. The equipment used a Morse key and was capable only of transmitting—it could not receive. The practicalities of early wireless telegraphy (radio) were rudimentary: a hole was cut in the bottom of the cockpit and the observer belayed over

100 feet of cable from a drum. This cable trailed behind the seaplane like a wagging tail and could only be belayed and recovered in flight. A Renzel set was bolted into each seaplane before flight and had a reputation for shorting and causing sparks, bringing with it the constant risk of an airborne fire. At that time the chapter on radio usage in the instruction handbook remained blank, except for a small typed note requesting 'officers to submit reports to the Air Department for later inclusion in the next publication'. Radio technology was still too new to allow any useful instructions to be written at this stage of the war.

Both seaplanes and aeroplanes could be equipped for offensive work. They carried a payload of bombs, darts and machine-guns. Two types of bombs were available: 100lb bombs containing 40lb of TNT and 20lb bombs containing 7lb of TNT. The seaplanes could carry two 20lb bombs and had specially designed bomb racks fitted under the lower wing. Steel spikes or darts were carried by the observer whose task it was to scatter these over enemy troops. They weighed 50lb per 1000 and could be carried as an alternative to a similar weight of bombs. The larger seaplanes with their 200hp engines could also be fitted with Lewis guns firing .303 ammunition.

The four Sopwith Tabloid aeroplanes had a maximum speed of 90mph with a fuel capacity for three and a half hours' flight carrying only a pilot. They could carry four 20lb bombs or 1000 steel spikes. In order to maintain sustained operations, a suitable aerodrome on land with level ground and an approach of 400 yards in every direction was required.

Ark Royal had her own organic armament as, just before leaving England, the ship was armed with 12-pounder guns and two Maxim machine-guns. The 12-pounder guns were placed on each side of the upper deck with a three-pounder anti-aircraft gun placed behind the wheelhouse. A .303 Maxim was also installed on each side of the lower deck for use as anti-aircraft guns. They would be brought into action for the first time when *Ark Royal* was off the Gallipoli coast.

As the ship had been despatched in haste, Clarkee had to organise his crew into separate flights while the ship was underway. Training of observers also began as these men had no prior experience and it was, for many, their first taste of flight:

> Every officer in the ship had to be an expert signalman both with flags, flashlamp, and semaphore—he must also be able to work the wireless . . . besides all that, the officers had to be trained as observers.

The first flight evolutions were conducted in the harbour at Malta, the halfway point to Gallipoli, and commenced with a bang:

> . . . Pussy tried to go up in his Sopwith: he started, thought he was going to foul a buoy when going along the surface at 60 mph, caught one float on a wave top, and went over with a horrid smash . . . it was a pretty narrow squeak.

The seaplane was badly damaged although the engine was salvaged. Five seaplanes were left in the hold.

Ark Royal arrived off the Gallipoli Peninsula on 17 February 1915. Carden, anxious to see this new invention, came aboard for a brief on her capabilities. He was given a written summary by Clarkee, which survives in the archives.

It provides an extensive description of seaplane types and includes a hand-drawn table showing the effective range of each seaplane. However, Clarkee did not include vulnerabilities such as the inherent fragility of seaplanes or the effect of sea states and wind strengths on seaplane operations. This would sting him later.

Clarkee was on his own. He was a gunnery officer without any helpful doctrine or directions to assist him with air operations. The *Naval Air Service Training Manual*, printed in November 1914, told the reader that 'the whole subject of the use of seaplanes was at an experimental stage, and that it was impossible in many cases to lay down hard and fast rules of procedure'. Every effort was asked of the practitioners of early flying to improve existing methods until some measure of finality could be reached. Individual chapters in the manual on the use of radio, night flying and workshops were left blank. These would be added as further experience was gained. This was the very cusp of technology and Clarkee, Buster, Bromo and Harry were riding along its sharp edge.

Clarkee separated his expectations of aircraft operations by basing his missions on seven recognisable roles: reconnaissance, spotting, photography, attack, patrol, transit and experiment. Spotting meant correcting the fall of naval shells onto enemy positions—up or down, left or right of target—by using the experimental radio. Harry recorded the pressing need to check the intelligence reports sitting on the Vice Admiral's desk. Carden was no fool, he knew that intelligence can be 'sexed-up' to meet some political need:

> On the following day we did reconnaissance flights
> along the coast and over the forts to determine whether

the Naval Intelligence Department information about the entrance defences was correct or whether any further batteries had been erected.

Three missions were attempted to verify the state of the guns but only one mission was successfully prosecuted before the attacks began as the sea was too rough for flight. But one flight was enough. Harry recorded in his own clear hand, 'Our flights only confirmed the accuracy of naval intelligence.'

With the escalation in hate on 24 February marked by the enemy sending 11-inch shells crashing into Channakale, Cemal bit back. He had attempted to get the Bleriot airborne again but it had steadfastly refused to fire. After stripping the engine and rebuilding the valves, Cemal successfully pulled his Bleriot into the air on 27 February and, at 500 feet, guided it up the Dardanelles to the open sea of the Aegean. The outdated Bleriot had a large wheel attached to the joystick; the cockpit resembled the product of an illicit affair between a motor vehicle and a Da Vinci sketch. It was all leather steering-wheel and bird-like wings. On his lap Cemal carried four round hand grenades. These were similar in size to a cricket ball except that each had a wick, was filled with explosive and was bound in a hard metal case. Cemal puffed on a cigar as he coaxed his Bleriot out to sea, both hands on the wheel.

Before long he had found it: a British warship, belching black coal smoke as it steamed out of range of the coastal gun batteries. In what can only be described as a David and Goliath moment, Cemal turned the wheel towards this grey monster. The wings warped in sympathy with the tension on its wires, the tail fin turned and the Bleriot gracefully pointed its nose at HMS *Majestic*. With his left hand Cemal picked up one of the bombs nestled in his lap and brought it towards his face. The fuse spat as it met the glowing cigar end. Like a pirate of old, he tossed the sizzling bomb down towards the ship below. With a crack, the metal ball split apart, but not over the wooden deck. Coolly, Cemal dropped three more bombs while flying in a large, gentle loop. Honour satisfied and both hands now back on the wheel, Cemal returned to the grass aerodrome outside Channakale. He had managed to eke out of the Bleriot a top speed of 60mph on his triumphant flight home.

Unsurprisingly, the British were outraged by Cemal's challenge to the Royal Navy's rule of the Aegean. The attack on *Majestic* was added to reports. Even Churchill read it in the daily despatch penned by Carden. The air war had begun in earnest.

Ark Royal's seaplane flight was given explicit orders to assist in the first naval attack. All the Turkish forts were individually numbered (1 to 35) and marked on both maps and naval charts. Further, a Russian spy ring had supplied Carden with photographs of each fort's blueprints. This was valuable intelligence indeed! Details of each flight mission were recorded:

Mission No. 4 on 17 February

Reconnoitre Forts 1 to 6 with special reference made to a battery known to be in the region.

Carden's naval squadron began Phase 1 on 17 February. It soon became apparent that, in order to conduct long-range bombardment with any hope of success, the warships had to be stable despite the choppy seas. At first, the warships were anchored at both bow and stern to improve stability and ensure greater accuracy. Carden reported poor results; the forts were certainly hit, but the enemy guns kept firing. Harry echoed this from his wicker seat 1000 feet above the conflagration:

> . . . a bombardment and attempt to force the Dardanelles—it was a wonderful sight. At daylight a reconnaissance flight of the coast for any concealed batteries unknown to the Naval Intelligence Department and to verify the position of guns in the known forts.

Harry and Joe Kilner flew in slow circles over the outer forts. They could look behind the concrete bastions and see the Turkish gunners loading 9-inch shells into gun breeches using gantry cranes, ready to fire back at the distant ships, lazily swinging at their anchors off the coast:

> Two things impressed me, the first was the pluck of the Turkish gunners in serving their guns in the face of the greatly superior volume of fire power directed at them . . . and no real damage had been done to any of the guns in the fort.

Despite the failure of the opening phase, Carden reported favourably to the Admiralty on Clarkee and Harry's work. Just having confirmation that the naval intelligence reports were indeed accurate was a boon:

> . . . air reconnaissance on 17, 18, and 19 February had confirmed previous intelligence reporting on Forts No. 1, 2, 3, and 6 allowing identification of additional guns in the eastern bastion of one of the forts.

Identifying the location and placement of enemy guns was of enormous value. Harry referred to this on many occasions, often when returning to his cabin after a flight. The maritime phase of the campaign did not fail because of faulty intelligence. It failed because a political mind—an incredibly bright and forward-thinking politician—was pushing Sackville Carden to do the statistically impossible. The probability of scoring a direct hit on a gun muzzle peeking from behind a bastion was around 10,000:1. And Carden was limited to 100 shells per day:

> It was easy enough to hit the forts, but to do any good, the guns themselves had to be destroyed and they formed very small targets. Long range fire, though impressive, did not seem to be effective.

Carden was forced to continue. What choice did he have? Had Carden refused, Churchill would simply have sought a more compliant replacement. So, with constant interruptions due to the weather, the naval squadron continued to bombard the forts on the good days, as Harry described:

> It was a gorgeous day with a wonderful clear light and from where I sat, I could see the effect of every shot. After the bombardment began we sent up four different seaplanes at intervals, to report on the damage done to the forts and to try and spot for the ships. But after *Vengeance* was hit, all arrangements went by the board. Fire was concentrated so much on certain batteries that it was impossible to say which shot came from which ship, so spotting was useless.

February closed for Sackville Carden. The Dardanelles remained defiant. A powerful naval squadron had been unable to batter its way even into the mouth of the Dardanelles. The outer forts (Sedd el Bahr on Cape Helles, Fort 1, and Kum Kalessi on the other shore, Fort 2) hit back hard. Carden's cautious assessment was proving correct; it was a very difficult prospect. Given the impact of the weather he had few choices remaining.

Echoes of Carden's problems reached senior British Army officers in London. The impressively moustachioed Secretary of State for War, Lord Horatio Kitchener, directed Lieutenant General William Birdwood to leave his headquarters in Cairo, hop on a warship and consult with Carden on the possible deployment of troops. William Birdwood was the General Officer Commanding the Australian and New Zealand Army Corps (ANZAC), then training on desert sands beside the pyramids. General Birdwood conducted his own reconnaissance on HMS *Doris* and sent his recommendations to the Secretary of War, including the likely deployment of his corps.

While William Birdwood did not visit *Ark Royal*, Clarkee and particularly the ever-curious Harry would later become very familiar with 'Birdie' and his staff. In his ignorance, or perhaps hearing that the seaplanes were struggling with the weather conditions, Birdie recommended the despatch of a balloon and aeroplanes to assist in the destruction of the many concealed gun batteries that troubled the navy. London responded to his suggestions, and more air power was warned for immediate departure. Harry ended his journal with a summary for the month:

So far we have done 16 hours flying time in 3 days—not bad considering all things. The *Agamemnon* was hit three times . . . so far we have not had any casualties on our side.

The first day of the new month started well for Harry:

It was quite a cheery day, when it dawned snow could be seen all over Imbros and the hills about the Dardanelles. Therefore did we take the law into our own hands and proceeded up the mouth of the Dardanelles. Howitzers and field gun shells were popping all around us . . . We got away a seaplane, Seaplane 172, which reconnoitred the Asiatic shore and reported continuous trenches with field gun emplacements. Guns were firing all the time from both shores and we replied by dropping a bomb on Mount Dardanus Fort and some spikes on a camp near it.

Then the capricious weather intervened again. Throughout the entire month of March, the seaplane flight found only 17 days suitable for flying. Even on these 'suitable' days when flight operations were attempted, mission aborts were frequent. *Ark Royal*'s log shows variable winds from the north and east gusting to gale force on a number of these days. Furthermore, even moderate sea states, up to sea state 3, prevented the flight of two seaplane types on *Ark Royal*'s order of battle. The inclement weather meant that engines needed to run at full revolutions, causing extra fatigue on temperamental tappet, race and guide rods. Reports of mission failure cite frequent engine breakdowns (sometimes simply from the effects of sea spray) and the requirement for overhaul. After another failed attempt, Harry simply wrote, 'When we arrived we tried at once to do reconnaissance flights, but after three weeks' buffeting things did not go right.'

Mechanics aboard *Ark Royal* worked diligently to improve engine reliability. In the event of mission failure, seaplanes were returned to the hold and immediately overhauled. Often, multiple attempts were made to prosecute a single mission. Once their fragility became apparent, Carden contacted the Air Department in London to request more seaplanes. He reported that only three of his seaplanes were fit to fly in the prevailing weather conditions:

> Seaplanes did good service on 18th and 19th. And they will be invaluable in the later stages. Please provide more machines to replace wastage. Commanding officer ARK ROYAL would like Short No. 161 and other Wight and three in number of 135 or 200 hp Canton short with liberal supply of spares. ARK ROYAL 4 seaplanes cannot be used under conditions prevailing here.

Carden badly needed eyes in the sky—irrespective of the difficulties.

By mid-March 1915 Erich Serno had four new aircraft under command. Three Albatros B1 two-seater biplanes and Frank Siedler's Rumpler B1 represented a significant improvement and, although small in number, brought Turkey into line with European powers. With German technical expertise came German efficiencies. A propeller workshop was established to address the effects of a stretched supply route from Berlin to Istanbul. Serno planned to establish seven aircraft companies in defence of the vast Ottoman Empire. Fortunately, he was ably assisted by a cadre of young Turks who had taken their pilot licences in France prior to the outbreak of hostilities. They provided the perfect cultural bridge as their keenness in flight and willingness to bring the air war to the enemy were now met with the latest technological advances.

Serno now entered the war in the Dardanelles. He arrived with Frank Siedler, several German mechanics and the Rumpler on the deck of a steamer. It was 17 March 1915. The aircraft had its wings removed and, once hoisted onto the docks, was pushed to a large customs shed that had been requisitioned as a hangar. It was assembled in haste; enemy warships could be seen prowling outside the mouth of the Dardanelles. Serno founded Abteilung 1 or 1nci Boluk (1st Aircraft Company) of the Turkish Air Service at Channakale.

In London, Churchill, as First Lord of the Admiralty, indulged his pet project by sending more scarce air resources to the Dardanelles. He acknowledged Carden's telegram and requested the Director of the Air Department to despatch reinforcements that same day. The Director agreed to send two more seaplanes, bringing *Ark Royal*'s complement of seaplanes to a total of seven, Pussy's seaplane having been destroyed in Malta. Communications were now the major problem.

Clarkee and Harry, with two serviceable seaplanes, struggled to assist Carden. In the monthly flight returns, comments on seaplane capability tell of their lamentable climbing rate and their susceptibility to rifle fire from Turkish soldiers, the seaplanes often returning riddled with bullet holes. Harry and his aircrew kept a running tally of their near misses:

> Our job was to fly over the surrounding country to try to estimate the strength of the defence and where their troops were firing from . . . We came close to the ground in order to try and find out, with the result that our machines were splattered with rifle fire. Bromo and Buster Brown had the record for the day with twenty-eight bullet holes in the planes, the floats badly shot

about, two holes in the propeller and a number in the tail.

The situation was also deteriorating in a seemingly quiet part of the peninsula. On Friday morning 5 March, HMS *Queen Elizabeth* was tasked with firing her huge naval shells to hit the forts from a new direction. The flying orders for the day required Harry's seaplanes to spot (correct) *Queen Elizabeth*'s 15-inch shells into the rear of Fort 17 on the other side of the peninsula. *Queen Elizabeth* dropped anchor just north of Gaba Tepe and opposite a small sheltered cove:

> Pussy and [Hugh] Williamson had just reached 3,000 feet when rifle fire burst the propeller, carrying part of the wing away. She went into a vertical spinning nose dive from which she did not recover and came down with a sickening splash into the sea. Contrary to all expectations, when our motorboat reached the wreck, Pussy was found on top of a float holding Williamson's head above water. Both were rather badly injured.

Queen Elizabeth waited patiently for another seaplane. Her gunnery officer in her tower could not see over the 400-foot cliffs surrounding the small cove so he was completely in the hands of the seaplane's observer. The ship was to fire along a bearing and the observer, flying over the fort on the other side of the peninsula, was to correct the shells onto the target:

> Immediately we got a second machine away, but she came back in half an hour, 'Sholto' Douglas the pilot having a bullet in the leg. Both *Queen Elizabeth* and *Ark Royal* were heavily fired at by field guns and

howitzers. The *Ark Royal* was not hit, but *Q.E.* being closer to shore was hit sixteen times. She had to shift billet further out.

Harry then went up (mission No. 34 since arriving) as the last flight of the day. His pilot took him over the small cove where the ANZACs would land in a month's time. This dangerous piece of coastline held a resolute enemy that could shoot down a seaplane, and hit another, while smashing artillery rounds into a warship off the coast. Harry's seaplane ran the gauntlet and circled the enemy fort on the far side of the peninsula. *Queen Elizabeth* belched flame, sending her shells in a parabola over the land and into the fort on the other side, aiming to hit the guns (and their gunners) from behind where they were not protected by thick concrete walls. There was much smoke and dust, but no guns were destroyed. This tied up the Royal Navy's newest and greatest warship in a fruitless exercise.

Harry's seaplane flight had little success in spotting naval gunfire onto targets. Of the six spotting missions attempted, they were rewarded with only three partial strikes. For Carden's blind ships which were attempting to destroy the guns mounted in the Dardanelles forts, the consequences were enormous. The technological advantage of airborne spotting was at the mercy of the experimental Renzel radio. Harry, or a less experienced observer, was expected to tap out on his Morse key the distances short of or beyond the target, followed by distance to the left or right of target. This was abbreviated to a simple alphanumerical sequence: 'A. 150 O. B. 200 L.'—meaning that the shot was 150 yards over and 200 yards left of target. An acknowledgement and repeat of this information was returned to the observer by semaphore or lamp from the firing warship. It was a cumbersome, inaccurate and difficult process that often failed:

Spotting results seem generally to have been unsuccessful owing to several causes:

Engine reliability, rendering the carrying out of the prearranged operations with the ships uncertain.

W/T [radio] gear unreliable. Frequent breakdowns were recorded.

Too many ships firing at the same target, though no doubt this was mainly due to insufficient number of seaplanes being available for separate targets to be engaged.

Smoke or dust from adjacent objectives affecting observation.

Inexperience of aerial observers.

Inexperience of ships' personnel in regard to co-operation with aircraft.

Unsuitability of ships' W/T receiving instruments which had not been adapted to meet the requirements of aircraft.

On reading this report, staff officers in London bullied Clarkee to improve his crew's performance, reiterating that 'aerial reconnaissance [was] necessary for successful fleet operations'.

In Iraq we referred to this as 'the application of a 16,000-kilometre-long screwdriver'. No doubt it was handled at the far end by an equally frustrated officer back at home. It does not work. The officer in place must be allowed to make the decisions. At Gallipoli a simple pattern emerged: a steady stream of suggestions became requests, which then morphed into demands. The four Sopwith Tabloid aeroplanes that were carried in *Ark Royal*'s hold remained unused. The '16,000-kilometre-long screwdriver' bullied Clarkee to fly them off the deck and ditch them in the sea. Clarkee fought back, telling London on 15 March that:

> As regards use of the 80hp tabloid Sopwith aeroplanes, an examination of the whole of Tenedos island was carefully made [and] a landing ground suitable for machines of this type was not to be found. They are, moreover, not suitable for regular work of the type in hand, being unable to carry a passenger for observing and their entire flights being overseas, when engine failure means complete loss of machine.

The Sopwiths could be launched from the deck, but their immersion in seawater would destroy them. They were a one-shot wonder.

Clarkee later reported that he had eventually found a suitable site on the island of Tenedos and was having an aerodrome built. A vineyard was leased from a Greek farmer at great expense and native labour was employed to pull out the vines and level the field for an aerodrome. The leasehold negotiated with the Greek farmer for six months was equal to a general's annual salary.

But not all the news was gloomy. In March *Ark Royal*'s seaplanes prosecuted 17 reconnaissance missions, the lion's

share of duties. For each day of 'flying weather' a reconnaissance mission was conducted and, from 14 March, two
or three reconnaissance missions were conducted per flying
day. Reconnaissance duties became the preferred mission
profile when 'spotting' duties failed to provide decisive
results.

After each mission the pilot and observer would report to
Harry in his little cabin where he would type out a formal
air intelligence report. I did a similar thing in Iraq. The aircrew would file into my tent and share a pot of tea, followed
by gentle but methodical questioning. There is no surviving
photo of Harry's cabin, but it was probably tiny and would
have contained a typewriter and a small desk. His aerial
intelligence reporting focused on Turkish defences blocking the naval squadron: forts, gun batteries and, in the latter
stages, the location of sea mines:

FLYING ORDERS NO. 53

No. 172—Flight Lieutenant GE Bromet and Lieut.
AG Brown RNR

Reconnaissance to locate minefields

REPORT OF FLIGHT

No. 172 Left 11.21 am Returned 12.36 pm GMT
Tuesday 16 March 1915. Visibility good until rainstorm
started. Height 2,500 feet.

Ten out of the 11 mines previously reported running
south east from 8 N. 57 are still in place and in approximate same positions as before. No isolated mines were

seen to the southwards of this. Mines to northwards of this line not examined due to rainstorm over that part. A sketch map of mine positions—as located today and as located yesterday—is attached.

RH Clarke Hall
Squadron Commander
In Command

Ark Royal and her seaplanes had the ability to range widely along the coast. Harry supported operations northwards into the Gulf of Saros, Xeros Island and the Turkish defences on the Bulair Lines (a line of old Crimean forts). On Wednesday 10 March, Carden ordered *Ark Royal* to reconnoitre the Bulgarian border and the Kavak River. The railway bridge over the Kavak River (on the Turkish side as Bulgaria was neutral) was shelled by warships in an attempt to disrupt the movement of supplies to the peninsula. By mid-afternoon the shelling had ceased and the bridge was found to be intact, despite reports that a French battleship had destroyed it. The next day, defensive works at the Bulair Lines were reconnoitred and reconciled with Naval Intelligence Department reporting. The earthen banks of the forts were found to be in disrepair. At times Harry's air intelligence reports also featured topographical information, which was of marginal interest to a naval squadron. In such cases, a heading was included indicating the provision of information, such as the location of fresh water and roads. The inclusion of such information supported Birdie's belief that his ANZACs were about to land on the peninsula.

Harry made certain that results from each low altitude reconnaissance mission were captured on naval charts and maps. His hand-copied map entitled 'Works Located by

Seaplanes to 19/3/1915' shows Forts 1–25 in detail; two new minefields on charting; the location of camps, field guns and trenches; that the inner Fort 19 had been reconnoitred; and the location of a cruiser and two torpedo boat destroyers as fixed on 18 March. Each feature linked to a corresponding mission report providing further details. It was a very effective method of compiling intelligence information. Harry was keen to describe the perils his aviators saw from the air to as many interested officers as he could. He also made frequent visits around the fleet. His first job was to smooth ruffled feathers. The loss of faith in spotting flights had to be remedied:

> . . . the result is chaotic and much ammunition and temper is wasted before the gun is laid truly on the target. Such misunderstandings were frequent and only after the observer and the Gunnery Jack met over a pink gin co-operation in indirect gunfire became truly efficient.

Turkish gunfire during Phases 1, 2 and 3 was only temporarily reduced as the exposed Turkish gunners found shelter; the guns themselves were not destroyed. As a consequence, Carden assessed that his warships were capable only of dominating the forts rather than causing their destruction. This prompted a reappraisal and a change in seaplane orders from fire correctional duties to reporting which forts were manned and firing.

During Phase 4 *Ark Royal*'s seaplane squadron was ordered to identify a safe channel up the straits towards Channakale. Harry now focused on locating sea mine positions and mapping these on Admiralty charts. Carden was learning how to make the best use of Harry and his pilots. He had discovered that the natural advantage of a seaplane was its ability to fly over contested space and report on defences or activity rather than correct shelling. From this point on, the seaplanes provided substantial support to naval operations. Carden reported to the Admiralty on the success of sea mine identification and their fixing on charts and his intention to identify an area for sweeping that would create a safe channel for his ships. Clarkee and Harry were now at the centre of Churchill's attempt on the Dardanelles. Experiments were conducted with deactivated mines sunk near *Ark Royal* which were observed at depths of 5, 10 and 18 feet, while the seaplane flew at 1500, 1000 and 3000 feet respectively. The mine, seen at various depths from various heights overhead, had a similar appearance to objects seen in the waters of the Dardanelles.

In preparation for the final stage in the destruction of the Dardanelles defences, Harry recorded in his diary the fact that his orders came from face-to-face meetings with Carden and his senior staff. On 15 March he was ordered aboard *Queen Elizabeth* and had long conferences with Carden, his deputy, Rear Admiral John de Robeck, and his Chief of Staff, Commodore Roger Keyes. The Admiral's plan was to send battleships through the channel on the course Harry had mapped as clear of mines. A signal came later from *Queen Elizabeth* ordering reconnaissance to see whether any mines had been found by picket boats and trawlers the previous night, with four flights undertaken to confirm known locations.

After debriefing the aircrew and typing his reports, Harry presented his charts to Carden. Minefields, gun batteries and forts were clearly marked on a single sheet of paper. Harry marked out two courses clear of mines. The first course was 800 yards close inshore on the Gallipoli or

European side, while the second course took the form of a channel up the very centre. Harry emphasised that these passages were:

> . . . clear on the strength that no mines were seen, and that 'No mines seen' was written directly onto naval charts. The naval staff was willing to risk there being no mines there.

During the decisive battle of 18 March the seaplane flight was given the task of reporting on the forts once the fleet was engaged: 'Reconnoitre Narrows defences during bombardment, reporting by W/T.' Three reconnaissance missions were flown over the Narrows and Channakale with the observers signalling which forts were engaging Carden's warships—except that Carden was no longer in command. The stress of operations (and the inevitable feeling that he had been correct from the very beginning) had proven too much for him. He had locked himself in the lavatory and refused all entreaties to come out. A leading gastrointestinal specialist recently offered his opinion that the poor chap was suffering ulcerative colitis brought on by massive stress. His staff, at a loss as to what to do, kept pushing orders under the toilet door. Carden was medically repatriated and replaced by another competent naval officer, his deputy, John de Robeck. The battle continued regardless of the change of commander and Harry described his bird's-eye view of the engagement:

> Few people can have seen such a spectacle as the attempt to force the Dardanelles on the 18th March, 1915 as viewed from the air. From 1500 feet—all the old Wight Seaplane was capable of—[I looked] over Gallipoli to

the sea beyond. In the clear weather the whole course of the Dardanelles stood sharply—like a silver pencil. First of all steamed the big ships, *Queen Elizabeth, Inflexible*, and two others, to engage the big forts at the Narrows at long range. The forts replied merrily, most ably assisted by numerous batteries of howitzers concealed in the mountains. Soon the water around the ships was one continuous succession of high flung columns of water where the big shells fell. Hits were frequent.

The 18 March attack was an all-out effort to break through the Dardanelles and send the fleet steaming along the two channels Harry had reported clear of mines. De Robeck's combined British and French fleet was given clear instructions and tasking. Harry's orders were listed in Flying Orders No. 58. As opposed to the private thoughts written in his diary, his report, strict in its brevity, reflects his professional persona:

FLYING ORDERS NO. 59

No. 922—Flight Lieut. R Whitehead and Lieut. H Strain RNVR

Reconnoitre Narrows defences during bombardment, reporting by W/T

No. 173—Left 10.35 am, Returned 12.15 pm GMT, Thursday 18 March 1915. Height 2,000 feet. Visibility good except over forts, which were being heavily shelled.

Forts 13, 16, 17 and 19 were all manned and firing rapidly. Fort 20 not manned. Forts 13, 17 and 19 were observed to be hit repeatedly, but damage could not be estimated owing to smoke. Mount Dardanus and Kephez Point Forts were not manned, but troops were in immediate vicinity with many field guns. Fort at Saundere River firing, and forts with four guns on ridge to southwards of Saundere River firing rapidly. Field guns firing from around, and half a mile inland from Aren Koi village.

A line of small boats across the stream immediately above the Narrows, lying broadside to stream. It is possible that these may have been engaged in mine laying. A large cruiser at Nagara Point. Practically all this information was transmitted by W/T during the course of the reconnaissance. Engine trouble necessitated return to ship.

RH CLARKE HALL
Squadron Commander
In Command

The French squadron was ordered to steam through the larger British warships, watched by Harry in his wicker chair 2000 feet above, to engage the forts at close range:

Next four French ships steamed through the lines of battleships. The Frenchmen looked very gallant as they tore up the straits, firing at a tremendous pace and constantly smothered in the white water of shell. The *Gaulois* was hit by something big: it seemed to stagger for a moment. It was next to impossible to report on the damage to the forts, as a dense cloud of dust and lyddite hung over each fort and all one could see were the flashes through the dust. The Frenchmen were having a hot time, principally from the howitzer batteries, whose shooting was good. As the Frenchmen turned to come out the *Bouvet* quickly disappeared. At one minute she was firing away gaily, next she was gone—dived under, without fuss or explosion.

The naval attack faltered. After steaming through the centre of the mouth of the Dardanelles and the large bite that is Eren Keui Bay, the lines of warships were subject to accurate shelling from the forts and plunging fire from concealed howitzer batteries. First the French warship *Gaulois* was holed below the waterline before *Bouvet* struck a mine and sank after turning to starboard, outside Harry's channel, and steaming close to the Asiatic shore. The squadron continued her mistake of turning to starboard and heading towards the Asiatic shore when the first line retired. Later that afternoon, Harry watched *Inflexible, Ocean* and *Irresistible* all repeat *Bouvet*'s error and strike mines close inshore:

> The exit of the fleet was an impressive sight: the wind had got up and was increasing dangerously. *Gaulois* came reeling out like a drunken man and was beached on Rabbit Island (outside mouth Dardanelles) to prevent her sinking. *Bouvet, Ocean, Irresistible* all sunk and *Inflexible* with a pain in her belly which nearly finished her off before she gained the quiet waters of Tenedos.

Harry and his Wight seaplane have been criticised for not locating the mines that caused the loss of a third of the naval squadron. But Harry identified only two passages clear of mines which did *not* include Eren Keui Bay on the Asiatic shoreline where the ships struck. The departure of the squadron from the identified safe channel and its sub-sequent movement into a minefield recently laid by the Turkish tender *Nusret* was an error committed on the day.

Indeed 18 March was also an active day for the mixed crew of Turkish and German pilots who shared a single-roomed house on the outskirts of the port. It was a homely affair: coffee on the boil, naval charts on the wall, and kept scrupulously clean. An intelligent arrangement had been reached: German pilots would take a Turkish officer as observer. This would end the problems of speaking through a translator, or via a third shared language such as French.

Early that morning a runner came with a message that the fortress at Gaba Tepe had reported enemy warships collecting out to sea. Erich Serno went up in the Rumpler with a German naval captain in the observer's seat. *Kapitan Leutnant* Schneider worked as a staff officer for Admiral Ernest von Usedom, the German naval adviser to Channakale Fortress Command. The Rumpler was a biplane of a design that all would recognise. An upper and lower wing with a Mercedes engine at the nose, the Rumpler could roar ahead at over 100mph while carrying both pilot and observer. This was a modern war machine with under-wing racks that carried bombs of over 25lb. *Kapitan Leutnant* Schneider held a book with silhouettes identifying each class of British warship. At 5000 feet the Rumpler flew over three lines of grey enemy ships, their coal smoke reaching up to the pair flying over-head. A total of 19 major warships were identified, including several French and a Russian ship in the second and third lines. The pilot and his observer knew they were looking down on an attempt to fight through the Narrows, although they could not see any transports, which suggested a landing was not yet contemplated; this was a naval affair:

Early in the morning we climbed to altitude. Beneath us spread out the lands behind Channakale. We saw in the secret filled channel the oyster shaped towers of Kilid Bahr. White shone the road that led through the sparse undergrowth of the plains of Gallipoli. We flew at 1600 metres altitude. At Tenedos we encountered forty vessels laying at anchor. All types were represented. Below were the heavy ships of the line and light cruisers, ponderous transports and aircraft tenders. The shadow of a submarine could be seen right below us, the wash of her propellers stretching out like a white streak behind her. Now six battleships in line astern sailed in the direction of the mouth of the Dardanelles. The armoured cruiser *Inflexible* with her Admiral's flag. Next following her was the *Queen Elizabeth*, *Lord Nelson* and *Agamemnon*, *Majestic* and *Triumph*. All valuable ships of the Royal Navy. Suddenly shrapnel clouds sprung up all around us. The French battleship *Bouvet* had sent up this greeting. We landed and reported to Admiral von Usedom. Soon, in all the batteries drums and bugles sounded the call to the cannons.

Serno dropped the nose of the Rumpler and pointed towards home. He pushed the controls forward and was rewarded with the air speed indicator pointing to over 90mph. With a tail wind he calculated that they were making 110mph over the sea. *Kapitan Leutnant* Schneider had circled the ships in his notebook and added names to the classes of warships. A quick addition told him that more than 100 heavy naval guns would be trained on the forts and gun batteries lining the shores. Losing height over Sedd el Bahr at the toe of Cape Helles, Serno shot along at 1000 feet over the surface of the sea. On either side gun batteries were hidden behind the crest of hills or in washaways. He was pleased to note that they could not be identified. Even their muzzle flashes would be hidden by intervening crests; the shells would be thrown in an arc over the crest and down onto the wooden decks of the enemy ships. Serno had enjoyed working with the Turks, warming to their easy manner and respecting their depth of experience. Their gunnery, he was about to discover, was superb.

The Rumpler circled over the broken town of Channakale before he reduced his airspeed and bounced onto the grass strip, coming to a gradual standstill. Serno brought the machine as close to the pilots' hut as possible. Already a knot of pilots stood at the door to greet his return. *Kapitan Leutnant* Schneider had unbuckled and was out of the rear seat and onto the grass as soon as the machine stopped. It was a rare sight to see a naval captain run and Serno enjoyed the moment. *Kapitan Leutnant* Schneider loped towards the hut, loudly demanding a horse to take him to see the commander.

Kapitan Leutnant Schneider's news was immediately telephoned to all the forts. Men ran from the messes to their guns. Canvas was pulled off and ammunition and charges brought up on hoists. Claxons roared the challenge. Battery commanders in the hills were warned. Last-minute preparations were made, ready shells stacked, telephones tested, slide rules pulled from leather covers. An impressive 35 forts were now prepared for action. Several batteries of howitzers were cleared for firing, the camouflage pulled from overhead. All they had to do now was wait. Gunnery observers looked towards the mouth of the Dardanelles. Shapes appeared in range-finders.

At 11 am the British warships entered the Narrows and sent their shells towards the inner forts. The noise bounced and boomed up the Narrows. A fort at Channakale was hit by the shells of several large calibre guns; bricks and dust were thrown high into the air. A message was handed to Serno by a soldier covered in brick dust, his eyes unusually bright: orders for another flight to determine the direction and intentions of the enemy fleet.

Cemal was ordered up in the Bleriot with Captain Osman as his observer. Cemal knew that an enemy seaplane was circling over the straits. Both Cemal and Osman carried pistols; however, their objective was not to engage the seaplane but to report on enemy movements. Cemal took the Bleriot low over the southern Asiatic shore, avoiding the seaplane and its ringside view of the battle. Osman was concerned that the enemy might have other intentions, such as landing a force. Flying inland they had a clear view of three lines of warships. The first line had entered the mouth and was a mile off Channakale and the Narrows, firing its guns at the stone forts clustered along the shoreline. The ships' progress had slowed; it was now a battle between modern warships and stone forts. One or two were aflame, hoses snaked over their ruptured wooden decks as damage control parties worked to extinguish the fires. A glimmer of hope arose in the two men; the warships were suffering. Osman hissed with delight as a howitzer shell struck the upper deck of a warship; smoke and flame belched and a snake of white steam told that some internal pipe had been ruptured. Further out, closer to the mouth, they flew over Orkanie Fort, and Osman could clearly see the second wave, French tricolours streaming in defiance, making for the Narrows. Evidently, the enemy's focus was on fighting through.

Not wishing to become a target with so much metal piercing the air, Cemal soberly brought the Bleriot in a circle further inland and away from the contested waters. He knew that information on the enemy's intentions was a prize worth taking. He made a simple bearing back to the grass strip and landed smoothly, despite a brisk crosswind.

The aircrew were kept away from the town and the water's edge. Serno could not afford to lose a pilot or a mechanic to military tourism. He had the men prepare both aeroplanes for further flight. The scream of shells and the concussion of explosions made each feel slightly ineffectual. A major battle was in progress. Serno was correct in anticipating further reconnaissance missions. His small flight flew two more that afternoon.

At 4 pm Admiral Ernest von Usedom demanded another reconnaissance over the fleet. Reports of several successes had to be investigated. The problems with translation were a constant barrier. For this task Serno sent the same pair aloft again: Captain Osman spoke reasonably fluent German and could thus speak to both parties in the headquarters. The flight followed their previous path, the Bleriot performing tolerably well during the short flight. But this time Osman was struck speechless. The French warship *Bouvet* had gone under, an oil slick and bubbles on the surface marking her grave. Similarly, two British warships were burning fiercely, lifeboats and men struggling in the water grave portents of an unfolding naval catastrophe. Wood, cork, lifejackets and upended cutters told of a Turkish victory. The hissing of steam and sirens were audible sighs between the punches of gunfire. Three battleships were sunk, three seriously damaged.

In the late afternoon the silence confirmed the Turkish victory. The great fleet had limped away. As many as three ships had been sunk. Another was burning fiercely and out of control in Eren Keui Bay. Smoke hung over the forts. The wind was still blowing dust and a yellow grit over all.

Cordite and sulphur from heavy explosions remained in pockets. The call to prayer was close, a nation defiant. The dead were collected for washing and burial as is the Turkish custom. The German pilots and mechanics watched as carts pulled the painfully silent wounded through the streets to the hospital at the edge of town. But it was evident to all that the quiet Turk had won.

Serno gave the most difficult task—the long cross-ocean flight to the island of Imbros—to Frank Siedler. They had to know what had become of the fleet. Were more ships waiting for first light? Frank had flown the Rumpler on the lengthy overland flight to Turkey. He deserved this honour. He took as his observer Huseyn Sedat—his eyes for this long journey.

The overseas flight took more than two and a half hours. They arrived to find Mudros Harbour a scene of utter chaos. A warship was beached on tiny Rabbit Island outside the mouth of the Dardanelles. Two warships were limping towards the lee of Tenedos. Even these clues did not prepare them for the sight of the broken fleet in Mudros. Black smoke and grey steam again told of ships in pain. They flew over the bay in the gathering dusk; they were ignored. Hoses, jets of water, oil and flames indicated a fleet heavily handled. It was clear from the vantage of 6000 feet that the fleet was not likely to tempt the straits again. So much damage and they had not even approached the first minefields or the main defences at the Narrows.

John de Robeck was unsure of the cause of this terrible destruction. Harry observed several small vessels moored across the Dardanelles and guessed that the Turks had drifted sea mines on the current. Harry's report of the mines moving down the straits on the strong current and striking Allied ships made sense. De Robeck signalled a withdrawal;

the cost of this engagement was significant. It effectively marked the end of the naval operation and, for Birdie as General Officer Commanding ANZAC, the beginning of the land campaign.

On 22 March, following a conference on *Queen Elizabeth* between General Sir Ian Hamilton and Admiral John de Robeck, the plan for a renewed naval attack was abandoned. It was now time to plan a land offensive. Harry's seaplane flights continued over the peninsula reporting that the Turkish Army remained in effective defence and warning of the deployment of further gun batteries. An extract from the flight report of 26 March describes an invigorated defence:

> Great activity south of Kephez Point; two new emplacements . . . contain six guns or howitzers each. A third new emplacement on coast south of lighthouse but only one gun yet. Fort 19—many shells had evidently burst in centre of fort. All guns, except second from southward, appear intact. A hundred men or more working in front of fort and many inside. Fort 16—buildings in rear destroyed otherwise intact. Fort 17—undamaged.

A renewed naval attempt would achieve little and only add to the mounting death toll.

ANZAC was already committed to the Gallipoli battlefield. The Australian 3rd Brigade had finished its desert training and by 4 March had arrived packed into steamers on the island of Lemnos. The brigade practised landing in rowboats and launched mock assaults. It waited for orders to join battles it could so clearly hear across 30 kilometres of sea. Birdie knew he had another role to play. Believing the navy would ultimately fail, he had anticipated that his men would be next and now looked for additional assets that would assist them in this new venture:

> I strongly recommend immediate despatch of man-lifting kite or captive balloon for use of Navy as this would not only give assistance in helping spotting long range fire but I should be able to detect concealed batteries which already trouble the navy. Message Ends.

Lord Kitchener considered Birdie's advice favourably:

> From Secretary War Office London
>
> To General Officer Commanding Cairo
>
> Received 8. 3. 15
>
> Your last paragraph. Admiralty sending out 12 aeroplanes and 12 pilots. Also 1 Kite Balloon Section. Ends.

Birdie's recommendation precipitated the hasty refurbishment and despatch of aircraft, and the Air Department selected Wing Commander Charles Samson's No. 3 Squadron, RNAS, to pack up and sail to the Dardanelles in support of the projected land campaign. Charles' squadron had entered the war flying over Ostend and Bruges in December 1914. Since then, according to squadron records, its aircrew had conducted 27 anti-aircraft patrols with five recorded aerial engagements. The pilots had enjoyed a busy time with 24 bombing raids on targets ranging from the submarine sheds at Bruges and Zeebrugge and, famously, the zeppelin sheds in Germany. No. 3 Squadron, RNAS, was sent to assist Birdie's ANZACs, not the navy:

> The following officers, aeroplanes and transport pro-
> posed for service to the Army as requested. Nine
> pilots, 4 observers, 12 aeroplanes, 100 of 100lbs
> bombs, 300 of 20 lbs bombs, 3 Lewis guns, 6 Maxim
> guns, 13 tents, 10 lorries, one ambulance, 2 workshop
> lorries and eight cars.

The movement order followed, directing Charles Samson and 'No. 3 Squadron to Turkey, with authorisation to despatch 17 officers, 160 men, 12 aeroplanes in packing crates, 8000 gallons of petrol and an armoured car squadron'.

Charles Rumney Samson was a brilliant aviator, albeit a headstrong individual. His service record reveals that he joined the Royal Navy as a boy of 14. He soon qualified as a gunnery officer before being bitten by the aviation bug. He was a risk-taker and quick to make decisions. To others, Charles was a man straight from a popular cartoon. He resembled a 16th-century buccaneer with a pointed goatee beard and a swagger to match. His men called him 'Captain Kettle' after a figure of fun and brassy derring-do serialised in *Pearson's Magazine* and sold as bound volumes as *The Adventures of Captain Kettle*.

Despite his resemblance to Captain Kettle, Charles Samson was a formidable pilot and on 10 January 1912 the first to fly an aeroplane off a ship—HMS *Africa*—during aircraft experiments at Sheerness. A 100-foot (30-metre) downward-sloping runway had been installed on *Africa*'s foredeck, running over her forward turret to her bows. Her crew then held the Wight pusher seaplane, with the engine mounted at the rear, by its tail as Charles clambered into its cockpit to attempt the first British shipboard aeroplane take-off. The aeroplane was released, sped down the ramp, dipped alarmingly, but then pulled up. Charles circled

Africa several times to the cheers of the crew, although on one pass he came uncomfortably close to the bridge. He climbed to 800 feet and concluded his historic flight by landing safely at an aerodrome ashore. In the first weeks of the war he was awarded the *Croix de Chevalier* for his pioneering aviation over Lille. By 17 October 1915 Charles had been Mentioned in Despatches for the second time: '3rd Wing has rendered splendid service under all conditions of weather, and by his gallant example he has, without doubt, set the highest standard which prevails in the 3rd Wing.'

Once again, Churchill was behind the despatch of aircraft. He also pressured Lord Kitchener for an approximate time-line for the concentration of troops now that the naval campaign had formally concluded. A tentative date of 20 March was discussed with up to 40,000 troops (mostly ANZACs) involved. This fitted in with No. 3 Squadron's expected arrival at the prepared aerodrome on Tenedos. Charles wrote:

> As our presence on the scene of action was urgently required, I was ordered to proceed overland across France and embark at Marseilles, where we would pick up the new aeroplanes. Bill Samson [Charles' brother— the squadron was a family fiefdom], [Henry] Butler and myself then went onto Paris in the Rolls. I went to the Ritz, and after a good dinner I went to bed in the best bedroom . . . We then drove on and we stopped the night at the Louvre et Palais, and drove down to the SS *Abda* at 6 am. I found the last of the cars being hoisted in, and two Maurice Farman and eight Henri Farman aeroplanes were taking up the whole of the upper deck. We were the sole passengers, as she had been especially detailed by our Allies to take us to the Dardanelles.

Fittingly, Charles went to Gallipoli with his Rolls Royce tourer and a charger, renamed 'Nigger', that he had taken from a dead German Uhlan at a skirmish near Aniche.

CHAPTER 2

April, the cards are dealt

To prepare for war is an unusual thing. It happens rarely, usually only once in a lifetime, and often skips generations. First you receive a warning order in the form of a signal, advising that you will be attached to a formation committed to overseas service. Then you complete the specific training required for that theatre of operations: perhaps jungle training or, in my case, training for Iraq and the potential use of biological and chemical weapons. Then there is a terrific rush; essentials are packed and the goodbyes begin. Desert camouflage uniforms, civilian underwear, books, spare reading glasses, webbing and various packs littered my apartment. Added to this were the tools of the intelligence trade: wax pencils (a sign of being 'old school'), coloured markers, a pointer, CIA books on the Iraqi order of battle and my CD collection. On receiving orders for departure the next day, I walked into a map shop in Pitt Street in Sydney and bought five large (metre square) maps of Saddam's fiefdom. Later I joined them with sticky tape and mounted them on an easel hammered together by a carpenter at the aerodrome. In the rush I forgot to claim the maps as an expense. Nothing much has changed since 1915.

Commanders (and to a much lesser extent their intelligence officers) fold into their packs a unique burden. A commander has responsibility for a campaign. The lives of all the men and women listed on the warning orders are theirs to carry. They are given a set of military objectives and the human and industrial means to achieve them. Rarely do the two match.

General Sir Ian Standish Hamilton was a blend of intellectual, free thinker and soldier. He was one of the first supporters of the use of aircraft in the coming war. He was taken aloft by Charles Samson just after Charles received his pilot's licence in 1912. Hamilton then infuriated his army contemporaries with his prophecies on the demise of cavalry on the modern battlefield. At 62 years of age when war broke out, he remained in England as less imaginative officers galloped off to France sharing a simple orthodoxy that would result in death on a scale never previously imagined. This intellectual remained marooned in the Horse Guards until his summons arrived.

Lord Kitchener appointed the whippet-like Hamilton as Commander-in-Chief of the Mediterranean Expeditionary Force on 13 March. Kitchener's impressive visage loomed from posters affixed to walls in dingy stations across England exhorting men to join the army. Now he sat behind a large wooden desk and failed to meet Hamilton's eyes. Again the characteristic rush and, five days later, Hamilton witnessed the Turkish victory as John de Robeck's warships shuddered below the Narrows on 18 March.

On 22 March, a grey, windswept Monday, a joint naval

and army conference was held in the wood-panelled ward-room on *Queen Elizabeth*. The army was committed to the fight. Hamilton telegraphed Lord Kitchener warning of a military siege rather than a battle, and including requests for trench mortars and periscopes. Kitchener's vision of flag-waving troops frightening the ignorant Turk into a stampede was false hope indeed; such hopes had sunk with the *Bouvet*:

> I told them too that my intelligence fold fix the num-bers of the enemy now at the Dardanelles as 40,000 on the Gallipoli Peninsula with a reserve of 30,000 behind Bulair: on the Asiatic side of the Straits there is at least a Division, but there may be several Divisions. The Admiralty information tallies and so, Birdie says, does that of the Army in Egypt. The War Office notion that the guns of the fleet can sweep the enemy off the tongue of the peninsula from Achi Baba southwards is moonshine.

Hamilton telegraphed Kitchener again the next morning describing these enemy strengths and reiterating his belief that he must land *all* of his army. It was slow cooking—first one ingredient then the other. With the worst behind him, Hamilton left de Robeck for Cairo in order to co-locate him-self with the Egyptian War Office and meet his new army.

And now to dig for the truth—intelligence detailing the Turkish defence of the peninsula was sound. Hamilton, and just about every general since, has used the 'faulty intelli-gence' wild card to explain away failure. It was obvious that Carden and de Robeck did not play this card because they had high grade intelligence, including the blueprints of each Turkish fort. But Hamilton would later have no choice—he was the type to blame some*thing*, rather than some*body*. In his published diary he left a hint of this:

> There is nothing certain about war except one side
> won't win. The winner is asked no questions—the loser
> has to answer for everything.

Only by picking apart the weft and warp that shrouds this campaign are the heady roles played by our aviators revealed. If the generals had acknowledged the work of Harry and Charles, it would also amount to a confession that they had all the intelligence they needed. So it was buried.

When news of the wonderful Turkish victory reached Istanbul, General Otto Liman von Sanders was appointed to command the Turkish 5th Army for the defence of Gallipoli. Now that the Allies had lost at sea, it was obvious that they would land an army. A mole, a spy in the Turkish Headquarters in Istanbul, began revealing to his agent plans for the defence of the peninsula: 'Turkish Staff officer told informant on March 5 . . .' Three days later, the Egyptian War Office published a secret Daily Intelligence Bulletin announcing the appointment of Liman von Sanders as the enemy commander. Hamilton now knew the name of his opponent and how many men and guns his opposing force possessed. De Robeck remained on *Queen Elizabeth* while his squadron continued the fight, informing Churchill that aeroplanes were a precondition for the success of the landings: 'in preparing the decisive effort in conjunction with the Army [with] systematic reconnoitring [of] both shores.' Harry and Charles would soon wield a strong influence on the shape of the landing.

More help was on its way. Following Birdie's request, the Air Department purchased the tramp steamer SS *Manica* and remodelled her to accommodate a kite balloon in her forward hold: she became the world's first tethered balloon ship. This bizarre concept involved attaching a sausage-shaped balloon to a ship by steam-winch. A wicker basket holding two gunnery officers would swing below the balloon at heights ranging from 2500 to 3000 feet. The gunnery officers could then direct artillery fire by speaking over a simple telephone line to the warships below. Flight Commander Philip Mackworth was appointed commander, assisted by a complement of six officers, one warrant officer and 57 ratings. Philip received orders on 22 March to steam immediately to John de Robeck's squadron. HMS *Manica* and her Experimental Kite Balloon Section No. 1 was rushed to the fight. Mr Herbert Hillier, the official war artist, was also accommodated onboard:

> Our small section of the Mediterranean Expeditionary Force is on the way to Gibraltar. But the chief topic is, will the fleet have got through without waiting for our invaluable help? Many of us are certainly very new to this sort of thing, as yet.

As Philip ordered *Manica*'s anchor pulled from the Sheerness mud, SS *Abda* with her crated aeroplanes dropped her anchor into the grey Aegean. Charles 'Captain Kettle' Samson was in his element:

> . . . daylight found us off the south coast of Tenedos. I landed with the whole of my party with two collapsible hangars in which we intended to live as a howling gale was blowing. Ashore we had a miserable time, lying huddled under the canvas hangar, which continually threatened to blow down. We had practically no

equipment and very little food. The weather improved and we disembarked the aeroplanes. The whole job took two days; and by nightfall I had at the aerodrome No. 50, two Maurice Farmans and eight Henri Farmans fitted with 80hp gnome engines. Next day we started work properly. We soon got used to continually flying over the sea.

With the arrival of SS *Inkosi* carrying the balance of Charles' squadron, the ground crew set to work assembling the remaining 18 aeroplanes. Following trials, Charles considered that only five were fit for war service, the rest incapable of making the long flight over the sea to and from the peninsula each day even before engaging the Turks. The eight new Henri Farman 80hp pusher biplanes, delivered straight from the factory, were too underpowered and easy meat for Turkish gunners. Only aeroplanes with an engine power greater than 100hp were used over enemy lines. These aeroplanes could fly at least as high as 5000 feet, thus reducing the risk. One of these exceptions was Charles' personal biplane BE2 (No. 50), which he flew solo. Like all air power units sent to Gallipoli, the squadron was moved with more urgency than planning. Charles' No. 3 Squadron, despite the efforts of its enigmatic leader, was not battle efficient.

Before the landings, and in spite of his difficulties, Charles' squadron prosecuted 50 successful reconnaissance flights over the contested southern end of the Gallipoli Peninsula. Locations and descriptions of enemy defences, seen from 5000 feet, were listed in post-mission reports, sent to each headquarters within 24 hours of each flight. Following their arrival at Mudros Harbour, the British 29th Division, Royal Naval Division and ANZAC received printed copies with supplementary mapping showing graphically where these formidable defences were located. Their war diaries have dozens of air intelligence reports filed in their appendices. How this was achieved and what effect it had on the landing is worth exploring. Even with only five war-fit aeroplanes, Charles' squadron had a much higher success rate than Harry's struggling seaplane flight. Taking off from a muddy aerodrome instead of thrashing about on a choppy sea had its benefits. Charles' five aeroplanes were grounded by inclement weather for three out of 25 days before the landings and flew an average of five missions a day, with a peak of ten missions on three separate days.

Harry and his mixed crew on *Ark Royal* were ordered to keep an eye on Turkish activity while Charles' squadron unloaded its crated aeroplanes. The Turks were indeed busy, digging trenches and stretching barbed wire across the few beaches that could attract an invading army. Then the tables turned:

> An aeroplane was seen approaching the ship from 6000 feet and the black crosses could clearly be distinguished under her planes. Anti-aircraft Maxims were quickly manned and we opened fire just as she dropped her bombs. The first fell about 100 yards ahead, and the second within six feet of the port side of the ship, abreast the hold, and gave her a nasty shaking, covering the bridge with splinters, and embedding bits of the bomb in the ship's side. The aeroplane then turned and made off over the Asiatic coast. In paying us her first visit, she paid us a delicate compliment, as there were many other ships nearer to her home.

The ship's flight log records that a seaplane on the deck was damaged. If the bomb had entered the open hatch and burst in the cavernous hold with its drums of petrol, *Ark Royal* would have enjoyed a Viking funeral.

The biplane with black crosses was the Rumpler from Erich Serno's 1st Aircraft Company. Serno's aeroplanes flew a number of successful missions that day, including the attack on *Ark Royal*. But poor weather affected Turkish air operations just as it did Harry's seaplanes. Two flights were prosecuted in the Rumpler on 26 March. The morning mission ended quickly with strong winds and rain obscuring much of the sea. A break in the weather allowed Frank Siedler once again to attempt the long overseas flight to Lemnos Island. There the enemy fleet remained, working parties painting and refitting broken superstructure. No reinforcements had arrived from Malta.

Two days later a pair of Albatros was delivered to the Channakale docks by steamer. New crews also arrived and found accommodation in the west of the town. The Albatros was more powerful than the Rumpler with a Mercedes engine punching 150hp and a ceiling approaching 8000 feet. It was the most powerful aircraft at Gallipoli. It also carried an observer, but Serno saw no need to arm him with a machine-gun. The back seat was for an officer, not an air gunner.

The aerodrome was causing problems as it was wearing down to its stone base rather than remaining grassy and even. Attempts to flatten the grass had removed the cover, revealing sand and more and more pebbles. Within days, the wooden ends of the propellers were splitting from slashing through airborne grit. The Albatros were grounded until new propellers could be crafted locally or sent from Germany. The Rumpler, with its stronger laminated wood propeller, remained the workhorse. Both the Turkish Air Service and the RNAS were hostage to a stretched supply line. They had a great deal in common.

The Turkish Rumpler made a nuisance of itself as Frank Siedler began a series of bombing attacks on the fleet. He had access to a small supply of 60lb bombs smuggled through Bulgarian customs that were fitted to under-wing racks. The days of Cemal's cricket ball bombs were over. These German-manufactured bombs had a nose detonator and tail fins as stabilisers—they even whistled as they fell. On 1 April Siedler attacked a warship outside the mouth of the Dardanelles. The problem was a lack of bombsight. Aiming was pure airmanship. Added to this, a ship was not a stationary target and tended to move out of harm's way. On 15 April a slower moving collier was hit; as a merchant vessel she had no anti-aircraft guns so Siedler conducted a low and steady approach. Black dust was kicked up and the effect of the explosion was muffled. She did not sink but plodded on wearing a thick coating of black. But the attack on *Ark Royal* was significant; it heralded the opening of the air war.

Ark Royal's and later *Manica*'s versatility (as ships capable of transiting the Aegean) allowed the conduct of flight operations from as far north as the Bulgarian border to the southern port of Smyrna (Ismir) on the Asiatic shore. Harry's seaplanes conducted 11 reconnaissance flights across this vast arc of enemy coast. By 10 April, de Robeck reported to Churchill that there had been effective progress with *Ark Royal* as she 'has been doing excellent reconnaissance work around the coast'. De Robeck included aerial intelligence reports on Turkish military preparations in his daily précis of operations to the Admiralty.

Meanwhile, Charles wisely appointed Bernard Isaac as his Squadron Intelligence Officer to provide the same level of reporting as Harry on *Ark Royal*. Charles wrote:

Bill Samson and Bernard Isaac were put in charge of intelligence, which soon became a big job, and they had plenty to do, as well as a good bit of flying.

Charles, as a blue-blooded naval officer, then cleverly recruited two army artillery officers to fly as observers. This was to ensure the capture of intelligence relevant to an army about to engage in battle having waded ashore from rowboats. When Captain Jenkins or Major Hogg flew as an observer (as opposed to an RNAS officer) it was recorded in the report as a form of reassurance. Charles began flight operations as soon as his personal biplane was assembled:

> I started bombing the Turks, dropping three small bombs from No. 50 on the Sogun Dere minefield batteries. I didn't hit anything; but it was good practice, and it was time the Turks realised that we had arrived on the scene.

Charles' squadron performed credibly owing to the particular geography of the Gallipoli Peninsula and the inability of the Turkish Air Service to mount a serious challenge. Clearly, an enemy pilot had shown considerable skill in his bomb attack on *Ark Royal*, but this needed to be a daily affair. Charles later briefed Hamilton, telling him that the topographical nature of the small peninsula, surrounded as it was by sea, was particularly suited to his aeroplanes as they could bomb the enemy and destroy supplies. But in this Charles boasted too much. He should have said that he could observe the enemy and provide Hamilton timely warnings, as there was nowhere for the enemy to hide large concentrations of troops before a battle.

On 1 April Bernard arrived off Tenedos aboard SS *Inkosi* with the remainder of Charles' squadron. He observed immediately that a war was in progress:

Passed quite close to *Inflexible*. She had a bad list and we could see where she had been badly hit in several places. At the time we passed she was getting out her dead 37 in all and lowering the bodies into launches for burial ashore . . . In the distance we see our new aerodrome. Presently a Maurice Farman flies over, then a BE and a Henri Farman, our first indication that Commander Samson and Co. have arrived safely.

(3 April) Weather atrocious, impossible to land. A French warship comes in to offer us assistance unloading and lowers a boat with four sailors, which overturns. We watch the unfortunate French sailors struggling. We rescue two, but one dies directly on the deck of *Inkosi*. The tender from HMS *Triumph* gets the other two but one was dead. Heard there is mail. I am more than anxious to hear from home.

Far across the seas in London, and at the same time the French sailors were drowning, Churchill sat in an Air Department conference expressing a positive opinion on the progress of aerial operations following the arrival of Charles' squadron. The First Lord of the Admiralty boasted:

The possibility of working a squadron of aeroplanes from an overseas base had not been foreseen and the operation was carried out with great success, and had materially altered preconceived ideas as to the means of employment of aircraft.

Despite *Ark Royal's* seaplane flight, Charles' squadron on Tenedos and the imminent arrival of the balloon, one important capability was still missing. None of the aircraft flying over the peninsula had the capability to attack

Turkish shipping with torpedoes. Two Sopwith 860 sea-planes were on their way as replacements but they too were underpowered and unable to carry the 700lb torpedo in active service conditions, despite successful peacetime trials in February 1914. On receiving this advice, Churchill considered sending a seaplane carrier with the sole pur-pose of sinking Turkish troop transports using the specially designed Short Seaplane Type 184 with its massive 225hp Sunbeam engine. HMS *Ben-my-Chree* was identified for this purpose and approval eventually granted to send her to the Dardanelles, where she arrived after the landings. But the idea was consistent. All knew they had to isolate Liman von Sanders' Turkish 5th Army from its supply bases along the Sea of Marmara.

Charles brought a number of committed aviators to the air battle. These men had accompanied him to Belgium in late 1914 flying a mixed dozen of aeroplanes. They had flown over the exposed left flank of the British Expeditionary Force from a landing ground at St Pol, near Dunkirk. Apart from reconnoitring German cavalry and advancing columns of infantry, they also had a role in preventing zep-pelins reaching England and attacking German submarine stations at Ostend and Zeebrugge. Four of Charles' aviators were awarded the Distinguished Service Order (DSO) in the first weeks of the war.

Flight Commander Richard Bell Davies was a Londoner like Harry. Richard joined the Royal Navy as a 14-year-old cadet. At 19 he took private flying lessons before he changed departments and joined the RNAS in 1913, where he met Charles. He and 23-year-old Flight Lieutenant Richard Peirse conducted a number of raids on German submarine bases at Zeebrugge in late 1914. Their citations tell of reso-lute and daring air attacks:

These Officers have repeatedly been subjected on each occasion to heavy and accurate fire, their machines being frequently hit. In particular, on 23rd January, they each discharged eight bombs in an attack upon submarines alongside the mole at Zeebrugge, flying down to close range. At the outset of this flight Lieutenant Richard Davies was severely wounded by a bullet in the thigh, but nevertheless he accomplished his task, handling his machine for an hour with great skill in spite of pain and loss of blood.

Likewise flight lieutenants Charles 'Herb' Collet and Reginald Marix were experienced aviators. Herb was an officer in the Royal Marines before transferring to the Air Department. He proved a courageous airman and was the first to attack the zeppelin shed located outside Düsseldorf. On 22 September 1914, he had flown the 200 miles to Düsseldorf and approached the zeppelin shed at an altitude of 6000 feet. There was a bank of mist below, which he had encountered at 1500 feet. He traversed the depth of this layer and emerged at a height of only 400 feet above the ground. His objective was barely a quarter of a mile ahead. Travelling at high speed he launched his bombs with what proved to be deadly precision and disappeared into cover almost before the enemy had grasped his intentions. Despite being hit by rifle fire, he returned safely and, for this extraordinary flight, he received the DSO. His citation highlights the remarkable nature of his feat:

On 22 September 1914, flying a Sopwith Tractor Biplane [Herb Collet] made a successful attack on the German Zeppelin Airship shed at Düsseldorf. Lieut.

Collet's feat is notable—gliding down from 6,000 feet, the last 1500 in mist, he finally came in sight of the Airship shed at a height of 400 feet, only a quarter of a mile away from it.

A few days later Reginald Marix flew a Sopwith Tabloid to Germany, dropping bombs on a zeppelin which was destroyed. However, his return flight was cut short owing to damage sustained in the attack and he was compelled to land 20 miles short of his base at Antwerp and complete his journey on a borrowed bicycle. He too was awarded the DSO for this action:

Flight Lieutenant Marix carried out a successful attack on the Düsseldorf airship shed during the afternoon of the 8th October. From a height of 600 feet he dropped two bombs on the shed, and flames 500 feet high were seen within thirty seconds. The roof of the shed was also observed to collapse. Lieutenant Marix's machine was under heavy fire from rifles and mitrailleuse and was five times hit whilst making the attack.

Charles also brought photographers Charles Henry Butler (known as Henry) and Gordon Thomson who were quick to discover the utility of aerial photography.

The aviators of Charles' No. 3 Squadron were equal to any of the Royal Flying Corps (RFC). The medal tally alone sets Charles' aviators apart. The despatch of his experienced squadron to the Dardanelles was a wise choice; they had proven themselves in the most difficult of circumstances and shown resolution in attacking heavily defended targets. They had an enigmatic leader who believed in air power and its ability to change the face of war.

John de Robeck was deeply concerned about the threat Turkish warships posed to his own troop transports transiting the Aegean in preparation for the landings. Turkish torpedo boat destroyers were based at the Aegean port of Smyrna astride the route from the port of Alexandria in Egypt to Mudros Harbour at Imbros. At 3 am on Easter Sunday, the day after Churchill's Air Department conference in London, *Ark Royal*, *Dartmouth* and *Usk* arrived off the entrance to the Gulf of Smyrna. Harry's seaplanes were ordered to conduct reconnaissance of the harbour and bomb any torpedo boats observed:

> No. 77 Pilot Lieutenant 'Bromo' Bromet; Observer Lieutenant Harry Strain
>
> Started in a nasty swell, which strained the chassis and injured the bomb dropping gear: stopped and repaired the chassis, taking the bombs into the nacelle—two were live!—and restarted. Batteries along the hillside on the south coast all contained high angle guns, and kept up a continuous fire. Proper A.A. guns on the hills behind Smyrna. There were three torpedo boats in the inner harbour, which came out as the seaplane approached, firing machineguns. One was attacked but dodged among the shipping, making accurate bombing impossible. Nearest bomb, thirty yards away, nearly hit a collier. Dropped the fourth bomb at a fort; just over in the water. Height 3,500 feet. Time: 1 hour 43 minutes.

Harry's private handwritten diary adds more colour than the officially typed flight log. He gave vent to his feelings later that night in his tiny cabin:

The Admiral wanted especially to smash the torpedo boats and the only way to do it seemed to be for the sea-planes to go in for 'frightfulness' and drop a few bombs on them. As soon as it was light (Easter Sunday too) my machine was got into the water. There was a nasty swell and our bombs were too low down in the water, and as we crashed from one swell to another the safety clips released and it was a miracle that we were not blown to Kingdom Come. I took the fuses out of the bombs very gingerly. I left 3 of the bombs, taking the other four in the nacelle with me.

Harry and Bromo were in a pusher seaplane. Bromo sat at the very front of the fuselage with his hands and feet on the flight controls while Harry sat immediately behind, cradling four 'live' 22lb bombs in his lap. It was an ideal aircraft for reconnaissance as they had uninterrupted views both forward and below with the engine situated behind them. Each bomb had a fuse cap in the nose, and if any one of the four had come into contact with something hard, their futures would have been bleak. Harry described the action:

Then we started and climbed well. We examined the shoreline for troops and guns and saw some new ship-ping, gaining height the whole way until we were nearly 3,500 feet and we needed it, for when we got within 15 miles of the city the alarm had been given—all the new batteries, AA guns, and big guns were loosed off. To those on *Ark Royal* 25 miles away it was a pretty show and somehow like a fleet action. Then we got over the harbour and I looked in vain for the torpedo boat—I had written a card 'I'm afraid the little blighter isn't here' and had handed it to Bromo in the front seat, when out from the inner harbour came not one but 3 Torpedo Boats all steaming at full speed. All the soldiers from the barracks and the esplanade kept up a constant fusillade of rifles, Maxim machineguns and shrapnel. But the little devils of torpedo boats underneath were dodging in sharp turns amongst the merchant shipping. I tried 3 bombs but did not get within 20 yards of my mark. As we were going out we had a pretty hot time because all the batteries had had time to alter the fusing of their shrapnel and readjust their mistakes and they got pretty close to us.

The seaplanes launched a total of five attacks against the three torpedo boats but all proved unsuccessful.

While Hamilton was in Cairo preparing himself for the difficult task ahead, de Robeck and his warships hit the enemy. The Turkish warship *Turgud Reis* (and her capable 9-inch guns) was lurking in the Marmara threatening the landings and so was listed as a high value target. Harry's seaplane flight made several bombing attempts in mid-April:

Mission No. 92 Wight No. 176

. . . proceeded to port of Gallipoli. Observed one battleship of the *Turgud Reis* class and three sailing ships in the bay south of Gallipoli. Attacked the battleship, one bomb fell 200 yards short. Also saw a gunboat and eight small craft lying on the other side of the straits . . .

During Hamilton's absence, de Robeck maintained his flag on *Queen Elizabeth*, allowing communication between both naval and army staff using SECRET signal cipher. They discussed the likely shape of the assault, with de Robeck informing the Admiralty on 25 March of his plans, including air attacks on Turkish supply depots at Maidos and vessels in the harbour at Channakale, and the conduct of reconnaissance and spotting duties against enemy artillery batteries.

De Robeck broadened his objectives to include a key aspect of Hamilton's emerging plan: a deception operation to convince General Liman von Sanders and his 5th Army Headquarters that the *coup de main* would be struck above the Bulair Lines in the very north of the peninsula. The concept of deceiving the enemy commander originated in a military appreciation 'Report of Landing Facilities Gaba Tepe and Cape Helles, Gallipoli Peninsula', which also recommended that aeroplanes should fly over Bulair 'so as to support the enemy in the theory that a landing is to be made in that direction'. This emerging deception plan was progressed with naval warships scouting the coastline of the Gulf of Saros and the Bulair Lines. *Ark Royal* also played her part, sent on 8 April to support the landing of Royal Marines on the island of Enos after a seaplane had conducted a low-level flight:

> Had a merry dinner with pilots from Samson's squadron—the first whisky and soda I have drank since Malta—after dinner we got the *Ark Royal* under way and went to rendezvous off Enos, where we undertook reconnaissance and reported it clear of troops and guns. Then the *Swiftsure* and *Majestic* sent in boats to explore the landing places (it is probably a blind). The Admiral wanted us to examine Gallipoli town for ships and drop bombs on them.

Picket boats conducted a reconnaissance of landing facilities while a seaplane circled lazily overhead. After its ruse over Enos, the seaplane flew over the Bulair Lines and the port of Gallipoli on the eastern side of the peninsula. Following this pantomime, de Robeck voiced his intentions to Churchill on 11 April, revealing that he would 'attempt to mystify him [the enemy] as to the main point of attack'.

The 'Report of Landing Facilities Gaba Tepe and Cape Helles, Gallipoli Peninsula' also called for Harry's and Charles' pilots and observers to fly reconnaissance missions examining the twisted ground from Gaba Tepe to Cape Helles to locate any Turkish artillery batteries likely to be concealed there. Harry and Bernard played a key role in providing Hamilton's expeditionary force with this vital intelligence.

On 9 April, Philip Mackworth and his No. 1 Experimental Kite Balloon Section aboard HMS *Manica* arrived off the coast of Gallipoli to assist in this search. It had been a mad rush to get the thing to Gallipoli and there had been no trials conducted to see whether this bizarre device actually worked. The balloon was still folded like an empty tent, defying belief that it might actually expand to 80 feet when pumped with 28,000 cubic feet of explosive hydrogen gas. On 16 April, the first day of its operation, Philip calmly fixed one or two holes then performed the balloon's test inflation before conducting the first successful flight. No. 1 Experimental Kite Balloon Section then reported itself 'battle efficient'. Looking to test this latest innovation in combat, *Manica* steamed off Gaba Tepe launching four prolonged flights, which first identified then targeted enemy camps and gun batteries.

While the balloon was slowly unfolding, Bernard finally came ashore at Tenedos. There he was confronted with a biblical scene from the days of the pyramids:

Watch working parties from the ships unloading our
stuff in splendid order. Five hundred seamen drag our
aeroplane cases up the temporary road from the beach
to the aerodrome. See and hear ships firing onto enemy
field guns on north shore Dardanelles. Collet, Pierse
[sic], and Commander are spotting.

Bernard and his tent-mate put up a bell tent and prepared
for flight operations:

(9 April) I spend morning joining up maps. I am given
charge of all maps and reconnaissance reports, and to
fly occasionally to verify and complete the maps etc.
First time in years that I have used any survey knowledge. It looks as if I will get all the information first
hand before even the admiral or the general staff. And
see most of the fighting too.

Hamilton's newly minted General Headquarters entered
Mudros Harbour on 10 April as First Class passengers
aboard the luxury liner RMS *Arcadian*. Hamilton met with
de Robeck before they drew up their separate orders. The
six seaplanes, the five aeroplanes operating on Tenedos and
the recently arrived balloon were all included in de Robeck's
naval orders for the landing. These were issued in the form
of a quality printed pamphlet sent to each ship on 12 April.
Hamilton published his army orders the next day. The general plan was to destroy the forts at the Narrows and secure
the Dardanelles to allow the naval squadron safe passage.
De Robeck's squadron was divided into several smaller
squadrons to support each of the landings. Under 'special
instructions' was a paragraph ordering Charles to spot for
the covering ships at Cape Helles and to respond to the

needs of the military officer commanding the landing. *Ark Royal* and *Manica* were both attached to the naval squadron supporting the ANZAC landing at Gaba Tepe. Separately, a single seaplane was directed to support the Royal Naval Division demonstration off Bulair, as part of the ongoing deception plan to fool Liman von Sanders. One seaplane was a small price to pay to give this pantomime landing some credibility.

Charles' squadron began work in earnest. His pilots and observers had clear objectives. Charles wrote:

> On 11 April a notable flight was made. This was our first attempt to locate all the trenches and gun positions at Helles and ANZAC. A fairly good result was obtained and a tracing was forwarded to the military authorities.

For Bernard, the work was less exciting. Sitting at his wooden desk in his tent, his maps hanging off an easel, he waited to question each man on completion of his mission:

> Start work immediately after breakfast joining up a further set of maps of Dardanelles for reconnaissance references. This should be the most interesting job of the expedition for I will know everything before the general. Everyone comes round for information. Spend whole day hard at it with observers making reports and recording results of spotting. Up late finishing reports which were typed at midnight. Sent copies of reports to Vice Admiral by orderly.

The aviators performed feats that were truly extraordinary. These men in their underperforming machines flew over the beach defences and returned with their bounty to where it was needed most. Reginald, Harry, Bromo, Herb and Charles identified trenches and fields of barbed wire simply by looking down from their aeroplanes. The accurate fixing of enemy camps, artillery batteries and entrenchments became priority intelligence requirements for Hamilton's staff. For a military commander, knowledge of enemy activity on the 'other side of the hill' was vital. And Hamilton had this intelligence confirmed on a daily basis.

Military planning defines the path a commander takes in order to achieve his objectives. Hamilton's planning in April 1915 was similar to our own Iraq planning. First, the objective was defined, then a means to achieve it was formulated that would take into account such constraints as terrain, weather and the enemy. In March, Hamilton's staff were supplied with 500 maps of Gallipoli in a series of three (1:40,000 scale) to assist with the planning process. These large, contoured topographical maps were printed with numbered red squares as a grid referencing system. This allowed identification and fixing of both topographical features and enemy defences. For instance, the Gaba Tepe promontory was fixed in artillery grid square 211 P. 1, which was an area of approximately 200 square metres.

Harry and Bernard typed air intelligence clarifying the Egyptian War Office intelligence bulletins, which were logged into unit intelligence diaries. Commanders were briefed on this reporting on a daily basis. Sergeant John McLennan worked in the ANZAC Headquarters Intelligence Section. John's diary records his concern over the state of the enemy defences: 'more aeroplane reports have been received and the map received along with them shows that the Turks have not been idle'. The headquarters staff were aware of emplacements, guns, lines of trenches and barbed wire, and their collective opinion was that Otto Liman von Sanders and his Turkish 5th Army had constructed capable defensive positions covering the beaches—except in the broken terrain north of Gaba Tepe.

Harry's and Bernard's typewriters were weapons, their metallic keys pounding information into the heads of Hamilton's staff aboard their luxury cruise liner. This is evident in Hamilton's concept of operations dated 13 April, which concluded that 34,000 enemy soldiers, comprising three Turkish divisions, had been identified on the peninsula. Hamilton's directions to Birdie and his ANZACs provide further evidence in the first paragraph:

SECRET

INSTRUCTIONS FOR G.O.C. A & N. Z. ARMY CORPS

General Headquarters

13th April 1915.

1. Information regarding the enemy.

The enemy holds the KILID BAHR Plateau in strength and is believed to have a number of troops concentrated in the neighbourhood of the ANAFARTA villages and MAIDOS. There may be two divisions (20,000 men) distributed in these areas. Gun emplacements have been located at KABA TEPE and NIBRUNESI POINT, but repeated air reconnaissances have failed, as yet, to disclose any guns.

2. Objective

A Landing in force is to be made by the A&NZ
Army Corps on the beach between Gaba Tepe and
FISHERMAN'S HUT. The objective assigned to the
Army Corps is the ridge over which the GALLIPOLI—
MAIDOS and BOGHALI—KOJADERE roads run,
and especially MAL TEPE.

While in Cairo and at Hamilton's behest, *Arcadian* had been
fitted with a lithographic press worked by contracted civilian
printers. This enabled distribution of his orders and printing of Harry's and Bernard's air reports. Multiple copies of
post-mission reports and map overlays were sent to each
of Hamilton's divisions, then onwards to subordinate units.

Amateur photographer Henry Butler was also one of
Charles' pilots. Henry flew 18 photographic missions,
apparently of his own volition, as there appear to be no surviving orders. Charles wrote:

> About this time [we were] told about the proposed land-
> ing, so we made every effort to get good photographs
> and drawings of all the beaches, with the positions of
> any defences.

At the operational level, Birdie's ANZAC Headquarters
learnt to value their eyes in the sky. Following their arrival
on 13 April in a string of 24 tramp steamers that processed
into Mudros Harbour, the senior officers who made up the
headquarters were briefed on Hamilton's orders to Birdie
and his ANZACs. The next day they conducted a beach
reconnaissance of Z Beach from the gunnery tower of HMS
Queen, steaming past Anzac Cove at five knots. Little could

be seen beyond the sandstone cliffs that framed a shingle beach. *Queen* then disembarked ANZAC's Intelligence Officer, General Staff Officer Grade 3 (Intelligence) Major Charles Villiers-Stuart, on the shore below Tenedos aerodrome. Charles Villiers-Stuart had taken the unusual step of asking to check the landing site from above.

Villiers-Stuart jumped from a picket boat and into the sea surging onto the beach. A muddy road wound up to a flattened area beyond the primary dune. The roar of aero engines made it quite clear that the line of bell tents defined the edge of an aerodrome. Villiers-Stuart, careful not to approach the strange biplanes that were in various states of undress (some had their cowlings pulled off to allow maintenance), turned to a naval rating for guidance.

Knocking on a tent flap prior to entry was ridiculous. So Villiers-Stuart followed military protocol. He cleared his throat, then saluted the middle-aged officer typing at his desk. Bernard looked up, stood up and saluted in return. A major's crown outranked the two gold stripes of a naval lieutenant. After polite introductions, a search for a signal (somewhere in the left-hand pile) and all was found to be in order. Flight Lieutenant Collet, DSO, was aware of the importance of his flight, and yes, they could begin as soon as they had finished the pre-flight briefing. A runner was sent to find Herb, who was making flight checks on a Maurice Farman biplane. Rubbing grease from his hands, Herb was introduced to the immaculately turned out major.

Herb Collet was an old hand. He was fiercely loyal to Charles Samson and followed his instructions as a point of honour. A list of Standing Instructions, with Samson's signature heavily penned at the bottom, was held in one hand as Herb gave a short, hair-raising brief on flight. It was a risky business. Biplanes often fell or rose sharply in mid-flight because of the various aerial currents that swept across land and sea. Further, his passenger should not be alarmed when he throttled back once they had clawed 300 feet of height so as to spare their (underpowered) engine from overheating. Sometimes the Renault engine coughed alarmingly, with a sudden drop in revolutions. Herb told Villiers-Stuart to ignore this event, as he would push the stick forward to keep the machine from stalling (or it would fall to the earth like a brick).

Herb continued his litany of the means of achieving instant death. The Renault had a nasty habit of cutting out in mid-flight. The Standing Instructions listed two solutions, one of which saw the pilot 'juggle the throttle in the hope that the Renault would pick up'. Nor was Villiers-Stuart to be a passive member of the flight; he had a role to play as well. As observer, his job was to reach under his wicker seat to the canvas floor of the cockpit and turn the petrol spigot clockwise. Sudden engine failure could be caused by the main petrol tap (located under the observer's seat) closing because of excessive vibration during flight. So while Herb pushed the control stick forward, and the Maurice Farman descended with a nose-down attitude, he, the major in the tailored uniform, had to put his head between his knees and . . . Villiers-Stuart was not looking forward to his maiden flight.

They walked across a muddy field to the biplane that sat like a giant dragonfly, its tail resting on a wooden box. It was a pusher (like Harry's seaplane) so the engine was mounted behind the aircrew. A skeleton of wood and bracing wire attached the wooden nacelle (or gondola) at the front to the tail at the rear. In between, at the point of balance, were the capricious Renault engine and its bat-like wooden blades. Unlike Harry's seaplane it had a pair of bicycle wheels with wooden spokes.

Leather flying jackets were folded on a pair of empty petrol cans. These they pulled on. Then, to Villiers-Stuart's astonishment, he was told to hang on to the empty tin. The squadron had been attempting to scrounge lifejackets from the fleet, but with all the sinkings, there were no spares available. The tin was the next best thing.

With slow guidance, like a child in his first dancing class, Villiers-Stuart placed each foot, in order, in various positions. Soon he was sitting in his chair. The upper and lower wings were spread behind him, giving him a lovely vista of his footprints below. Herb vaulted into place and began the incantation all pilots use to placate the gods of the air. First he moved the control column in a giant circle. In response, various pieces of the wing hinged up or down. Then he performed alternator checks and uttered some babble about oil temperature and pressure. Finally, the wooden propeller was spun by a mechanic and the engine roared into life. Herb directed the machine into the wind.

Wind. Cold. Tent rushing past. Then a lifting sensation and below the grey sea. Herb pushed back the throttle and climbed at a gentler rate over the sea towards the finger of land ahead. It was not unpleasant. Bumps here or there, a dropping of one canvas wing and a view of a mighty battleship. They flew through its coal smoke and towards the shoreline. Villiers-Stuart looked past Herb's head and shoulders to see a biplane circling over the land ahead. To his shock, the warship below fired its guns and, turning, he saw the grey toy disappear in spouts of flame. A few seconds' delay, then gouts of dirt erupted under the aeroplane up ahead. So this was spotting!

Herb lowered the left wing and Villiers-Stuart found himself on a bow bend, looking down into the Turkish fort of Sedd el Bahr at the very toe of the peninsula. Little pink faces looked up at him. Some were pointing up. A shriek, then an alarming bang above: anti-aircraft fire. Soon they were following the coast. Down below were onion fields cut by steep cliffs. Dirty lines cut through a farmer's holding—enemy trenches. Some were circular like defensible redoubts; some were in parallel lines to stop an advancing enemy. Some fields glittered, their crops tangles of barbed wire.

As they flew closer to Gaba Tepe they left the farmland behind. The patchwork of cultivation was overtaken by coarse bushland and crazy ravines. Gaba Tepe itself was an angry finger pointing into the sea. Its nose was a network of trenches. Herb seemed to know what he was doing. He was taking his passenger on a racecourse pattern over ANZAC's landing beach.

Villiers-Stuart had his map folded at the right place. The red squares of 212 and 214 framed Z Beach. A glint of metal below. Herb saw it too and they banked steeply. Mud. Fading brushwood. Four artillery pieces under a latticework of felled trees. Villiers-Stuart scraped his pencil from 212 L. 9 to M. 7 on his map. Herb continued, following the third inland ridge. A turn southwards and they tracked inland over the villages of Boghali and Kojadere. A division-sized encampment had already been reported, and there it was. Hutted encampments covered a quarter mile of cleared space with a further camp of 200 tents astride the road. The scale was breathtaking. Thousands of enemy soldiers scattered below. Horse lines. Mule lines. Limbered wagons. But this was known.

South of Gaba Tepe something new, perhaps constructed overnight. Two four-gun batteries could be seen dug into the ground as they approached from the north. Unbeknown to the gunners sitting inside, the wind had peeled back the cover exposing them to prying eyes from the air. The pencil scraped its course from P. 1 to O. 9 in red square 202. And then there was more. Clearly, these men had not paid attention to their orders; they must be new to the peninsula and the perils from the air.

More than an hour later they returned over the greying sea to their muddy home. Villiers-Stuart was exhausted. He was sweating despite the intense cold. His stomach was tense. His legs ached from attempting to gain purchase with his feet. The biplane joined the earth in a gentle swoop; he almost cried in his relief. The information he held in his hands was valuable and he was frightened that a cruel wind would carry it from his clenched fists. Now he could report the threat. Eight missions were flown that day. Herb completed the squadron's flight log in black ink:

April 14 M.F (2) Capt. Collet Pilot; Maj. Villiers-Stuart Passenger; 2.20-3.40; Military Reconnaissance to GABA TEPE.

Charles Villiers-Stuart had seen plenty that contradicted Hamilton's orders. On entering Bernard's tent he was welcomed with a cup of tea and a waiting typewriter. The result was a thorough intelligence report:

The following information has been obtained as the result of a scouting flight over GALLIPOLI PENINSULA with a military officer as observer:—

The following batteries and entrenchments were seen

One battery, with four large entrenchments (either roofed or empty) Square 212 L. 9 to M. 7.

Two four-gun batteries between P. 1 and O. 9 square 202.

All the coast strongly entrenched from 'g', square 193, to beyond GABA TEPE.

Field Work under construction in square 203. X. 8.

A strong defensive line runs along the high ground from the middle of square 194 to square 204. Q.

Two four-gun batteries. Square 193. O. 5.

One four-gun battery. Square 203. U. 2.

One four-gun battery. Square 204. R. 5.

Infantry Redoubt. Square 204. R. 8.

Camp at Square 225. M. 8.

On his return to his ship in Mudros Harbour, Villiers-Stuart filed his report in the ANZAC intelligence war diary: 'Aeroplane reconnaissance carried out by intelligence officer Army Corps. Information gained inlaid in sketch Map I.' All now knew that the ANZAC landing on Z Beach would be heavily contested. This changed the nature of the ANZAC assault from the 'open back door' represented in Hamilton's orders. A cold wind of apprehension swept through the headquarters.

Bernard did his duty. Later that night, under a pool of light from a kerosene lamp, he made his diary entry:

Henry Butler takes photographs from the air. Commander Samson and [Lieutenant] Osmond go spotting for HMS *Majestic*. Busy all day recording reconnaissances and writing them in on maps.

The situation was, in fact, far worse. More flights over the Gaba Tepe area from square 224 to square 195 (including Boghali and the port of Maidos) were conducted. The total number of Turkish tents climbed to 2817. Working on a figure of 12 soldiers a tent gave a potential total of 33,804 enemy soldiers camped in the direct path of the ANZAC advance from the beach. A Turkish camp of 400 tents (in square 203 T) hidden in an olive grove in the Peren Ovasi Valley increased yet again the estimates of the enemy size. This camp lay outside ANZAC's route but was of significant concern to Lieutenant General William Bridges in his planning for the landing of the Australian Division. It could hit his exposed right flank as his men advanced inland.

Meanwhile, life continued at Tenedos aerodrome with competing tasks juggled by Charles and his aviators:

> We were busily engaged from now onwards in spotting for the battleships and engaging shore batteries. We got some quite good results and several guns were hit. We were doing reconnaissance work in addition, and I made it a rule to carry bombs, and to drop them whenever a good target was seen. Thus I made economical use of my few pilots and aeroplanes, at the same time developing our full effort.

Harry and Bernard detailed the placement of enemy artillery batteries, fixing each against a grid reference with an estimate of the battery's arcs of fire. Their combined efforts told of 312 guns on the peninsula. Some 67 individual barrels were recorded on mapping, with 40 barrels capable of killing Australian soldiers as they sat inside their rowboats on their approach to the beach. Again, not included in this number was a mobile field artillery brigade identified in an artillery park outside the village of Boghali. These guns could be hitched to mules and dragged to face the enemy once he landed.

Sir Ian Hamilton peered at Henry's photographs on 15 April during his visit to Charles' aerodrome on Tenedos. He recorded the meeting in his breezy fashion:

> After lunch spent the best part of two hours with Samson and Keyes trying to digest the honey brought back by our busy aeroplane bees from their various flights over Gallipoli.

In Bernard's bell tent, Hamilton was presented with maps and photographs, which he took away with him and studied on *Arcadian*. Charles' impressions suggest that the photographs shocked Hamilton into saying something he would usually have kept to himself:

> I received visits at Tenedos from Sir Ian Hamilton and Sir Aylmer Hunter-Weston. They had a careful look at all our photographs, and thoroughly discussed the part we were to play in the 'landing'. I was greatly impressed by Sir Ian's remark that he expected to lose 50 per cent in casualties before he obtained a footing. Personally, as a result of all my constant flights over the peninsula, I thought the landing would be impossible.

Charles boasted to Hamilton that, were he to be given another 50 airframes, he could take the peninsula without a soldier having to land. Hamilton was helpless; aeroplanes were a scarce resource:

... the Gallipoli peninsula, being a very limited space with only one road and two or three harbours on it, could be made untenable ... So equipped [with aeroplanes] he reckons he could take the Peninsula by himself and save us all a vast lot of trouble.

Bernard completed a briefing pack containing two photographs of Sedd el Bahr fortress and maps with tracings showing the placement of trenches covering the landing beaches. It was another long day for him:

Called by sentry at 5 am after a terrible night of thunder and downpour. We are swamped out. Trudge down to aerodrome with orders for men. Trudge back again thoroughly wet through. Orderly comes at 2.30 for reports for Senior Naval Officer. Busy most of day digging drains around tent and camp. General Sir Ian Hamilton and others come up to see Commander. I gather from the interview that we are to go over to a new aerodrome at Cape Helles pretty soon, but my experience teaches that generals know very little about these things. They are merely fearless.

To be fair, Hamilton was typical of a generation of officers who had served in armies before the invention of powered flight, and he was probably viewing aerial photographs for the first time. He later recorded in the privacy of his cabin:

The photographs, etc., I have studied make it only too clear that the Turks have not let the grass grow under their feet since the first bombardment; the Peninsula, in fact, is better defended than it was ... Two of the Australian Commanding Officers dined and I showed them the aerial photographs of the enemy trenches, etc. The face of one of them grew very long; so long in fact, that I feared he was afraid, for I own these photographs are frightening.

Hamilton's grasp of this new form of intelligence changed the way he planned to execute the landings. He now sought to exploit a gap in enemy defences that Charles had found. Y Beach presented an opportunity to land below an unde-fended clifftop without being killed in the sea. It could be scaled, providing a flanking approach to the British objec-tive of Krithia. The day before the landing he requested an aerial photographic mission over Y Beach and photographs were taken to confirm that the clifftop remained unguarded. The photographic plates were quickly developed and sent directly to Hamilton, now on *Queen Elizabeth*. As the clifftop remained undefended, the amphibious assault at Y Beach went ahead as planned.

On *Ark Royal* Harry remained busy. His seaplanes were ordered to spot naval guns onto an important enemy ammunition magazine outside the village of Taifur Keui, midway between Bulair and Cape Helles. It was partially destroyed on 16 April with a seaplane spotting 14 shells of 9.2 calibre onto the No. 2 Magazine:

> For several days we have been roving about the Gulf of Xeros with the *Agamemnon*, *Lord Nelson*, and *Usk*— we have spotted *Aggy*'s gunfire onto a village with a supposed magazine—very successful as far as we are concerned but the *Agamemnon* shooting was so bad that after we had spotted her on she could not remain on the target.

This success was reported widely, even up the chain of command to London. A second attack by an aeroplane on 20 April struck the magazine, again resulting in 'some damage at Taifur Keui blowing up one of the magazines with a 100lb bomb'.

ANZAC planners used every scrap of information to get their men ashore alive. William Bridges and his Chief of Staff, Colonel Cyril Brudenell White, included Bernard's reports in their orders to their assaulting brigades. The first ANZAC orders set was published on 17 April with grid references and descriptions of enemy defences. Knowledge was shared.

ANZAC Headquarters had an affinity with the novelty of aircraft. Artillery staff met and discussed air support with the navy in a series of joint conferences on board *Queen Elizabeth*, resulting in the tasking of *Ark Royal* and *Manica* to support ANZAC's vulnerable flanks. ANZAC included in its Corps Operations Order No. 1 dated 17 April a drawn schematic 'diagram showing position and supporting ships and arrangements for Aerial Observation and Reconnaissance'. This single-page diagram shows *Manica* stationed opposite Gaba Tepe on the right flank and *Ark Royal* off the Fisherman's Hut on the left. Birdie and Bridges met Clarkee and Philip Mackworth to discuss flight operations. Then Harry was called:

> (21 April) In the evening just as I was having my cocktail before dinner a message came that I was to repair on board the military headquarters ship at once—I went, but the motor boat went slowly and by the time I got there everybody was at dinner and they kept a place for me among all the fat generals. It was a good dinner but I didn't have time to eat much as all asked me so many

questions that I had to talk all the time. Then we went up to the saloon and had a great pow wow as to what the seaplanes were to do during the coming landing. It was very interesting and apparently they depend upon us enormously—I hope to goodness that the weather is good.

At Z Beach the emphasis was on seizing the beachhead during the hours of darkness. The enemy gun batteries had to be captured by the first waves before they opened up with shrapnel in dawn's first light. Then ANZAC could be in a position to repulse an enemy counterattack on both flanks. Harry also felt the cold wind of fear:

We land 30,000 up by Gaba Tepe and from the camps, guns and trenches already observed we should have a pretty hot [chance] to make a good footing.

John de Robeck ordered the largest enemy camps destroyed. The camp threatening ANZAC's right flank in the Peren Ovasi Valley grew from a 'big camp about 400 tents 203 T' on 15 April to 700 tents four days later. Over the next three days, aerial reconnaissance identified four other enemy camps, including one of 450 tents and a smaller company bivouac guarding Z Beach:

SAILING ORDERS QUEEN ELIZABETH

18 April 1915

With BACCHANTE and MANICA with Tug you will proceed to rendezvous TALBOT at a position 6 miles west of Gaba Tepe at 4.30 am 19 April. On arrival you will take TALBOT under your orders and carry out bombardment of camps in neighbourhood of Gaba Tepe at daylight. The positions of the camps, as reported by aeroplane reconnaissance, which you should attack are:—

Camp of 700 tents at 203. T.

Camp of 450 tents at 194. P. to 195. Q.

Camp of 20 tents at 212. I. 9.

Camp of 20 tents at 224. N. 2.

Method of Attack

Ships are not to anchor or remain under fire from shore batteries. Range should first be obtained by a few ranging shots followed by a burst of rapid fire for about two minutes, using common or shrapnel shell set to burst or graze. Economy of ammunition is to be exercised, about 40 rounds being fired at each large camp and 20 at each small camp.

A seaplane has been ordered to be in position with TALBOT on camp 203 T at 6.30 am at which hour fire should be opened by BACCHANTE . . .

All was peaceful in the Turkish 27th Infantry Regiment camped in the shady olive grove. Dawn broke, welcomed by cooking fires and bubbling pots of lentil soup. Caught in the flare of early light was a large sausage-shaped balloon suspended against a backdrop of heavy grey clouds. For the two gunnery officers in the wicker basket the camp appeared as fields of mushrooms. The tents stood out sharply against the olive trees and earthen paths tramped by their inhabitants. Orders were spoken over a telephone; then the mushrooms were flattened. It was as though a wilful child had kicked and squashed the mushrooms into the red earth.

Official artist Herbert Hillier was confined to roaming *Manica*'s deck. This was no time for paintbrushes and gouache. Not wishing to waste the opportunity, he borrowed binoculars to observe the events unfolding around him:

> 0350hrs Gallipoli. Preliminary bombardments and reconnaissance. We are spotting gunfire for *Bacchante* trying to draw fire from the Turkish concealed batteries. Our fire is returned from some enemy batteries, but only a very small extent of those really there. In some places we can see newly made lines of Turkish trenches which are so easily discernible that our experts label them duds—cut to draw away from the real trenches and emplacements. So no shells wasted on those.

Official reports on this unequal engagement reached Hamilton:

> I believe the *Bacchante* today sent some shells onto the camp of 700 tents which is reported to be in the valley between Maidos and Gaba Tepe. There was a tremendous scattering of Turks.

John de Robeck now ordered Charles to attack the supply depots at Maidos. The squadron bombed Maidos in daylight, mustering all five serviceable aeroplanes:

April 23rd saw our first big raid. Five of us went off to attack Maidos, where large numbers of Turkish troops were quartered. We dropped seven 100lb and six 20lb bombs with fairly good effect.

A total of 840lb of bombs was dropped on the busy dock-side with the happy result that shipping and other traffic was temporarily suspended during daylight in the final days before the landing. A report of the bombing raid was sent to the Admiralty, recording that 'five planes had done excellent work and it has been of great value to our future operations'.

Harry's and Charles' constant flights were taking their toll on the enemy. Colonel Kannengiesser, staff officer to General Liman von Sanders, gave orders that all defensive works were to be constructed at night. Movement of large units would be by night march to conceal them from the hostile aviators circling above, namely 'the English, who, most indiscreetly, watched us with their aeroplanes and captive balloons until they could almost look into our trouser pockets'. The Turkish Air Service replied. A battle escalated between the two with Charles' squadron conducting its first anti-aircraft patrol on 2 April. On 16 April, the Rumpler bombed the aerodrome on Tenedos and repeated the 'hate'. Bernard wrote, two days later:

> (16 April) German aeroplane flies over and drops bombs, hits nothing. Warner's firing with 12-pounder anti-aircraft very erratic.

> (18 April) German aeroplane flies directly over our camp at 7.30 am at about 6,000 feet and drops three bombs, but missed us—no-one was hurt, the nearest being 20 yards away. Richard Davies gives chase

but never catches up. Richard and Herb go again and they did some damage to enemy aeroplane sheds near Channakale.

Destroying air assets on the ground is the most effective means of conducting offensive air operations. The Turkish pilots had a firm grasp of this concept. Charles' heated reaction to this attack was immediate, with three air patrols and two retaliatory raids sent to bomb the Turkish aerodrome. Six 100lb bombs were dropped on the enemy aerodrome behind Channakale.

The attack by Charles' aviators on the enemy aerodrome was devastating, with a burning shed collapsing on top of a grounded Albatros. But the Rumpler escaped damage. Fuel and stores were burnt in the raid, which then placed restrictions on flight operations. Petrol was difficult to procure; there were fears that the aeroplanes would be grounded unless a supply could be transported illegally by rail through Bulgaria. For the moment civilian supplies were requisitioned for military use. One advantage of a horse- and bullock-drawn army was that there was less competition for distillate. But the Turkish Air Service was effectively grounded until after the landings as it was now reduced to one serviceable airframe and vital supplies had been burnt. By default Charles had achieved 'air superiority'. Erich Serno returned to Istanbul appointing *Leutnant* Preusner as commander in his absence. A nucleus of efficient aircrew was forming: *Kapitan Leutnant* Hussein, a Turkish naval officer, proving a dependable observer, and *Leutnant* Frank Siedler, an efficient and aggressive pilot.

While the ANZACs planned a silent night attack on Z Beach, the British 29th Division was going in at dawn, landing on five beaches—S, V, W and X, and the clifftop at Y. They also knew what they were up against. Captain Creighton worked in Major General Sir Aylmer Hunter-Weston's Divisional Headquarters and later described his thoughts:

> It seems a perfectly desperate undertaking. The aerial reconnaissance reports acres of barbed wire, labyrinths of trenches, concealed guns, Maxims, and howitzers everywhere. The ground is mined. In fact everything conceivable has been done. Our men have to be towed in little open rowing boats to land in the face of all of this.

On the day before the landings, Charles' aeroplanes conducted four missions in the afternoon once the weather had cleared. Henry took photographs of the clifftops above Y Beach. All dealt with the coming action differently. Bernard, a happily married man in his mid-40s, thought of family:

> Thinking of home and getting desperate about having no letter. Wondering if Vi and the children are all right. Wondering if poor father is better or worse. Wind dying down: possibly the landing will take place tomorrow. Signal comes at dinner time that the landing will commence at sunrise tomorrow. Go to bed early. Suppressed excitement all around.

Both a seaplane from *Ark Royal* and *Manica*'s kite balloon were ordered to spot naval gunfire onto the Gaba Tepe garrison and conduct a final reconnaissance of Z Beach. The seaplane was unable to rotate (take off) due to the choppy seas, but observation from the balloon found no significant changes to enemy preparations. Herbert Hillier wrote:

Having now ourselves seen practically the whole of the coast on the Aegean side of the Gallipoli Peninsula, we cannot imagine whereabouts the troops can possibly land there. 'Action Stations' again off Gallipoli. Our last skirmishing action before the great battle. This being over satisfactorily we beat about the Aegean until keeping our rendezvous, time and place, when all is truly in the melting pot. A calm sea and a beautiful evening, moon only about half full but too bright for our liking, while it lasted. Then dark enough. In the night troops from Tenedos are on their way here, and ANZAC from Mudros.

Both ships belayed sea anchors in the evening in preparation for being 'on station' before dawn. Harry reflected on his experiences thus far:

> . . . there are some operations in which one has a sensation of almost Olympian omnipotence; spotting for a battleship is one. I spotted for *Queen Elizabeth*, then the very last word in concentrated power, with her eight 15" guns and a complement of a thousand men. Yet she looks like a toy down there; a marionette to answer my directions. I signal to open fire on a pre-arranged target. There is a flash, a cloud of smoke enveloping her, then a pause which seems never-ending until suddenly, ten miles away, a dark brown cloud shoots into the air. Death, havoc and destruction perhaps, but to me, on high, a purely impersonal matter requiring a spotting correction to get her onto her target; what happens to the pygmies down below does not enter my head— until the watches of the night.

CHAPTER 3

Flying over the bloody beaches: 25 April 1915

Three warships steamed past on the port side of *Ark Royal*. Through his binoculars, Harry focused on the irregular shapes of soldiers standing along the railings. His attention was caught by a hatch opening, casting a man in silhouette, a rifle slung over his shoulder. Harry looked again at the luminous dial of his watch; it was now a little past 2 am, 25 April 1915. The waiting before a flight is always the hardest part. Harry was conflicted with waves of excitement and nausea. His leg was also aching, the skin a mottled blue from frostbite. This was no scene from a Shakespearean play, 'no touch of Harry in the night'. Just fear, some pain, and the need to mask his inner feelings from his messmates.

Ark Royal remained at sea anchor, swinging gently five miles due west of Gaba Tepe. The moon still hung as a threatening presence keeping the invasion force below the visual horizon. The warships must not be seen by Turkish sentries on land. Now Harry sensed that more men had entered the darkened bridge; the greenish glow from the binnacle was hidden by an interloper into this private world. In the darkness he could not tell the identities of those newly arrived on the bridge; all lights had been extinguished to hide the presence of the ships from their enemies on land. Orders were passed in whispers; tension covered the men on duty like a suffocating blanket.

Harry had no business on the bridge; he held no watch-keeping certificate. But he had an excuse to stand with Clarkee and the lookouts, his double duty as the Intelligence Officer providing him a ready pretext. Clearly the three warships, *Queen*, *London* and *Prince of Wales*, were steaming towards Z Beach on time. Harry enjoyed the privilege of information; he knew that the first wave of ANZAC soldiers was soon to row themselves towards the shores of Gallipoli.

The men standing along the railing were from Colonel Ewan Sinclair-MacLagan's 3rd 'All Australian' Brigade. They comprised the covering force, ordered to row ashore in the first wave. The men had another hour to kill before they climbed into the rowboats wagging behind the wakes of the three warships. Harry saw the boats as lengths of sausages, strangely white against the darkness of the sea.

The corridor down to the wardroom was unusually busy. Officers' servants carrying bulky leather coats made their way to the flight deck in convoy. All five available seaplanes were rostered for duty—the ship's entire complement of aircrew would fly today. With a polite nod Harry squeezed past, making for the wardroom door, immediately assaulted by the warm fug of pipe smoke, cigars and alcohol as he entered the confined space. The officers were all up, unable to sleep. Four pilots were concentrating on a game of cards. A pile of drachmae and oddly shaped coins explained their interest. The other three observers were talking in a quiet corner, an open bottle of Napoleon Brandy their subject. Harry joined this group, welcomed with smiles and nods of recognition. A grimy glass appeared for his personal use. The bottle made its rounds. Talk was absurd; it changed at whim, punctuated by coughs of laugher. They had all flown over Gallipoli. Each had his pet stories of making it through. Harry still had the crowning tale with 48 bullet holes punctured through the fabric of his airframe. The door slowly opened. All turned. The steward spoke solemnly, 'Gentlemen, compliments of the flight commander and would you all please make your way to the flight deck. The first seaplane is ready to be hoisted.'

All the officers rose. They were an odd assortment: tall, short, rake thin and happily corpulent. They were united as a group by their navy uniform jackets. Gold loops on their sleeves denoted rank: two thick rings for a lieutenant, one ring for a sub-lieutenant. A figure of a bird—in the shape of a goose in flight—told that all belonged to the RNAS. Each pilot found his observer and, like lovers, they walked through the door into the corridor beyond in pairs. Joe Kilner and his observer were rostered for the first flight. Harry, partnerless, was the last to leave, knowing that his pilot, Flight Lieutenant Whitehead, was waiting for him in the hangar. Theirs was to be the third seaplane up.

The hangar was a large, well-lit compartment in the bowels of the ship. The time was now 3.32 am and Seaplane 161 was ready, its wings folded like a butterfly's. Five grey butterflies dozed under the closed overhead hatch waiting for the hook to be lowered and the machines winched out in turn into the darkness and placed gently on the surface of the sea. Pilots and observers carefully probed around their butterflies ensuring that oil and petrol levels were at maximum and the bracing wires were stretched at the correct tension. The butterflies were toothless; no bombs were attached to the racks beneath the lower wing.

Harry's orders were clear. *Ark Royal*'s seaplane flight was to patrol the northern end (left flank) of the landing beach. Intelligence from some 170 previous flights over the peninsula had confirmed the presence of an enemy division bivouacked outside the village of Boghali. Harry had flown over this pretty village, a tumble of tiny terracotta roofs in a sea of olive groves. Along the coastal road, hundreds of tents and upturned faces told of the threat. By simple calculation these enemy soldiers were only two hours' march from the landing beach.

Sir Ian Hamilton's Mediterranean Expeditionary Force began its amphibious assault on the heavily defended Gallipoli shoreline in the early hours of Sunday morning, 25 April. In reality, this meant heavily burdened soldiers clambering from ships, down cargo nets into rowing boats below. Sitting in order, they rowed towards beaches to be met by an enemy defending his home.

While the armada eddied at its disembarkation points out to sea, cloaked in a veil of silence, Charles' aviators attempted to find sleep in bell tents beside a muddy aerodrome. The aircrew aboard *Ark Royal* and *Manica* were already at their stations.

The ANZAC covering force was the first to land in a silent night assault, the boats grounding on the shingle of Z Beach at 4.20 am. An hour later—at dawn—and along the breadth of the Gallipoli Peninsula, heavy explosions hammered across the grey sea. All at once, warships shelled Turkish trenches at the toe of the peninsula to assist the landing of the British 29th Division on X, W, V, S and Y beaches at Cape Helles. Warships also pounded the Asiatic shore to assist a French 'feint' landing at Kum Kale, and further up north at Bulair to add drama to the Royal Naval Division 'demonstration' at the neck of the peninsula.

The gale of the previous days had abated overnight leaving a glassy smooth sea on that Sunday morning. Along the coastal fringe a heavy mist lay offshore, concealing the southern toe of the peninsula. The mist also lingered in the deep valleys behind Z Beach, surrounding the dominant terrain of Sari Bair Ridge, Chunuk Bair and Hill 971. By mid-afternoon the weather had closed in, bringing rain in the evening. Wind strength and sea states allowed full use of all aeroplane types including seaplanes, although visibility over land was obscured.

Each air unit had its own responsibilities, with Harry's seaplane flight and Philip's kite balloon supporting the ANZAC fight at Z Beach, as distinct from Charles' No. 3 Squadron, which supported the British assaults on X, W, V, S and Y beaches and the French feint at Kum Kale. John de Robeck placed each air unit under direction of each beach lodgement, resulting in 'shorter' reporting chains. ANZAC Headquarters, with direct support from Rear Admiral Cecil Thursby's 2nd Naval Squadron, was able to request changes to its air support as the day progressed into a nightmare.

Missions were conducted from first light until after sunset. Harry's seaplane flight, Philip's balloon and Charles' aviators spotted for the supporting warships, sending heavy navy shells crashing onto enemy artillery batteries and trenches. The air plan for the amphibious assault had three clear and simple objectives. The first was to keep aircraft above the beaches throughout the day to fight off the Rumpler and to keep enemy artillery fire to a minimum. The second was to provide naval gunfire correction in the morning until Allied artillery had been landed. This was extended into the afternoon as few guns were unloaded across the Cape Helles landing beaches or at Z Beach owing to an effective Turkish defence. The third objective was to reconnoitre inland for the movement of Turkish reserves and provide warning of any counterattacks. All the aviators worked hard to meet these objectives throughout 25 April until last light. The first and third objectives were achieved, while the second met with only partial success.

Hauptmann Erich Serno's 1st Aircraft Company at Channakale remained effectively grounded. The destruction of stores and the loss of the Albatros represented a significant drop in capability. They were unable to fly on the day of the landings. Given that they had flown four missions during the 18 March naval attack, this told that problems with logistics—spares, oil and petrol—had an immediate impact on operations. The RNAS was equally vulnerable.

Hamilton's placement on *Queen Elizabeth* gave him access to reporting from aircraft on the emerging shape of the battle. Air reconnaissance reports from all the landing zones were picked up by the flagship's signals department. Hamilton had a view of the beaches from the gunnery tower and from descriptions sent by his aviators. The communications plan between the air service (the RNAS, *Ark Royal*'s aircraft and *Manica*'s balloon) and General Headquarters had been formalised in a series of conferences on *Queen Elizabeth* prior to the landings. Provision was made for a radio network connecting ships, aircraft and shore operations, with *Queen Elizabeth* managing the radio net and procedures that were outlined in a pamphlet entitled 'Signal Organisation for Combined Operations'. Commander Cottrell, a member of de Robeck's staff on the flagship, was responsible for both telegraphic and intelligence duties, a position that facilitated the passage of intelligence information following its receipt on board.

Provision was further made for the communication of air service signals that allowed 'messages of extreme urgency' to be communicated directly to Hamilton's staff.

The air service task load surged to a total of 26 missions on 25 April. No. 3 Squadron was ordered to keep two aeroplanes aloft in support of the 29th Division and French landings across their six designated beachheads. This was achieved with 16 missions flown throughout the day. *Ark Royal* and *Manica* were ordered to keep the balloon and a single seaplane flying over Z Beach throughout the daylight hours. This task was also accomplished, with seven seaplane missions and the kite balloon up from before dawn until after last light. Harry was shot at as his seaplane flew over Hill 971 during a counterattack by the Turkish 19th Division. Sopwith 922 was 'parcelled out' from *Ark Royal* to the warship *Doris* to support the Royal Naval Division's demonstration off Bulair, and flew over the pantomime landing and the port of Gallipoli in both the morning and afternoon. Harry recorded:

Z Beach

Sunday, 25th April, 1915

Battle of the landings—A.N.Z.A.C.

Dawn, followed by the most glorious sunrise I have ever seen. But on this morning the moment is very tense, such as cannot happen very often in a lifetime. This great assault, [on] which our nation is staking so much. We have been cruising more or less about this locality, in a desultory sort of way, since midnight. Waiting for 'the boys' to arrive: and then waiting for this light, as without it we can do nothing. Ever since the darkness began to thin out a little, the stuttering rifle fire, more and more punctuated with enemy shrapnel bursts, shows us clearly enough where the killing is going on.

The ANZAC landing at Z Beach, north of Gaba Tepe, avoided heavy casualties with the use of surprise to seize its beachhead. The first wave of the covering force landed relatively unscathed, but the boats became intermingled in the darkness and landed across a small cove, later named Anzac Cove. The covering force's use of darkness had one advantage in that enemy artillery could not fire until after dawn, allowing the first boatloads of 1500 men to land without the deadly attrition caused by shrapnel. Harry's seaplane flight conducted seven missions throughout the day, the first at 5.45 am. Similarly, the kite balloon first ascended at 5.21 am, Philip waiting impatiently for sufficient light to allow him to rain explosives on any Turkish infantry foolish enough to be seen by him in his commanding position over Gaba Tepe. He completed his first flight at 2.20 pm. Herbert Hillier set up an easel on *Manica*'s lower bridge, his keen eyes trained on the action and determined to capture the battle in watercolour. As he painted, he kept a running log:

> About 5.20 am. The first boatloads of the Australians and New Zealand troops have landed here in the darkness and others are following as quickly as they can be got ashore. The 3rd Brigade is attacking here, 1500 troops under Colonel MacLagan with the 1st and 2nd Brigades following close after the 3rd. The men being taken from the transports to the shore by destroyers join in just as fast as they can touch land.

Daylight reinforcements, including the second wave that was landed from destroyers, were hit by accurate shelling. The ANZAC assault was stalled by enemy counterattacks from Boghali and the Peren Ovasi Valley and a fierce fight ensued for control of the second ridge. This lasted throughout the day. The swiftness of the Turkish response caused command difficulties as ANZAC units were thrown into action as soon as they landed. Reserves were being eaten up:

> It takes longer to get right into the shore than one expects at first sight. They are getting under heavy enemy fire before they even get into shallow water, especially rifle fire, which is very fierce. The Turks have swarmed across to the spot in great force. We are spotting from *Bacchante*. The enemy gunfire is getting very heavy now, as the light increases. And it is now light enough for guns to get to work better. Our expert spotters have been ready, up in the captive balloon, for some time now, waiting for sufficient light to direct the gunfire onto the right targets. *Queen Elizabeth* has passed close by to our port side, her big guns bearing on the land but not firing. The Commander in Chief and Staff are aboard her, and she is turning to take up a position further south.

Communication across the broken and twisted nullahs (dry watercourses) improved considerably once Australian signallers had belayed telephone lines between Divisional Headquarters on the beach and brigade positions on the ridgelines. They did so under extreme conditions—this is a story in itself. A detachment of Australian signallers (radio operators) boarded *Queen Elizabeth* to assist with communications on the other end of the radio net. Within an hour of the landing ANZAC was able to report, via radio, its success in taking the beach. Hamilton's headquarters war diary recorded:

> 4 a.m. QE got under way at IMBROS, reached SEDD EL BAHR 4.30 am and 5.10 am heavy firing was reported off Cape Helles. QE proceeded on and arrived off KABA TEPE at 5.20 am. At 5.35 am QUEEN (HQ Lt Gen. BIRDWOOD) reported 4,000 men had been landed at Z Beach. Heavy rifle fire was in progress about this time on the slopes of SARI BAIR and at 5.45 am some shrapnel was seen to fall in neighbourhood of BACCHANTE.

The Australian 1st Division was forced to fight off a spirited Turkish attack by Colonel Sefik Aker's 27th Regiment on its right (southern) flank. Then a concentrated assault from Mustafa Kemal's 19th Division was launched from over the high ground of Hill 971 on the left. The New Zealand and Australian Division was then thrown in to reinforce the line as each new threat arose. By evening they were exhausted, the infantry continuing its fight for the seaward slopes of the second ridge. Despite its success in taking the beachhead under cover of darkness, ANZAC did not gain any of its stated objectives, including the covering force's holding position on Third Ridge. The men of ANZAC were to remain in this position until the August breakout.

Harry flew over Anzac Cove twice. His first flight had a far greater impact than he could have realised and it is worth reconstructing these events from a range of diaries and official reports:

Off Gaba Tepe—we lay for the night off Imbros then went over in the dark towards Gaba Tepe, all the transports and fleet for this particular landing moving more or less at the same time. The first landing was made before dawn with comparatively little opposition, though there must have been some for we heard the rattle of small arms and found a boat floating about stove in, and a man's haversack and pocket book. As soon as it was dawn Joe Kilner's machine No. 161 was got up and off she went, but was very soon in the water again. One of the Schneider Cup machines (single seater) was also sent away but it also came down with a missing engine (Pussy Garnett). Then we were sent off, Whitehead and myself, in 176 and we prowled over the left flank to spot *Majestic* onto anything in the way of batteries but there was nothing showing though [there was] a hot fire on the other flank which was met by *Triumph*, being spotted by the balloon. I reported the *Turgud Reis* firing from over Maidos Bay and *Triumph* was ordered to fire on the *Turgud Reis* which soon changed her position. It was amusing in a way to be allotted to one flank— Whitehead was always wandering down to where the landing was going on and it was interesting enough there Heaven knows to keep me stuck there. They were met with a very stiff opposition and by heavy gunfire from the south flank which the balloon was supposed to be spotting—but we could do no good there as we were not allowed to direct the fire over our own troops (a policy with which I had heartily disagreed and which we now abandoned by virtue of necessity)—thereupon Whitehead went down there. I waved him away onto the left flank again and for 2 hours we prowled over the left flank reporting by W/T everything we could see of importance. Then when we were about 3 miles inland the engine gave up the ghost, but fortunately recovered sufficiently for us to struggle out of harm's way, the machine was badly damaged by rifle fire. I signalled as we were coming out and another machine was sent to take our place, and one of the tabloids was sent for a fast prowl to see if anything was moving on the roads further than we could see. However, he couldn't see anything more than I had reported, we were both handicapped by a low lying morning mist which obscured most things almost straight below one. Somehow too the ships and the fire seemed a secondary show, the real actors in the drama were these tiny ants on the shore and the little water beetles going to and fro between the ships and the beach.

Ark Royal's official flight log added:

No. 115 Wight No. 176

Pilot Lieutenant Whitehead; Observer Lieutenant Strain.

A thick cloud, low lying haze over the ground, interfering with observation. At 3,000 feet seaplane circled over left flank, intending to spot the *Majestic* on to any suitable target, but no movement could be seen. All the firing was from the right flank, where the *Manica's* balloon was spotting. Reported the *Turgud Reis* and two destroyers with ferry boats in the Dardanelles, and *Triumph* was in consequence to open fire at her, soon causing her to shift billet. Reported a number of trenches. Engine began to miss when the machine was well inland, causing a hurried return. Machine damaged. Chiefly in one float and the tail by rifle fire. Time: 1 hour 40 minutes.

Ark Royal's ship's log provides the timing for these events:

H.M.S. 'Ark Royal', Sunday the 25th day of April 1915

From, To, or At Kephalo, Gaba Tepe

1.30 Weighed anchor shaped course N12E 11 knots

3.10 Stopped up as requisite for seaplanes

3.15 A.S. Ratings employed about seaplanes

4.0 Destroyers commenced landing Expeditionary Force C. South N34E

5.17 Cap'n Kilner left in 161 5.25 Returned. Oil pump damaged.

5.43 Lt Whitehead left in 176 for reconnaissance flight over west line etc.

6.50 Lt Kershaw in 1438 left.

6.52 Lt Kershaw landed

7.22 Lt Whitehead landed

Harry flew over Anzac Cove from 5.43 am to 7.22 am. What he did not know is that his report on the lurking Turkish

warship *Turgud Reis* had been sent by radio to John de
Robeck and Hamilton on the flagship *Queen Elizabeth*. The
General Headquarters diary tells a story of ANZAC suc-
cess—with the enemy warship the only blight on the plan:

> 6 a.m. At 6 am enemy ship was reported by balloon
> to be on square 205 J SE of MAIDOS raising steam,
> at 6.15 am a returning destroyer reported good pro-
> gress on Z Beach and 300 casualties up to date. At 6.42
> Australian Brigade were making good progress up the
> hill. At 7.12 TRIUMPH ordered open fire on Square
> 205 J.

The records indicate that Harry's signalling was relayed or
picked up directly on board *Queen Elizabeth*. With Harry's
seaplane losing height, only harassing fire was sent in the
direction of *Turgud Reis*. Harry was not in a position to
linger owing to the pressing need to scrape over the high
ground (971 feet) that surrounded the coastal fringe and the
safety of the sea. But what little fire was sent in the direction
of the *Turgud Reis* was sufficient to persuade the enemy warship to seek shelter.

Manica was stationed on the right flank nearest the
Turkish garrison on Gaba Tepe. Philip Mackworth and a
gunnery officer climbed over the wicker sides and into their
eagle's nest at 5.17 am. They had maps, binoculars and a
basket with a coffee flask and rounds of ham sandwiches
wrapped in greaseproof paper. They had learnt from previous experience to eat once airborne—not because they
were hungry, but to prevent airsickness resulting from the
awful swinging momentum of the balloon. After checks to
ensure that the telephone was functioning, the balloon was
slowly belayed aloft. This was the most dangerous part.

If the balloon snagged on the superstructure, or a cinder from the coal smoke that belched from the funnel found a leak, then they were done for.

Once above the ship the tension eased. The steam winch belayed more cable allowing the balloon to wag behind *Manica* like a poodle's coiffed tail. The balloonists were soon swinging in the basket 3000 feet above the landing enjoying a panoramic view over the peninsula. The valleys were still cloaked in grey mist; the ridgelines ran before them like wave tops. The landing continued below them. Seven Beagle Class destroyers ferried the second wave of the covering force from the decks of *Queen*, *London* and *Prince of Wales*. The first wave, which had landed in the night, had already scaled Plugge's Plateau, dived into the valley beyond, and was emerging on the exposed crest of the second ridge. Their sleeves were rolled up, according to orders, to assist with identification from the air and from the gunnery towers of the prowling warships.

The mist presented a problem. At 6 am Philip and his gunnery officer reported by telephone that *Turgud Reis* was preparing for action. Steam and a dirty smudge of smoke gave her position away. Then a gun, literally at their feet, began firing from Gaba Tepe. Its position was identified as square 211 P. 3. *Triumph*'s guns smothered the position in shellfire; the enemy gun fell silent. Then *Turgud Reis* appeared on the other side of the peninsula off the port of Maidos, her sides consumed in smoke as she fired a broadside. Her 11-inch shells arced over the peninsula and fell into the sea just short of three transports loaded with soldiers. The grey water erupted into 100-foot geysers. In the wicker basket high above, the phone was whipped from its bracket and the Turkish ship's position in square 205 J once again called in. *Turgud Reis* shifted position. Now they could see a seaplane circling; then *Triumph* responded with the seaplane's observer directing the bearing for the shot. Its guns belched flame. Philip gazed at the enemy warship through his binoculars. His gunnery officer held the map and telephone. A ridge just inland erupted. Too short. Corrections were made, another salvo was fired, but *Turgud Reis* had moved off, seeking the shelter of the intervening ridges. Her new position meant that she was unable to bring her guns to bear on the transports. A respite had been gained, as recorded in Hamilton's war diary:

> 8.39 Australians reported capture of ridge 400 square 224 and advancing extending their right towards KABA TEPE. 3 Krupps guns captured in Square 224. Disembarkation proceeding satisfactorily and 8,000 men landed.

Flashes from rifles on the right flank—the balloon's area of responsibility—told that ANZAC was in contact with the enemy. The destroyers had unloaded their crowded decks at the base of the 400-foot plateau. The doll-like figures ran up its brushwood slopes to occasionally appear in breaks in the foliage. A four-gun battery was marked on the map from earlier air reconnaissance reporting; it was captured by the 3rd Brigade before it had a chance to open fire.

By 9 am artillery muzzle flashes told of something else—that Colonel Sefik Aker's attack was developing. Orange pencil sticks of flame licked from Third Ridge. A 23-year-old private from Sunshine on the outskirts of Melbourne recorded the landing in his diary later that evening. John Martin Fisher was a devout Roman Catholic who had enlisted in 7th Battalion, 2nd Infantry Brigade. He had waded from his rowboat before climbing into the fight on Second Ridge:

Grabbing what was practically my first meal since Saturday night. Yesterday we were allowed three minutes to have as many hard biscuits as we could and imagine how many hard biscuits you can eat in that time. Well, we got onto a destroyer and sailed as far inshore as possible and then took to smaller boats. I was in the first and pulled about 10 yards away when we were saluted with a shrapnel shell which struck the destroyer and several lads on deck. Then they rained ones on us till we landed. But, fortunately, their elevation was too high. Had to land up to our knees in water. A lad was lying on the beach who I thought might be just wounded, but found after inspecting him that he was dead with half his face blown away. Well, we fixed bayonets and started after the enemy and the country, which was very hilly and covered with scrub, made it very difficult work. Gotten tough with them about noon when the fun began, in fact, where I was on the right flank, it was hell's own work. Shrapnel bursting over us, machine guns pouring their deadly fire in and the explosive rifle bullets exploding all around us. Their work was deadly and the sights of some of our lads a nightmare you read about. They got right around us, enfiladed us with bullets flying everywhere. Then occurred a scene which I shall never forget and makes me shudder when I think of it. Was lying alongside a lad named Davis when something solid hit me in the face and splattered all over me. I looked and found a piece of his skull the size of my hand alongside me; poor chap he never moved. The sight upset me and I stood up to get a better view determined to avenge that shot. I fired one when an officer said 'Well lads, we are in a very tight corner but we'll die back to back, fix bayonets.'

Was still standing and in the act of drawing my bayo-net when something hit me in the hip and I fell. [2 pm annotation] A bullet had gone through my water bottle (letting out the water which I had been so careful not to touch) and the fleshy part of my leg, coming out on the inside. Well, I never expected to get out of that alive. Believing our retreat to be cut-off, and if I was to die, it was to be while fighting. So I fixed my bayonet while lying on the ground and some Lance Corporal pulled me up and helped me back with them, for we intended reinforcing a position in the rear. One chap took my rifle but I soon got it back again. We were in a gully into which the enemy had been pouring shrapnel, and I found it impossible for me to go with the others. I got that way with the pain I was suffering that I lay down on my face alongside a waterhole to wait for the finish.

But one thing put that out of my head. My dear Nina flashed before me, she who was waiting so patiently and with so much faith for my return; then I determined at all costs to get back to the beach. For two and a half hours I fought my way up steep hills and down gullies, through the thick scrub which pulled my puttees off. I was thinking only of her who is my only hope and to whom the life I was trying to save belongs. My leg was getting stiff and in spite of such exertion, getting cold. One chap who was giving me a hand wanted several times for me to rest, but I was afraid that if I stopped the leg would get stiffer and would not be able to move. So with the help of God I kept moving, where to at first I don't know, but providence guided me safely to the beach where, with hundreds of others, I had my wound dressed. After waiting about an hour, I was put aboard a kind of lighter and the sights of some of the poor fellows were just awful. They, who a few hours before were fine strong men in the vigour of life and who when small parts of humanity were treated with the utmost care, are now nothing but human physical wrecks. I can't help commenting on it. The fortunes of war shown in their true light. But Australia has good cause to be proud of her sons; they accomplished a task which men have not before been asked to do. To land in small boats in an enemy's country and whenever you looked, to see the shiny barrel of a gun staring at you, to hear bullets humming around you like so many bees and the boom of artillery, sending their deadly shells to greet you. Such was the lot of the 3rd Brigade, who smiling through it all said, as soon as they landed, 'Give them a bit of Australia boys—six inches of cold steel'; and they got it. Rather they would of had they waited when our boys charged up the hill. The Turk made good use of his legs, which was the result every time we showed the shining steel.

Well, after leaving shore we sailed from boat to boat trying to get aboard, but they were filled up. At last, after three hours, got accommodation aboard the 'Seang Choon', where the 14th Battalion still were. A better-hearted set of chaps you couldn't wish to meet, nothing was too much trouble for them to do for us. Brought us tea, bread and butter; my first since so called break-fast that morning. But I could only eat a small piece, it being 8pm. They wanted to carry me below, but I wouldn't let them. Their kindness was too much for me and I felt a lump in my throat. I hobbled down with their help and spreading a couple of blankets on the floor they put me to bed with a drop of brandy. It was then I realised what kindness was and thought of my

Nina and her kind sympathy which I so much needed then. I couldn't sleep for the boards were not too comfortable when you had to lie on your back.

Positioned above Private Fisher's personal ordeal on the 400 Plateau, Philip Mackworth was unable to join the fight because both sides were mixing on the right flank. They could not—would not—send 9-inch naval shells into the backs of their own men. Harry's second flight over the cove bore more fruit:

No. 120 Short 136.

Pilot: Lieutenant Edward Dunning; Observer: Lieutenant Harry Strain

Scouting down over the line of Maidos: a large number of carefully prepared trenches and redoubts seen high up near the crest of the ridge: could see no guns, but they cease when a seaplane is in the vicinity. Maidos road was clear. *Turgud Reis* was lying off Nagara Point, and small boats were ferrying supports over. Then proceeded north to Taifur, being met with heavy rifle fire the whole way, but no formed bodies of troops could be seen: back along the road line, but could see no sign of guns. One float was damaged by rifle fire, and engine trouble developed over Taifur. Time, 2 hours.

Harry's diary reveals a little more. Fatigue was setting in. The aircrew had been flying now for two months. With the loss of Hugh Williamson to hospital following a crash on 5 March, the workload increased for Harry as senior observer:

Machines were kept in the air until 3.30 when Edward Dunning and I went up in 136—I have seldom enjoyed a flight less: to begin with I was feeling ill. I have a vein swelling on my leg as a result of a bruise plus frostbite which has given me Phlebitis.

Phlebitis is a condition in which the veins close to the surface of the body become swollen and tender, often developing blood clots. When deeper veins develop blood clots, it is known as deep vein thrombosis. Flying in the open cockpit of a seaplane in wintry conditions had clearly affected Harry's health:

The Medical Officer had asked me not to fly—then Edward Dunning is extraordinarily slow in understanding what one wants and when he does, still slow in obeying one's orders, but he has any amount of pluck. The worst of him is that he thinks of himself as observer and never flies the machine into such a position that his observer can see. However off we prowled to try to spot the *Majestic* onto a battery which I found not to exist— I couldn't see anything firing near the spot where her shot was falling and told him so. I couldn't see any field guns about there as they stop firing when one is over them and they are all concealed in the brushwood. Accordingly we went on a trip to Maidos to see if any troops were advancing, then we went over the line and up to Taifur, 30 miles away, after which we came back, being always met with rifle fire. Small transport units could be seen here and there in the scrub, but before one could spot the ship onto any one it had disappeared into a ravine or over the shoulder of a hill, while the larger units hurrying up along the Bulair road or from

Kilid Bahr were out of range for the ships. Sari Bair itself was alive with troops by 11 am as we found out in an uncomfortable manner. The seaplane was in a pig-headed mood and would not climb beyond 1,400 feet. As Sari Bair was 971, that left some 430 feet between the machine and the reserve troops lying there. And Turkish soldiers cannot miss at that distance: first little white specks began to appear in the floats, then things began to happen in the cockpit, including a head rest being shot away. When the machine touched the water she collapsed with a tired sigh: how she had stuck together I don't know. We were away 2 hours and then there was one final reconnaissance before dark which ended our day. Our troops seemed to have made good their footing but have suffered severely in the process— some of the signals we got were disturbing at the time.

At Z Beach the air service was tasked with watching the roads the enemy would use in their counterattack. *Ark Royal* and *Manica* were directed to report all enemy movements to enable *Triumph* and *Majestic* to smash enemy forces in the open with heavy naval gunfire. The roads from Taifur and Maidos were observed in each successful flight, but enemy soldiers became lost to view in the scrub and mist-shrouded valleys. Joe Kilner, flying a Sopwith (No. 1438), noted that at 5500 feet nothing could be seen owing to poor visibility, twisted topography and overhead cover. Scattered troops were observed, but not in a position that would allow shelling by warships as they were on the reverse of slopes or in valleys. Few guns were identified because of effective camouflage. Hearing various radio reports, Rear Admiral Thursby reported to De Robeck on *Queen Elizabeth* that Turkish soldiers from the 3 Corps encampments seen at

Maidos were not moving southwards to smash the British *coup de main* at Cape Helles; instead they were advancing across the peninsula towards Gaba Tepe to fight ANZAC.

Lieutenant Colonel Sefik Aker, Commanding Officer of the Turkish 27th Infantry Regiment, was now in a position to exact his revenge. His men had suffered the effects of naval shelling on 19 April and it was his men who first punched into ANZAC's right flank. He knew his troops would be seen advancing in column as they marched northwards, inland of Gaba Tepe, before deployment into line on the third inland ridge. But they survived the day and he later recorded the battle in terse soldierly facts:

0545 received the movement order: 'Take the mountain battery which is at CAMBURNU, halt the enemy landing which is being attempted between Ari Burnu and KABA TEPE, proceed to Kaba Tepe and throw the enemy forces which land there into the sea.' Ordered a fast march along newly made road to the side of the main road in NW direction. Concern with naval gunfire and [order men] to march in leaps and bounds.

I knew Ari Burnu and the country behind very well. My purpose in the march was to occupy before the enemy, artillery range [the third inland ridge] which dominates the Ari Burnu range and all around. Our situation on the march was precarious and dangerous, for the sun had risen and was beginning to get high in the sky. Over the whole plain from BOYUN we were exposed to attack from enemy naval gunfire and bombing attacks from aircraft. It would have been possible for the regiment to march safely on this road before sunrise. Our reasons for the battalion being made to march along different roads were in order to pass quickly over the dangerous area.

We continued to march and reach BOYUN. In the sea at Ari Burnu we saw masses of battleships and other big and small ships. From one of the battleships off Gaba Tepe an observation balloon had been sent up. At any moment they might spot us, for we were in range of strong binoculars. It would take almost another hour before the last columns of the battalions had passed the area. All this time enemy aircraft were operating and they too worried me. But they passed by without doing anything. Before the aircraft came overhead, I made the marching columns take shelter in a ditch at the side of the road. Perhaps it was this reason that they could not see us. Since the land along the coast was high we were not exposed to the navy. But a balloon was looking down on us from above. The firing which we expected did not materialise.

We considered it our good fortune and an act of providence that although we had been in sight of the navy, the balloon and the aircraft for almost one hour they had not fired on us. They could not see us for three reasons: our marching column was in the same direction of the sun relative to the navy and the sun had not got up very high. The season of spring vapours which rises from the sea and land in fine weather makes the atmosphere misty. And the clothes of our troops were khaki colour. I did not take the major roads but side roads. I suppose their eyes were turned on the Maidos direction either from the navy or from the balloon [and] must have come to rest exclusively on this road. We took another. The men had to march single file or two abreast, the length of the marching column which was the security echelon, was not able to arrive [until] after 0800. First shots fired 0830. Men requested to leave their packs behind. Left on ground in formation. They changed into clean underwear. Dominant high ground reached. MG [machine-gun] fire and single gun firing at 1,500 metres at own battery. 1030 locked in battle.

Sefik Aker's dispersal and the separation of his regiment into small groups delayed his damaging counterattack against the ANZAC right flank. Colonel Sinclair-MacLagan, the commander of the covering force (3rd Brigade), had halted on the second ridge allowing his men to form a line just in time to meet the delayed arrival of the 27th Regiment. Minutes mattered.

Harry's seaplane flight and Philip's balloon failed to find Aker's men in the scrub. But they did perform valuable service. *Turgud Reis* and her 11-inch guns posed an immediate threat to the movement of men from the decks of transports to the beach in open boats. *Turgud Reis* played a game of 'cat and mouse' by steaming back into range to send salvos towards the ANZAC anchorage off Gaba Tepe.

Major John Hamilton of the 6th Battalion, an Intelligence Officer, was aboard the SS *Galeka*. He penned a note to his wife, fully aware of the risks he faced:

Dearest,

I am writing this in the hope that it will get to you in due course. Dearie, this may be my last to you, so cheer up, if I fall . . . I will be only one of the many brave fellows who have died trying to do their duty for King and country.

We are about to undertake a task which is extremely difficult and we are to land in the face of the enemy.

They have any amount of artillery in hidden spots, so our airmen tell us, we have to face that in our boats. If they get a shrapnel into them we will sink and of course we have a poor chance to swim with all our equipment; but then we have the consolation of knowing that the fleet are behind us and will pepper the Turks if they can only see their guns. Well dare I hope that by the time you are reading this letter that I am still in the land of the living and may have got into communication by cable or otherwise, after we get ashore. Anyhow, Dearest, there is one consolation that we are the reserve battalion of a brigade, and the last of the 4 to get ashore. And then another aspect to look at it is that we will have alarmed the Turks with our first shore party and as it will be in the morning by the time we are putting off from the ship we may cop all their artillery fire whilst we are in our boats.

Anyhow, Dearest, I hope that this will not be my last letter by any great long chalks, we are all bustle each man has 200 rounds, 3 days rations, 1 quart water, a waterproof sheet, his greatcoat, officers the same. We will have to live for 3 days without any supplies. I cannot conscientiously tell you any more about myself or what is going on, but as you will have it in the papers long before this reaches you it would be useless telling you. Anyhow believe me this, if I fall . . . be happy in the thought that I have done my duty to you and my country. Dearest, I have been a true hubby since we met and Dearest, it is comforting that I can face God and be pardoned for my sins. The only thing I can say is that being a soldier for so long, 19 years, I felt that if I didn't come on this I would not be worthy of my name as a captain in the Intelligence Corps.

Good love and God bless you and my darling little Boyne

Your loving and true hubby
Jack

Xxxxxxxx from Daddy to Boyne and her mother.

At 9 am *Queen* retrieved her anchor and steamed from her covering position to avoid *Turgud Reis* and her accurate shelling. The unarmoured troopships, including *Galeka*, also steamed out of range as their ships' captains, who were in fact merchant mariners, were reluctant to risk their livelihoods. At 10 am Charles Bean, the official war correspondent, saw five shells detonating in the sea by the transports, one narrowly missing a destroyer.

The transports were ordered to disembark the soldiers further out from shore just as Colonel Sefik Aker's men attacked from Third Ridge. *Turgud Reis*' fall of shot was corrected by a forward observer on Gaba Tepe via telephone line across the peninsula. The Turkish ship steamed away three times to avoid counter-fire directed by Philip and three times she steamed back into range. Sailors were responsible for rowing the wooden boats across this widening gap. Midshipmen—boys as young as 14 years old—stood at the tiller:

10.40 am. By this time some of the high ground over the Cove has already been captured. The 2nd Brigade is fully engaged. 1st Brigade following up with New Zealanders and an Indian Mountain Battery.

10.50 am. More transports are arriving here. They have to keep further out from the shore owing to the enemy gunfire at them, many big shells coming over from the Asiatic side now.

By 3 pm Philip's balloon and the presence of the Australian submarine *AE2* had forced *Turgud Reis* to seek shelter in Gallipoli Harbour. The transports were then able to steam close to shore to deliver their troops. John Hamilton landed on the beach alive.

The infantry recognised the respite provided by a sea-plane overhead. Birdie wrote a signal to *Ark Royal* in the afternoon as pauses in the incessant bursting of shrapnel told that enemy gunners held their fire when they saw the prowling seaplane: 'General Birdwood therefore requested that, as far as possible, seaplanes should fly constantly over our lines.' The final seaplane flight was launched at sunset, as the aviators knew they would see the telltale muzzle flash from enemy guns in the darkness. As a result, an artillery battery which had fired on the exposed backs of men on the ridgelines was spotted in a cypress grove outside the village of Kojadere. Naval shells burst around it; it fell silent.

At the end of that dreadful day, Clarkee submitted a typed report to the Air Department in London:

REPORT OF OPERATIONS No. 13 HMS ARK ROYAL Sunday 25 April 1915.

In accordance with instructions ship arrived close to HMS *Majestic* at daylight to endeavour to spot her gun-fire onto batteries or troops on left flank until military observers were in position themselves to control ship's fire and also to reconnoitre country around for the advance of reinforcing troops.

Flying started at daylight and continued through day seven flights being made and a machine being kept in the air for over eight hours.

The nature of the country—interspersed with ravines and gullies and covered with brushwood—renders the location of troops or guns extraordinarily difficult and few results were obtained. Reports of the roads from TAIFUR to MAIDOS leading to the landing place, and movement of TURGUD REIS and other ships in the straits were signalled from time to time throughout the day. The ship remained under way for the night.

COMMANDER

Manica also lay out to sea. Her balloon was winched down after dusk. It remained inflated, sitting like an overstuffed pillow in the open forward hold. Philip had spent over 12 hours on duty calling fire onto the gun batteries in the hinterland behind Gaba Tepe. Herbert Hillier maintained his artist's eerie vigil on the lower bridge:

> The light is fading fast, and the struggle going on hard as ever. There is an increasing roll of rifle and machine gun fire ashore. Everyone knows that our losses have been very heavy. The fighting area is flickering all over with the sharp splashes of rifle fire. We can do no more of our job until the dawn lets us again. Each man is asking the question—'can the boys hold out?'

The French feint landing on the southern Asiatic shore at Kum Kale achieved its objective. A brigade was landed and advanced to the Saundere River, capturing over 400 Turkish prisoners. In the late afternoon it was stopped by a Turkish counterattack and a fierce battle fought across a cemetery. The French feint tied up two Turkish infantry divisions, drawing them into the battle. This prevented the Turkish troops taking boats across the Dardanelles and deploying against Hamilton's main effort, across the Narrows at Cape Helles. The French feint also diverted the attention of artillery battery commanders and kept a portion of them from exploding shrapnel over the exposed British landing across the mouth of the straits. The French remained on the Asiatic coast for two days before they were withdrawn to land on the British right flank. Charles' aviators divided their attention between the two. Aviators also identified howitzer batteries and brought fire to bear once they betrayed their hidden locations.

The Royal Naval Division conducted a 'demonstration' just after dawn at Bulair. My grandfather, Staff Sergeant Charlie White, Royal Marine Light Infantry, was involved in this ruse. He lived for another 23 days. Warships shelled the northern beaches before Royal Marines climbed into boats and conducted a pantomime landing. The boats approached the shoreline but did not land. Again, Hamilton's purpose was to ensure that two Turkish divisions remained in reserve in the north of the peninsula and away from the main landings in the south. This was accomplished. The Royal Naval Division remained on its transports off the northern coast for another two days until the Royal Marine Light Infantry was disembarked at Anzac Cove. They then reinforced the right of the line before being withdrawn and redeployed at Cape Helles.

The Royal Naval Division demonstration off the Bulair Lines held the attention of General Otto Liman von Sanders throughout Sunday and into Monday 26 April. Liman von Sanders abandoned his headquarters to lie on his belly on a ridge overlooking the transports and warships waiting off-shore. His first reaction was to send a division northwards, up into the Gulf of Saros, rather than southwards to assist his hard-pressed soldiers at Gaba Tepe and Cape Helles.

Hamilton's deception plan worked well and his various feints caused a paralysis of command in Turkish 5th Army Headquarters at Gallipoli. This in part explains the delay in the movement of infantry reinforcements to oppose the British 29th Division at Cape Helles. Liman von Sanders was fixated, following the movement of warships and transports that appeared to threaten his northern area. From his position overlooking the transports, the German general witnessed the lowering of seaplane No. 922 onto the sea from its place on *Doris'* aft gun turret. The seaplane conducted two reconnaissance flights, one in the morning and one mid-afternoon. Clarkee reported:

Sopwith No. 922 was returned from the 'Doris'. With Lieutenant Douglas as pilot, and Petty Officer Brady as observer, she assisted during the feint landing near Bulair Lines in the Gulf of Xeros, and made the following flights—

25th April 1915

No. 145 Reconnaissance of Bulair Lines, Kavak and the northern end of the Gulf of Xeros, reporting a battle-ship off Gallipoli, and several small camps in district. Time: 1 hour 30 minutes.

No. 145 A similar reconnaissance carried out in after-noon: no movement of troops or transports seen. Time: 1 hour 37 minutes.

The lone seaplane fulfilled the requirements of the earlier military appreciation and, to some extent, may have also contributed to the delay in the despatch of Turkish reserves to counterattack ANZAC and the British landing in the south. Although Hamilton's ruses—the feint and demonstration—occupied the attention of four Turkish divisions, it was only a matter of two days before they were exposed and Turkish reserves were sent to deal with the enemy invaders. The Turkish response was characterised by good leadership and planning at 3 Corps Headquarters and at the divisional level. The loss of Liman von Sanders due to his fixation at Bulair had no real effect on the Turkish response to the invasion. After all, he was unable to speak Turkish and would have been a wallflower in his own headquarters. Turkish senior officers used telephones for quick situation reports; Liman von Sanders would have had to interrupt conversations for translation into German. He was also unable to pick up the phone himself to speak to Turkish commanders in battle. So the loss of the 5th Army commander had little effect on Esat Pasha, the 3 Corps commander camped at Maidos. Esat Pasha ordered counterattacks by Sefik Aker and Mustafa Kemal at Gaba Tepe. He also ran the defence at Cape Helles, having organised a series of interlocking defences that would turn the sea red with blood.

As Hamilton's headquarters staff saw no viable alternative, the British 29th Division attacked in daylight on five beaches around Cape Helles. Hamilton had considered all options, but the most effective way to clear the Turkish Army from the Kilid Bahr Plateau and from along the shores of the Dardanelles was a direct approach. The Turkish 9th Division, defending the southern tip, also recognised this and prepared its defences accordingly. Hamilton attempted two flanking attacks on S and Y beaches where he knew the enemy defences were weakest.

The *coup de main* of the British 29th Division was stopped dead by the veteran Turkish 26th Infantry Regiment—detailed for this task by the 9th Division—from prepared trenches. The strength of Turkish resistance prompted Lieutenant General Sir Aylmer Hunter-Weston, the British divisional commander, to abandon any hope of an advance towards the village of Krithia and the dominant hill of Achi Baba. The objective was reduced to simply getting ashore. The covering force approached the coast in daylight after a preliminary naval bombardment. It suffered heavy casualties, caught in open wooden rowing boats.

The grounding of the SS *River Clyde* represented a precursor to the use of modern landing craft. *River Clyde* was a 4000-ton collier converted to a modern Trojan horse, carrying 2000 soldiers from the 1st Battalion of the Royal Munster Fusiliers and Royal Dublin Fusiliers hidden in her holds. Large doors were cut in her steel sides to allow men to step out and run along a suspended gangplank to the beach, a stream of soldiers yelling Gaelic war cries. Eleven machine-guns were manned by members of the RNAS Armoured Car Squadron who had disembarked at Tenedos and been given a new job. A machine-gun nest was mounted behind the boiler plate at the bow, a sort of Ned Kelly affair with the men peeking through small slits towards the enemy.

But *River Clyde* was beached too far, coming to rest beneath the imposing sandstone ramparts of Sedd el Bahr castle at V Beach on the tip of the Gallipoli Peninsula. Soldiers ran down the gangplank like tin ducks at a shooting gallery, with up to 80 per cent cut down by Turkish machine-guns, rifle and artillery fire. Their hunched forms carpeted the gangplanks and small boats brought in to bridge the gap to shore. Six Victoria Crosses were awarded for work in the blood-soaked sea. The force commander, Brigadier Napier, attempted to land by boat. It was sent silently drifting back out into the Dardanelles with bodies lying in crimson bilge.

The only exceptions to the bloody carnage were the landings on the far flanks on Y and S beaches. Y Beach, as expected, was completely undefended as 2000 troops scaled the cliff and waited through the first day for a link-up from the south which never came. The Plymouth Battalion, Royal Naval Division, was under the command of Lieutenant Colonel Godfrey Matthews, and the 1st Battalion, King's Own Scottish Borderers, was commanded by Lieutenant Colonel Archibald Koe. Godfrey Matthews and Archibald Koe argued over who was the overall commander while their leaderless troops mingled aimlessly on the beach and the clifftop. They did not begin to fortify their beachhead until 3 pm when Matthews finally agreed with Koe to dig in. As a consequence, when the Turks launched a counterattack at dusk, their trenches were mere scrapes. They were attacked through the night and re-embarked the next morning, having achieved nothing. The landing on S Beach, in Morto Bay on the British right flank, was opposed, but resistance was overcome by direct assault. Here British soldiers also waited in position for a link-up which did not occur until the next day. The British were still fighting for the beach environs into the second day, leaving the objective far out of reach.

The landing was met by fierce Turkish resistance. Overall the Turkish 9th Division defence was far more responsive, resilient, and achieved more than Hamilton's expeditionary force. The Turkish defensive plan met all its objectives: the enemy infantry were contained and could be pushed into the sea by reserves when they arrived.

Charles' squadron flew missions from 5.15 am to 6.30 pm with two airframes over the cape throughout the day. Sixteen missions were flown—nine spotting and seven reconnaissance—with nine 100lb and four 20lb bombs dropped on enemy troops and gun batteries. Charles wrote:

> We were to be up in a position over the beaches before the tows left the ships, and were to spot certain ships' fire onto any bodies of the enemy who were resisting the landing. After the landing had been effected we were to spot the ships onto any large bodies moving down to reinforce. In addition long range reconnaissance had to be carried out to Bulair to watch for possible movements of Turkish reserves.

Flights overlapped, with missions launched every hour and lasting 90 minutes. Charles' team of aviators and observers cycled through three missions each. Charles was above X Beach when the Lancashire Regiment rowed ashore:

> It was a splendid morning for air work, also for the ships' boats. The ships started firing at the beaches and beyond to various positions that were thought to be held by troops or occupied by guns. I saw the tows leave the ships, and they finally broke off from the steamboats and rowed for the shore. Just before the tows were slipped the Turks started firing. I saw Hell let loose.
>
> The sea was literally whipped into foam by the hail of bullets and small shells. It seemed practically impossible that the boats could get in through that tornado of fire; but still they came on, and we saw the troops jump out and reach the beach.

I saw men fall the moment they reached the shore. But others charged on, some going straight up the slope, others making for the cliffs on the right flank. We located some Turks and guns quite close to the beach. Osmond signalled their position; but the ships disregarded our message, and kept their fire too far inland. We dropped our bombs at these Turks, but unfortunately missed them.

My next glance of the beach showed it covered with bodies of our dead. But I could see the landing had been made good. Reinforcements were arriving and the naval beach parties could be seen hard at work regardless of the fire.

No. 3 Squadron reports on enemy activity were recorded, almost hourly, in the General Headquarters war diary. In contrast no aerial reports were entered in the 29th Division Headquarters war diary. Its commander, Sir Aylmer Hunter-Weston, was deaf to aerial reports describing the difficulties experienced at the other designated beaches including the failure of *River Clyde* at V Beach. He was blind, losing effective control of his various landings. Sir Aylmer was ensconced on *Euryalus*, a warship circling off W Beach, ensnared by events around Teki Burnu. Hamilton, thanks to *Queen Elizabeth*'s monitoring of the radio nets, received nine aerial reports throughout the day, the first at 6 am. A progress report on V Beach, including the fate of the Royal Munster Fusiliers and Royal Dublin Fusiliers, was reported by Reginald Marix with Major Hogg as his observer: 'An aeroplane reported gap of 50 feet between *River Clyde* and lighters and that troops cannot disembark.'

Perhaps only minutes later, Charles, with his friend Herb Collet as observer, banked southwards for the short flight to the toe of the peninsula. They also caught sight of the disaster 5000 feet below:

> As our time was up, and we were relieved by another airplane, we returned home. Passed over the fortress of Sedd el Bahr where I could see the landing was being held up. The *River Clyde* was fast ashore; but the lighters ahead were not in the right position. Gaps occurred. These lighters were full of corpses. The beach and water close to the shore were strewn with bodies. It was an appalling sight for us to look at from our safe position in the air. It made one think we were not doing our bit.
>
> The Turks were keeping a hot fire on the *River Clyde*. It seemed impossible for anyone to get ashore from her. Some shells were arriving from the Asiatic side; but undoubtedly the most serious obstacle was the rifle fire from Sedd el Bahr village. The sea for a distance of about 50 yards from the beach was absolutely red with blood. A horrible sight.

Charles' flight log tells the story of morning missions over the contested beaches:

> Commander Charles Samson (P); Lieutenant Osmond (O): 5.15–7.50 am, spotting and bomb attack.
>
> Flight Commander Reginald Marix (P); Major Hogg (O): 5.30–8.30 am, military reconnaissance.
>
> Lieutenant Henry Butler (P); Midshipman John Sissmore (O): 6.30–8.30 am, reconnaissance on Krithia.

Lieutenant Gordon Thomson (P); Lieutenant Richard Peirse (O): 7.30–10 am, spotting for HMS *Vengeance*.

Commander Charles Samson (P); Captain Herb Collet (O): 9.10–10.30 am, spotting flight and bomb attack.

Squadron Commander Richard Davies (P); Midshipman Erskine St Aubyn (O): 9.20–11 am, spotting for HMS *Prince George*.

Flight Commander Reginald Marix (P); Major Hogg (O): 10.30–12.20 pm, military reconnaissance and bomb attack.

Lieutenant Julian Newton-Claire (P); Captain David Jenkins (O): 10.50–11.50 am, military reconnaissance.

Lieutenant Wilson (P); Lieutenant Bill Samson (O): 10–12 am, reconnaissance.

Lieutenant Gordon Thomson (P); Lieutenant Richard Peirse (O): 11.30–2.50 pm, spotting.

Midshipman John Sissmore was taken aloft by Lieutenant Gordon Thomson in the old Maurice Farman (tail no. 1241) which had been with the squadron since August 1914. It was old but known as a reliable machine. John was scanning for the movement of Turkish reserves onto the battlefield. He tapped through his message while over Krithia. It was taken down by a radioman and entered into Hamilton's war diary not 30 minutes later. It is very likely that the original 'flimsy' or wafer-thin radio message was passed to Hamilton in the gunnery top: '8.30 am body of troops in gully 700 yards south west of Krithia moving south.'

Richard Peirse, Herb Collet, David Jenkins and Bill Samson called in targets representing points of fierce Turkish resistance over the radio to warships cruising off-shore. Only reports that were of immediate interest to the 29th Division's frantic assaults on Hill 138 were recorded in the war diary:

> 9.10 report from aeroplane battery F.2 (N. 29 Division map) still firing.

> 11.20 a.m. trenches abreast Gulley Beach occupied by Turks.

Hamilton was kept abreast of evolving problems and opportunities from the air. After talking to aircrew while their aeroplanes were being refuelled, Bernard Isaac, the squadron's Intelligence Officer, used the naval wireless station on Tenedos to relay important information on a possible Turkish counterattack: '11.21 aerodrome TENEDOS reported 2000 troops seen in 169 A moving South East.'

Square 169 A on Hamilton's map shows a deeply etched nullah that stretches southwards from the village of Krithia to the toe of the peninsula. Turkish reinforcements were using 'dead ground' that hid them from view of the ships out to sea. In the confusion of battle, these enemy troops moved past the British soldiers sitting peacefully on the clifftop of Y Beach. Lieutenant Henry Butler flew a solo mission back over this dead ground to report on any further movement. He called in naval fire, but the steep-sided nullah protected the Turks from shrapnel. Missions continued into the afternoon:

Commander Charles Samson (P); Captain Herb Collet (O): 12–2.45 pm spotting for HMS *Goliath* and *Triumph*.

Lieutenant Henry Butler (P): 11.15–1.15 pm reconnaissance over Square 169 A.

Flight Commander Reginald Marix (P); Midshipman Erskine St Aubyn (O): 1.30–4.15 pm spotting flight and bomb attack.

Sub-Lieutenant Julian Newton-Claire (P); Lieutenant Whittaker (O): 1.30–3 pm reconnaissance and bomb attack Magram.

Squadron Commander Richard Davies (P); Lieutenant Osmond (O): 4–6.30 pm spotting flight.

Lieutenant Wilson (P); Captain David Jenkins (O): 4.55–6.33 pm military reconnaissance.

Y Beach was not shelled during the preliminary naval bombardment because it was known from aerial photography to be undefended. Sir Aylmer Hunter-Weston confirmed this in his own report on the landing, later making up for command deficiencies in his personal version of events:

About 2½ miles further up the coast and west of Krithia arrangements were made to land the King's Own Scottish Borderers and the Plymouth Battalion Royal Marine Light Infantry. This force was to extend in a southerly direction down the coast and effect a junction with the Royal Fusiliers. They were to be put ashore as soon as it was light, as there were no works on the cliffs above this landing.

Hamilton again had his air intelligence confirmed on the day of the landings by a report from *Goliath* at 6.40 am. With his own observations framed by powerful range-finding binoculars in the gunnery top, Hamilton radioed Sir Aylmer at 9.21 am, asking whether he should exploit the opportunities presented at Y Beach. He received a reply from Sir Aylmer at 10.45 am that diverting troops to Y Beach would delay disembarkation elsewhere. The opportunity hung in the balance. Turkish troops moved silently through a deep gully not 500 yards from British positions. Neither party was aware of the other's presence.

At midday Charles and his team of aviators saw soldiers from the 3rd Battalion, 27th Infantry Regiment, emerge from the nullah and rush forward to reinforce the broken Sedd el Bahr fortress on V Beach and dominant ground over X Beach. Sometime before 4 pm, Charles' team observed another tranche of reinforcements sent by Turkish 9th Division Headquarters:

> 2.30 pm 1500 infantry on road from Krithia to Maidos, marching towards Krithia, head of column 4,000 yards from Krithia.

> 5 pm 300 infantry on Maidos Krithia road going towards Krithia head of column 2 miles from Maidos.

Now realising that the enemy was using this approach as it hid them from Henry Butler's solo flight, the air service responded. Perhaps out of the loop and in the confusion of the busy operations room, with many messages being passed around, this was transcribed into Hamilton's war diary as:

> 4 pm TENEDOS aerodrome reported 1500 troops on Krithia-Maidos Road Square 15 (?). proceeding KRITHIA 2.30 pm

Following Henry's return, Bernard had marked on his map the approach of enemy reserves and where best to destroy them in the open. As a matter of course, all pilots reported to the Intelligence Officer's tent for questioning and the collation of intelligence and pre-flight briefs. Bernard was now in a position to recycle 'live' intelligence for the following flights. Reginald Marix and his observer Midshipman Erskine St Aubyn spotted for *Prince George*, catching the troops on the exposed road *before* entry into the deep nullah. These soldiers had been ordered to move southwards towards Krithia and engage the enemy, but instead had advanced into deadly naval gunfire once in the open onion fields. Heavy 9-inch shells burst over the men advancing in column. Thousands of small lead balls ripped into their exposed upper bodies. Mercilessly, Erskine, who was just a 15-year-old 'snotty', corrected each shot until the men lay in broken red heaps on the landscape. Charles and Herb kept observing the road for more men caught in the open, finally bringing HMS *Goliath* and *Swiftsure* into action once again. Halil Sami, Commander of the Turkish 9th Division, halted all movement along the roads, waiting for the cover of night.

Reports of isolated enemy infantry formations from the air also told Sir Ian Hamilton that the large 3 Corps camps identified in the Maidos region were not moving to counter-attack at Cape Helles, as only 3800 men were seen by Charles' aviators. This information was gold: on that first day, an advance to Krithia, once past the beach defences, would meet with only scattered opposition. But with the difficulties of securing an effective beachhead, little could be done and the situation could not be exploited, as Charles noted:

> After an hour at Tenedos refuelling, I set off once more, this time taking Herb Collet as observer. We were fully occupied spotting for the warships' fire. I saw that everything was going all right at the Lancashire landing; but we were still held up at Sedd el Bahr. The *Queen Elizabeth* had arrived, and was firing salvo after salvo of 6 inch at Sedd el Bahr fort and village. I could actually see the shells passing through about six walls before they burst.
>
> On my last flight, again accompanied by Collet, we had to spot for HMS *Goliath* and *Swiftsure*, who were firing at Krithia and Achi Baba. Our propeller was hit by a rifle bullet during this flight. We got safely back to Tenedos although the vibration had us worried. I felt that the old squadron had done its bit that day.

But Charles' squadron had initially suffered a number of problems with spotting. Spotting flights covering the first hours were of little value as supporting warships paid no attention to their wireless reports. Charles wrote later that he and his aircrew were ignored in the early morning as he believed the naval gunnery officers in their towers already had sufficient targets framed in their range-finding binoculars:

> We worked hard that day and most of us made three flights; we practically all found that the ships took little notice of our signals until too late.

It was in the afternoon, when the battle advanced past the beach (except at V Beach) and into the fields beyond, that the supporting warships took notice of spotting instructions. The gunnery jacks were then blind. Warships lost visual targets as the men fought beyond the first escarpment, and thus observers' frantic signalling was answered with naval gunfire support onto targets further inland. The best results came from catching the enemy in the open. The movement of enemy reserves along the roads provided a plum target.

Bernard pulled no punches. His diary entry reveals that Charles' pilots were partially responsible for their own failure in spotting in the bloody dawn phase:

> The landing at Sedd el Bahr fort was disastrous. Blood in the sea: boats and bodies and gruesome debris were seen all along the beach even at 6000 feet. I was kept busy all day taking reports and signalling results to Vice Admiral and ships firing. A task made more difficult by the sudden swelling of the heads of pilots except Collet, Marix, and Osmond. The other four landings were more successful. Achi Baba Hill was to be gained tonight but this does not now look very helpful. I quarrel with everyone. Vice Admiral signals that our spotting is of very little value as we don't know tables. A natural event of employing pilots who know all about oil and flying machines, but nothing about wireless telegraphy. I miss dinner. I work till 9.15. We have no casualties. Enemy too busy to shoot at aeroplanes.

But Charles must have the last word:

> All my pilots were full of admiration at the behaviour of our troops. But we all felt rather depressed as it was

obvious that the landing was a failure. We were held up and unable to advance.

I must here place on record my humble opinion that the Dardanelles landings have been mainly spoken about as an ANZAC show, with not enough credit given to the British 29th Division. I mean no disparagement to the Australians and New Zealanders, for whom I am proud to say I flew many thousands of miles. But I do think that the landings at Helles were feats of arms showing, if I may so vulgarly put it, sheer guts and fighting powers totally unsurpassed.

The main landings at Gaba Tepe and Cape Helles stalled for different reasons. The infantry of two ANZAC divisions established themselves ashore but were hard pressed defending their beachhead from counterattacks by Mustafa Kemal's 19th Division and Sefik Aker's 27th Regiment. The British 29th Division was halted on the beaches surrounding the cape by companies of the Turkish 26th Infantry Regiment fighting from deep and well-placed trenches. During the landing, 29th Division Headquarters concentrated its covering force and its succeeding echelons where beach defences were strongest. The result was that the highly trained regular soldiers of this division were brutalised by a numerically inferior force fighting with the advantage of redoubts and trenches and supported by wire entanglements. The bodies of Fusiliers were pulled from the sea, bloated, ripped apart by the ferocity of the fire. They were buried in deep sandy pits along the shore. A carpet of maggots paid homage to the cream of Irish and English soldiery. But behind this slaughter, the intelligence picture—supplied by spies in Istanbul and eyes in the sky—was first rate. The cause of failure lay elsewhere.

Hamilton deliberately excluded Harry's seaplanes, Philip's balloon and Charles' aviators from his official despatch. It was as though they did not exist. He told Lord Kitchener and the Horse Guards in London (in a précis below) that his intelligence had been limited to what he could see through a telescope:

From the General Officer Commanding the Mediterranean Expeditionary Force.

To the Secretary of State for War, War Office, London, S.W.

General Headquarters, Mediterranean Expeditionary Force, 20th May, 1915.

My Lord, I have the honour to submit my report on the operations in the Gallipoli Peninsula up to and including the 5th May.

. . . What seemed to be gun emplacements and infantry redoubts could also be made out through a telescope, but of the full extent of these defences and of the forces available to man them there was no possibility of judging except by practical test. Altogether the result of this and subsequent reconnaissances was to convince me that nothing but a thorough and systematic scheme for flinging the whole of the troops under my command very rapidly ashore could be expected to meet with success; whereas, on the other hand, a tentative or piecemeal programme was bound to lead to disaster.

. . . Needless to say, the difficulties in the way of previous reconnaissance had rendered it impossible to obtain detailed information with regard either to the locality or to the enemy's preparations.

This would cause serious ructions in London with consequences for our aviators struggling to support the land forces in the Dardanelles.

CHAPTER 4

Holding on . . .

An aviator's experience of war is unlike that of the soldier. In some ways it is abstract: he flies over the battlefield and looks down on the carnage below. He is part of it, but somehow remote, like watching television at home. There is danger of course, but risk comes with ascending into the air. Pilots and aircrew have a natural self-belief; they all have a personal mantra that wards off disaster. Their eyes constantly scan instruments, the horizon and dangers to the aircraft (from anti-aircraft fire or enemy aeroplanes, for example). Aviators are vigilant, keyed up, and talk in clipped tones while in the air. On the ground they behave like Japanese schoolgirls; they are incredibly cliquey and driven to consensus. Their shared experiences in the air set them apart.

On several occasions in April 2003 I flew across the desert into Iraq in a Hercules. I sat behind the pilot on a bench, completely helpless and useless to the mission at hand. But there was clear value in an Intelligence Officer making the flight; there was much to learn at the other end. One thing became obvious: military flying was exhausting. After each mission the aircrew would enter my tent sweat-soaked, their faces quiet masks of exhaustion. They knew that it would take only one slip-up for the four-engine aircraft flying at 200 feet across the desert floor to auger in. I learnt about this level of fatigue after my first uneventful flight. It took me an hour to type a simple post-mission report of two lines. Nothing dangerous had occurred, but it was as though my body was so charged with the 'flight or fight' survival instinct that I was left like a rag doll in the aftermath. And then afterwards it was back to the creature comforts of a large American air base: Baskin Robbins ice cream, Pizza Hut, air-conditioning, three beers at 'the wagon wheel bar', a movie theatre and a bucket of popcorn.

Clearly infantry and all combat arms deserve the highest praise. They have no relief. They remain in location in the field as a close-knit group for weeks or months on end. But not aviators. They return to modernity and phone calls from their partners about the missing dog. Or to say that a daughter is being bullied over the internet. Or that a phone bill is due. They have one foot in the war and one foot at home.

Aviators suffer a different stress. They have a bird's-eye view of the battle. They look down like Olympian gods on the unfolding drama. They become brittle. Some become too engaged and suffer for their empathy. Later in this story Sub-Lieutenant Harold Kerby joins Charles Samson's squadron; he lasts eight weeks before he has a mental breakdown. Yet soldiers suffered daily bombardments and the loss of mates for over eight months and continued on regardless. Hints of Harry's personal decline are found in his diary. Whimsical stories, the collection of bullet holes and near misses should be seen on another level.

Unlike the ANZACs caught in drenching rain ashore, Harry Strain returned to a three-course meal in the wardroom. He changed before dinner. In fact *Ark Royal* was unique among Royal Navy ships in that she had a bathroom with *four baths* and an endless supply of hot water. Her designers considered that aircrew required the therapeutic qualities of baths to restore blood circulation after flight. After cocktails, Harry retired to his snug cabin and wrote in his diary, describing the events of 25 April. Then he was up at 4 am on 26 April for the dawn flight:

> Again it was a case of getting ready at the first peep of dawn. I went up with Edward Dunning, but just as we were getting into position and had located the enemy trenches, not to mention *Turgud Reis* over the other side, our engine went fluff. We had to make a forced landing not too far from shore. In fact the morning was one of disaster: none of the machines would fly. I was feeling rather rotten and glad in a way to be out of it: I kept my leg stuck up and lay in a coil of rope in the sun watching all that was going on through my glasses.

The first four weeks after the landings saw a number of bloody infantry assaults as each army sought decisive gains. Neither side managed to break through enemy trenches and both won little ground despite appalling casualties. Both Anzac and Cape Helles were subjected to repeated Turkish counterattacks 'to drive the invaders into the sea' while Hamilton's expeditionary force sought to enlarge its cramped beachheads. The Allied focus was on Cape Helles where the onion fields and vineyards begged large-scale infantry attacks. After a short period of rest following the brutal shock of that first day, the surviving soldiers from

the British 29th Division attempted to advance in a series of
daylight infantry assaults. These became known as the First
and Second Battles of Krithia. Two brigades were stripped
from ANZAC to assist in these battles. The 29th Division
slowly moved its front lines 200 metres across a carpet of
bodies towards the broken tumbledown of terracotta-roofed
houses that had been the village of Krithia.

The Turkish defence was professional and displayed
flexibility in command. Despite their inability to crush
the beachheads, the Turks mounted an effective defence
and divided command and control of the army into a
Southern Group, facing the British 29th Division, and
a Northern Group opposite ANZAC. Both groups were
supplemented with newly deployed artillery batteries and
infantry divisions.

Overall, air activity from 26 April to 18 May was particularly vigorous. Harry, Philip, Charles and their aviators flew
a total of 284 missions over Anzac and Helles during this
period, with the balloon up for some 13 days. On average,
Charles' aviators flew ten missions per day, Harry's seaplane
flight two missions per day, and Philip's balloon an eight-hour
flight a day, weather permitting. The enemy was reinforced
with a new Albatros, flying a mission every second day.

The aviators were given specific responsibilities with
Charles' No. 3 Squadron undertaking all aerial duties at
Cape Helles, leaving Harry's seaplanes, with the support of
Manica's kite balloon, to assist Birdie's men clinging to the
cliffs above Anzac Cove. Charles' squadron also flew long-
range reconnaissance missions across the breadth of the
peninsula, patrolling as far north as Bulair. Telltale signs of
Turkish military intentions were easily seen from the air:
troop movements at ports and roads, camps, the location of
reserves, and the movement of transports in the Marmara.

Ark Royal's seaplanes conducted 66 successful missions in support of General Birdwood from 25 April to 18 May: 42 reconnaissance, 21 spotting, one anti-aircraft patrol and two trial flights. Monday 26 April was an extremely difficult day. *Ark Royal* cruised off the cove attempting to provide what support she could:

> The Turks appeared (we could see them), turned our left flank at the same time making a heavy assault on the centre. We saw our men falling back. In the centre, where the firing was strongest and where shrapnel was constantly blasting over them, our men were falling and being driven back. A signal came to the ships to support them with gunfire, and they did. But things were critical—then up came *Queen Elizabeth* and opened fire with her 15 inch—the effect was appalling and she saved the situation. A signal came through, 'QE range and time correct, give them beans.' Our own casualties must have been very heavy as the fighting became very close—so close that there was no demand for our services. We made two successful reconnaissances later that day.

Following Hamilton's directions to hold and dig, General Birdwood, General William Bridges and his Chief of Staff, Lieutenant-Colonel Cyril Brudenell White, all knew that the 'tables were turned' and that they were, in fact, under siege. The swiftness and decisiveness of twin Turkish counter-attacks from 25 to 27 April left ANZAC units intermingled and disorganised. After a few days each battalion was retired from the line for reorganisation before climbing back up the slopes into hastily dug trenches. Birdie directed small-scale tactical assaults to improve the security of these forward trenches. The 4th Battalion was able to push forward onto the 400 Plateau; otherwise the men literally had their backs to the sea. Both General Bridges as divisional commander and General Birdwood as corps commander became dependent on Harry's seaplanes to assist in every minor skirmish. They were not afraid to use seaplanes; in fact they became adept.

Clarkee and Harry were ANZAC's eyes. Clarkee summarised this activity succinctly, writing that:

> The duties allotted to seaplanes included reconnaissance of all roads leading to the enemy's positions from Maidos on the east to Taifur Keui in the north, the location of the enemy's battleships in the Dardanelles, permanent fortifications and field gun positions and flying over the enemy's lines to keep down gunfire.

Clarkee's meticulous flight records reveal that more was achieved. He grouped the distribution of pamphlets, reconnaissance over Smyrna, anti-submarine patrolling and coordination of missions with infantry movements under the broad banner of reconnaissance flights.

The pattern of cooperation between ANZAC Headquarters and the air service continued. Birdie included in his orders the coordination of air missions in support of several hard-fought infantry battles. He described in detail where he wanted naval shelling to explode over the enemy's heads to support his men when they left the cover of their trenches:

ARMY CORPS OPERATIONS ORDER NO. 5

ANZAC Cove 30/4/15.

1. The Army Corps maintains and consolidates its position. No further news from the South.

2. The Army Corps will occupy tomorrow a general line in advance of its present position to include the knoll 224 d 5 and thence South by West along the western bank of gully . . .

3 (d) The 2nd [Naval] Squadron will co-operate with fire:—

i From the south west up the gully 224 O S W

ii On the knolls 224D 5, 237 Z 238 q-v and area to the west thereof

iii on villages Biyuk and Kojadere.

4. Reports to Army Corps bivouac.

Birdie and his staff were comfortable with the joint coordination of air activity and had stepped beyond the infantry tactical doctrine of the time. He included orders for aircraft to assist in each attack. Corps headquarters directed the Naval Brigade, 1st Australian Division and New Zealand and Australian Division to advance their lines at 5 pm with the overt presence of seaplanes and Philip's kite balloon. Rear Admiral Thursby's naval squadron ordered Harry and Philip to correct naval shells onto squares 224, 237 and the villages behind Third Ridge. Each target was beyond visual range of ANZAC artillery observers in the trenches and naval gunnery officers out to sea. Clarkee recorded in his flight log that three missions were flown on 1 May, with one in particular fulfilling the requirements of Birdie's orders:

Examined the roads north of ANZAC, and flew over the Turkish lines at request of the General Officer Commanding [Birdie] during attack of our troops keeping shrapnel fire down materially. The *Manica*'s balloon was attacked by aeroplane with bombs, both yesterday and today while spotting for Q.E. Time: 2 hours 39 minutes.

Turgud Reis threatened ANZAC's fragile supply chain—supplies were vulnerable to shelling as freighters approached an open coast and transhipped goods onto small craft under direct Turkish observation. Enemy artillery observers directed intense shelling on the movement of stores from ships to smaller craft and the manhandling of goods onto the open stretch of Brighton Beach. Soon the navy became suspicious of enemy movement on Suvla Point, a finger of land on the northern left flank with a clear view of Anzac Cove:

> We made a small landing on Suvla Point and discovered a Turkish Observation Station with 3 officers and 14 men—we captured the lot except 8 were killed. We lost no men.

Turkish artillery observers still had a clear vista of ANZAC movements from Hill 971 and the Sari Bair Range. Gaba Tepe also provided observation along Brighton Beach to the cove. They had no need of aircraft to spot for them. All they had to do was pick up a telephone and speak directly to the battery commander in his camouflaged dugout. But for the Allies, enemy shipping movements at the ports of Gallipoli and Maidos were beyond visual observation and the range of Allied artillery. The only method of disrupting the enemy's supply movements was by aerial spotting and bombing or the presence of Allied submarines in the Sea of Marmara.

Life at Anzac Cove was extraordinarily difficult. No. 981 Private Richard Farley Bulkeley, 2nd Battalion, 1st Infantry Brigade, waded ashore on 28 April and joined his mates in the 3rd Battalion after helping to unload ammunition from one of the steamers off the cove:

> Volunteered with 19 others for stretcher bearer work ashore. Got ashore about 7pm on a destroyer & found when we landed that we were to reinforce the battalion. Given ammunition & marched down the beach to camp for the night. Came on to rain. Very cold & miserable. Got settled in a dugout in the sand & the damn thing fell in & nearly buried me. Bullets whizzing round all the time. The firing line is just up the ridge. How our boys took this place I don't know, the hills run straight up from the water.
>
> 29 April. Hardly got a wink of sleep last night. The 3rd came down from the firing line this morning. They have been badly cut up. Digging trenches practically all day & all the time under fire, chiefly stray bullets & shrapnel but also there are a good few snipers about, & I had a few mighty close to me this morning. In the evening expected to be shelled from the south so all had to turn to & dig trenches. At night had to go up to the trenches in the firing line & bring down a Maxim. Plenty of bullets up there. Too cool to sleep at night. The hills & banks all round the shore are a wonderful sight as everyone has to dig himself in, & in consequence they are just a mass of burrows.
>
> 30 April. Very heavy rifle & shrapnel fire during the night & a good dose of shrapnel at dawn to wake us

up. A man shot within a few yards of me at breakfast. Making my dugout safer & more comfortable & had a good sleep. All day long there is a constant shower of bullets, a good few got hit. The wonder is more don't. Each man does his own cooking & one has to go out under fire & gather sticks to boil one's billy. Got bacon, jam & raisins served out for tea. Saw a couple of our guns going up tonight. They will get some more Turkish delight tomorrow, as the boys say.

1 May. The usual dose of shrapnel at reveille. Given a place in the battalion this morning—C Coy, No. 9 Platoon. Had a great dinner, fried up bully beef, bacon & onions. The base is a wonderful sight now. Saw General Birdwood this morning when I went up for water. About 4pm we moved up behind the firing line. Such a night, the Turks were only 300 yards away & we were waiting with fixed bayonets all the time expecting them to charge. We got a good go at them with rifles about dawn.

2 May. Very heavy shrapnel fire first thing but we are pretty well dug in. My mate isn't up to much. Spent the day digging in for shelter against shrapnel & occasional sniping. It is very cramped in the trench & one dare not put your head up for more than a couple of seconds. They have a machine gun which just has our range. Heavy shrapnel fire in the afternoon but we are pretty safe from that. A chap in the next trench got shot badly through the throat. An extra man came into the trench about 7 pm as we are expecting a heavy attack tonight. We were firing hard all the night.

The Turkish supply chain was shorter, its base at Istanbul a day's steaming away. There was also a longer overland route by railway. The Turkish 5th Army enjoyed the breadth of the peninsula with more space and infrastructure, including access to potable water from wells, to support its men in the front lines. On the other hand, Hamilton's expeditionary force was further from its supply bases, confined to small beachheads and reliant on potable water sent from Egypt in barges. It was far more vulnerable to having its supplies cut as Turkish gunners had the advantage of observation from the high ground and constantly shelled the disembarkation piers. The Turkish warship *Turgud Reis* and many well-sited gun batteries targeted Allied transports off Anzac Cove throughout this entire period.

As their sole response Harry and Philip were ordered to keep *Turgud Reis* out of effective range by directing naval shelling over the hills of the peninsula and down onto her decks. *Turgud Reis* was a credible threat to supplies, mentioned over 25 times in Clarkee's flight returns as shelling transports off Anzac Cove. On most days *Turgud Reis* steamed along the Narrows to a point where her 11-inch guns could effectively engage the transports. Once return fire was directed at her (with the assistance of a seaplane or the kite balloon) she broke off the engagement and either sought shelter in the lee of the cliffs lining the Narrows or steamed northwards out of range, as Harry reported:

> Then we have got a little of our own in the battleship duel across the Straits. The *Turgud Reis* or the *Goeben* is in the habit of appearing on the other side at dawn and loosing off half a dozen 11 inch shells, generally at the *Ark Royal*, which she has taken an intrusive dislike to— some of them have fallen very close. Well, the fleet got tired of this game and on three successive mornings I was sent up before dawn to where the battleship was, then

gave the order to *Queen* to fire and all opened their big guns on her at my direction—it was like a glorified sporting gun with 12 inch shells instead of No. 5 Shot. The unfortunate thing was that the Turks were quite alive to the game and as soon as they heard me in the air the fact was signalled to their battleship and she steamed away. It was a question of time before we had her.

Ark Royal's seaplane flight conducted 20 spotting missions in an attempt to sink her, with *Triumph* providing the gunnery in most cases. Two representative flights illustrate this process. On 27 April, 11-inch shells burst among transports in the anchorage off Anzac Cove before a seaplane spotted *Triumph's* fire onto *Turgud Reis*, forcing her to move out of range after a few shots:

> Yesterday I spotted the *Triumph* onto *Turgud Reis* getting one shot just over, about 20 yards. Meanwhile *Turgud Reis* went fast under a cliff and bolted northwest.

This was repeated on 30 April with two shells fired from *Triumph* straddling *Turgud Reis*, again forcing her into a hasty retreat up the Narrows. Without the capability of the air service to counter *Turgud Reis*, a stranglehold on ANZAC was begging. The complete dependence of the Allied forces on the shipping of potable water by barge suggests that continued disruption to supply would have had an immediate effect.

For the infantry, few gains could be made in the face of accurate rifle fire and heavy artillery barrages. A pattern emerges in which seaplanes flew over enemy gun batteries hidden in the scrub simply to reduce the terrible effect of shrapnel on men caught in the open:

As for ourselves, we have been going on doing the same thing, patrolling over the lines and now the Turks cease firing altogether with their field guns when we are up. We have also spotted various battleships onto different forts and burned Maidos.

Private No. 13 Yanni Ilia of the 1st Battalion, 13th Regiment, 5th Division of the recently deployed Turkish 2 Corps, was captured by a digger on 2 May. Ilia told Lieutenant Pirie of the Royal Navy Volunteer Reserve (a Turkish-speaking Intelligence Officer attached to ANZAC) over tea and biscuits that:

> They were marching along gullies and water courses to escape observation. They have standing orders to cease fire and hide whenever a seaplane is sighted. The Turks are quite nervous about the seaplanes and our shrapnel. The proclamations scattered by seaplanes have been picked up and read—the news of German non-success has had a depressing effect, the 13th had no rations at all since Friday when they had bread and German soup.

Australian Headquarters was keen to learn as much as possible about the enemy. After capture, each soldier was given first aid, interrogated and then interned in a stockade at the beach. The prisoners were fed and treated well. The majority were privates and were happy to talk with polite Lieutenant Pirie:

> The Turks had no complaints about food. Only 150 rounds per man . . . reasonably well fed, water brought by horse transport . . . considers his officers to be very bad. Thinks quality of food deteriorating—officers

neglecting the men . . . prisoner has diarrhoea from water—was harried about and made to work—hence desertion. This man has been sent to hospital . . .

Birdie had given his intelligence officers a set of priority intelligence requirements—a list of facts he needed to know *now*. After identifying the prisoner's unit (and the name of the commanders all the way up to corps level), the prisoner was then asked the route his unit had taken to get to Gaba Tepe, details of contact with German officers, the amount of rations and ammunition provided, and the locations of Turkish gun batteries. Then an officer was captured and the situation became just that little bit clearer:

Prisoner of War 6 May 1915

Major Hadji Ali—Yuzbashi Tripoli in Africa, Adana Regiment 2 Army Corps. He was 5th Division Transport Officer.

Shells and a bomb fell quite close to their HQ—animals hit also a few soldiers. His stores are coming up by way of Biyuk Anafarta village from Gallipoli. There they take to a new concealed road through the hills—on this his battalion of 800 men are working. All tents concealed by branches. This road is covered by trees to mask it from seaplanes. Used to come from Constantinople to Gallipoli but owing to shelling and bombardment 5 days ago the base has been transferred to Sharkeui and Hexamul (where there are now important stores). Stores still pass through Gallipoli. There are 3 or 4 transports coming from Sharkeui: barley, oil, rice, wheat, grain, sugar and butter. They have

commandeered all cattle and are serving fresh meat at
the rate of 4 beasts per battalion per two days. Men get
a hot meal once every two days. Heavy gun ammunition is plentiful, but distributed in hidden dug outs at
the bottom of hills. They fear to centralise it for fear of
seaplanes. Has been 25 years in army—served in Italian
and Balkan wars. He dislikes Turks, says that troops
have now to be driven into action at revolver point.

An unusual feature of the ANZAC approach to the use of
Harry's seaplanes was the attachment of an Australian artillery officer to his flight. This practice, although marginal to
the activities of an army corps numbering many thousands,
was indicative of Birdie's flexibility and his grasp of new
technologies. Harry could not find the hidden guns:

We have flown slowly backwards and forwards over the
Turkish lines while our troops were attacking in order
to prevent their using their field guns and it has the
effect of keeping their fire down. The Turks are quite
cluey enough to realise that if they fire they will be
discovered; and if they don't fire, they are so well concealed in the brushwood that we can't find them except
by fluke.

Perhaps an artillery observer would help—perhaps they
could use a thief to catch a thief.

Lieutenant Graham Davies of the Royal Field Artillery
flew missions over the Gaba Tepe area to locate the hidden
gun batteries. He flew on nine spotting and reconnaissance
missions, with post-mission reports specifically including
his name and position as a Forward Observation Officer to
add credibility. His first flight was on 28 April. He then flew

as an observer in support of ANZAC Orders No. 5 during the ANZAC push on 1 and 2 May. The flight records noted that, in support of the battle, Davies conducted a 'reconnaissance over Gaba Tepe district: observed a suspicious place in the olive grove, which might be an emplacement'. Harry, of course, was more direct:

> Two reconnaissances were made and Whitehead took up a gunner to see whether he could find the enemy's batteries, but he was no more successful than we were. He said that things were so critical on the second day that Birdwood seriously thought of abandoning the landing.

Davies rejoined his battery on 8 May. The perspective gained from his flights proved enormously valuable to ANZAC and Davies corrected the artillery range cards from sketches he had made. Lieutenant Colonel Edmund Nicholson's original brown cloth-covered field service book (held in the Australian War Memorial) has a copy of Davies' sketch map showing enemy trench lines on the 1:40,000 scale and the possible placement of Turkish artillery batteries attributed to air service reporting.

Harry's seaplanes continued to assist the infantry, particularly when troops had to move in the open. On 7 May, Flight No. 170 was just such a mission:

> Patrolling in front of lines to keep down fire, while landing of additional troops was going on. Time: 1 hour 42 minutes.

Some three missions were conducted to keep shrapnel bursts from tearing into the heads and shoulders of the men as they rowed ashore. Significantly, the Turkish Air Service Rumpler swooped on this plum target, with a 'German aeroplane' dropping two bombs among the packed transports.

Private Herbert Reynolds of the 1st Field Ambulance was a keen diarist. His first aid station had a vista out to sea and he often recorded *Manica*'s balloon or one of Harry's seaplanes flying overhead:

> There has been practically no wounded at any of the dressing stations today. About 5pm the battleships put a number of shells into the fort on Kaba Tepe while our field guns burst a few shrapnel around it. Just at sunset all the battle ships commenced a terrific bombardment of the enemy. A seaplane was circling around overhead evidently directing their fire.
>
> 3 May. The *Goeben* sent over a good number of shells this morning and succeeded in hitting one of the transports anchored off our position. It evidently did no great amount of damage, though a huge sheet of flame went up when it exploded, as it steamed off with the rest of the boats and anchored further off shore. There have been a fairly large number of casualties today.
>
> 7 May. The enemy's artillery has been very active, especially from Kaba Tepe, but the damage done was very slight compared to yesterday. They put one of our field guns out of action and disabled the crew. One of our seaplanes has been very busy attempting to locate the enemy battery behind Kaba Tepe. Reinforcements have been arriving all day in destroyers.
>
> 9 May. Early this morning the *Goeben* sent over a few large shells with the usual result, only causing a splash. The enemy's artillery has been very active

again, they did not cease firing today like they usually do when the captive balloon on the [*Manica*] or a seaplane went up. About 3pm the enemy ceased his artillery fire and things became unnaturally quiet for the rest of the day.

Birdie's requests for help were answered. Orders for Harry's seaplanes at Z Beach went via Cecil Thursby as Commander of the 2nd Naval Squadron to *Ark Royal* or *Manica*. Birdie's request for Charles' assistance, which was outside Thursby's chain of command, was also effectively answered. Birdie wrote a letter to Sir Ian Hamilton which was forwarded for action by Charles' aviators. It was to save ANZAC from annihilation:

May an aeroplane reconnaissance be made of the area in my immediate vicinity, with orders to clear up the following:—

Enemy concentration in 224 N 9 6

Enemy concentration in 224 J 7 9

Enemy guns, especially in 224 N 9, 224 J 6, 4 gun battery in olive grove . . .

General information as to location of camps, stores in KAJADERE, BOGHALI, BIYUK ANAFARTA would also be useful. Such a reconnaissance every few days would be desirable.

This request was sent to the aerodrome on Tenedos and several scouting missions were launched in response.

To further promote cooperation, a landing ground and a seaplane base were reconnoitred at Anzac Cove. Lieutenant Geoffrey 'Bromo' Bromet went ashore on 8 May while *Turgud Reis* was once again shelling ANZAC transports, to meet Birdie and scout for a suitable position. The confines of the cove and steep terrain made this impossible. A seaplane station held greater potential, but there was no suitable cover. A few days later a seaplane base was built across the sea on the island of Imbros.

Hamilton's headquarters also attempted to influence Turkish morale through the aerial scattering of propaganda pamphlets. The genesis of this program lay in an intelligence report sent by Birdie's ANZAC Headquarters to Hamilton describing the low state of morale of Turkish troops. In response, 'I' Branch (Intelligence) was ordered to draft proclamations. Proclamations were printed in both Arabic and Turkish for scattering by aircraft over the front lines in the first week of May, and attempted to persuade the hardy Turkish soldier that he had been duped by German leadership into a war that would lead to misery, death and failure.

Harry scattered the first propaganda pamphlets over Turkish trenches on the 400 Plateau at Johnston's Jolly on 1 May:

> One flight I had was amusing—I became a tract distributer. If all else fails I shall apply to the National Bible Tract Society for a job, hanging in the air and dropping tracts to the unfaithful below. This time it was experimental. The Germans have been spreading stories among the Turks that we starve and torture our prisoners, so General Birdwood got some of our prisoners to write letters in Turkish saying how well they were treated, and then told us to drop them. It seemed a

pity to let them go alone so I mustered all the Arabic I could remember and issued invitations to food and wine aboard the *Ark Royal* to all and sundry, spouted some pretty home truths about the Germans calling them pigs and sons of immoral dogs, then wrapped them up with a sixpence each, enclosed them in weighted bags with the Turkish letters, and long streamers attached to the bags to attract attention. I labelled the lot 'frightfulness' and proceeded with Joe Kilner to drop them.

Yanni Ilia had seen the packets flutter to earth. Harry's sixpences were not mentioned, no doubt quickly disappearing into soldiers' pockets.

Charles' squadron was also ordered to drop two packets of proclamations over Krithia at the southern end of the peninsula. A similar order was given to the Commanding Officer of HMS *Minerva*, which had a seaplane aboard, requiring 40 copies each of the Arabic and Turkish versions to be dropped by the seaplane over infantry positions in the Gulf of Smyrna. On 13 May repeat orders directed a seaplane to 'drop proclamations in the Turkish trenches' at Anzac but the seaplane failed to claw sufficient height and the tracts remained in the hands of the observer. They were later thrown into the Turkish trenches from ANZAC trenches by the infantry. On 29 May a third batch of proclamations exhorting the Turkish soldiers to surrender was scattered by a seaplane and a copy of this proclamation (translated into English) was included in the ANZAC intelligence war diary. It urges the 'deceived Turks' to reconsider their faith in German leadership.

The tempo of operations soon wore down *Ark Royal's* flight capability. Clarkee reported to Rear Admiral Thursby his concerns over poor use of his dwindling assets, requesting stricter economy of effort in the employment of flights. Clarkee cleverly quoted a recent report on the RFC in France (published by Sir John French on 4 April 1915) to illustrate the amount of effort required for each mission. He followed this letter the next day with a more detailed request, noting that the present arrangements for three daily flights at 5 am, 11 am and 4 pm dedicated to spotting on *Turgud Reis* had, at times, proved fruitless as she had been out of range. Clarkee's solution was to hold a seaplane on standby to prosecute a mission when *Turgud Reis* opened fire. He held grave concerns over serviceability: only one aircraft was fit for active service, two aircraft were erected awaiting trial, two were in overhaul, and the two single-seater scouts were parcelled out for operations off Smyrna. Clarkee warned that he would be unable to conduct anti-submarine patrolling and reconnaissance duties in the near future unless he was able to husband his resources. His recommendations were adopted.

On paper, Harry's seaplane squadron comprised ten seaplanes on 14 May. In practice the seaplane flight had one twin and two single-seaters fit for service. Clarkee was given a collier, SS *Pemmovah*, as a depot ship on which seaplanes could be erected and overhauled in Mudros Harbour. After almost every flight over Anzac structural repairs were required, including patching a 'collection' of bullet holes sustained from rifle fire. The fate of Seaplane No. 136, a Short, is worth exploring as it illustrates the fragility of the canvas and wood seaplanes:

I remember a very hot flight with Edward Dunning when we explored all the roads to Maidos and North to Taifur Keui (and fired at the whole way). Then over the Turkish lines and behind them trying vainly to locate their cleverly concealed batteries—we were only some 1500 feet above them and the machine was riddled with bullets besides a lot of shrapnel being fired around us. Edward and Martha Park tried to do the same thing and got a little lower and did not get off so cheaply. The butt of Edward's revolver was shot away, Martha's headrest was blown off. Two shots came just beside his two feet, two others went through the petrol tank.

Landing on a choppy sea completely wrecked the seaplane. The mission lasted a mere one hour and 45 minutes.

The seaplanes were required to operate over a wide area. One serviceable seaplane was parcelled out to *Doris*, another to *Minerva*. Following operations off Bulair, Sopwith No. 922 was returned to *Ark Royal* on 29 April 1915 in a state of disrepair as it had been stored on the aft gun turret. Firing of the gun had caused the wings to warp and the fabric to strip from the machine. A fast single-engine scout (Sopwith 1437) was then placed on *Doris* and another (Sopwith No. 1478) on *Minerva*. Two flights were conducted from *Doris* over Smyrna in an attempt to locate Turkish torpedo boat destroyers. During operations from *Minerva*, three maritime patrols and one bombing mission were conducted against the Sanjik fort.

Philip's kite balloon was in such demand off Anzac that prolonged inflation, plus the effects of salt and sunlight, soon caused the envelope to deteriorate. Philip decided to deploy a Boer War veteran, a spherical balloon which had remained stored in *Manica*'s hold. It was attached to the tug *Rescue* under command of Lieutenant Hartford. A number of flights were attempted, but its fabric was also in poor condition. So the spherical balloon was scrapped and the tug was used to store hydrogen bottles, reducing the risk to *Manica*. A request for a replacement envelope was sent to the Director of the Air Department. Rear Admiral de Robeck supported this with a signal to the Admiralty describing the valuable assistance lent by the air service:

> Spotting by aeroplanes steadily improving. The mere sight of a kite balloon rising often causes enemy batteries to cease firing . . . A kite balloon ashore would be useful; but a second kite balloon ship is most desirable.

Anzac Cove turned into an ants' nest with the men living and sleeping underground. Private Richard Bulkeley adapted to his new life. An infantry soldier's day was spent digging, carrying water, on trench duty, or sleeping. It presented a marked contrast to the life of aviators who enjoyed safe billets:

> 14 May. Off work at 6am. Got a bit of breakfast & turned in for a sleep, on again at noon digging a trench. There was an awful stink in it & had a look over the top & there was one of our boys dead & nearly stripped & as black as a nigger & swelled up, an awful sight, but one is so used to these things now that you don't take much notice. A German spy was shot early this morning, also a letter was sent in saying that we could not take the Dardanelles & had better surrender. Off digging at 6pm & went in the trenches in the main line & in a good posy. One bad casualty only in the night & a lot of heavy firing on the left.
>
> 17 May. Came out of the trenches at 5am but had to go back in reserve about 9. Back in the firing line at noon. The enemy had an 18 pounder about 300 yards in front of the trenches & all the afternoon they were knocking hell out of us. All we could do was to lay in

the bottom of the trench while they knocked the top & sand bags in on us. Came out at 7pm & went down to the beach & had a swim. Saw a lot of 2nd Battalion who have just come back from helping the Tommies down south. They were badly cut up, only 1,800 came back out of 5,000. Were to have had the night off to sleep but were called up twice.

At Cape Helles Turkish soldiers hidden in the stone fortress of Sedd el Bahr and its broken village fought on. Hidden behind broken walls, they sighted their Mauser rifles, levelling the foresight on the heads and chests of advancing British soldiers. A squeeze of the trigger and the figure fell. But the British kept coming and soon they were within the broken castle. War became medieval. Soldiers hunted one another in small groups. Bayonets thrust into bellies. Too much blood was spilt for quarter. Turkish soldiers became trapped in storerooms and in dark corners where they died. It was not until late afternoon on 26 April that the castle was taken. The village behind fell to a series of punishing assaults. Men died in empty chicken coops. Soldiers from both sides lay in agony on the floor of stone huts, soup bubbling in the corners of kitchens. This punishing action delayed the 29th Division as it attempted to consolidate its beachhead, even before an advance to Krithia could be attempted. Over the following two or three days, the British division lay exhausted in huddled groups around the clifftops, unable to exploit its brief numerical advantage. The nameless dead were buried in pits, officers interred separately in marked graves.

Charles' aviators flying over the peninsula reported that only company-sized units moved southwards from regimental camps. The British 29th Division had successfully landed, but was now cut off from Charles' observers—it was operating blind. In effect the British division had only a small window of opportunity to advance towards the village of Krithia and the high ground of Achi Baba as the enemy required two or three days to assemble to meet this threat. The ruse at Bulair was now exposed. The division's commander, Sir Aylmer Hunter-Weston, was unaware of this opportunity and planned an assault at 8 am on 28 April. By this time the first fresh battalions of Turkish reinforcements, first the Bursa Jandarma Battalion, then the 20th Regiment, had occupied the high ground after a gruelling march from Bulair to replenish the hard-hit Turkish 9th Infantry Division.

In the first two days the 29th Division was ashore, Charles' aviators conducted 18 missions with 11 reconnaissance flights, including two photographic missions. These all told that the path to Achi Baba was clear of enemy troops. Seven spotting missions were flown, directing naval shelling of roads which significantly delayed the Turkish reorganisation. The officers hesitated, afraid of being caught on the open road where naval shells would tear apart their young men. They wrote a complicated set of movement orders which involved men moving southwards in alternate leaps and bounds to reduce casualties, but which caused considerable delays in the movement of reinforcements.

British radio communications were now under severe pressure given the amount of signal traffic. Aerial reconnaissance reports were picked up by Hamilton on *Queen Elizabeth* but not by Sir Aylmer on *Euryalus* which monitored a different wavelength. Then Sir Aylmer joined his troops ashore. A small knoll, now cleared of enemy, became the Divisional Headquarters. Trenches and dugouts were constructed and a mole city was created to house red-tabbed officers. The communications gap between Bernard Isaac and the head-quarters widened. The eyes in the sky became abstract; reporting from brigade positions relied on breathless runners and assumed greater importance. Sir Aylmer's appreciation of the battlespace was further hampered by the terrible confusion on the crowded and heavily shelled beachhead. The problems for divisional staff officers on land and under shelling were multiplied by competing priorities and casualties, and subject to the confusion that follows all major engagements in war.

A loss of situational awareness is the norm in war. Communications are the first to fail; disruptions breaking the chain of command are a constant feature of battle. Sir Aylmer's staff were no exception. Importantly, Charles had been tasked to reconnoitre their objectives: the village of Krithia and the dominant hill of Achi Baba. Henry Butler flew two photographic missions on 26 and 27 April, identifying Turkish trenches at the base of the hill and in front of the village, forming a defensive line some distance from the congested Allied shell-scrapes clustered around the cape. There was a gap—an uncontested no man's land of three kilometres. This critical information was passed to Hamilton, but because of the gap in communications, it was not received by Sir Aylmer and his staff. The death of Lieutenant Colonel Charles Doughty-Wylie while leading a charge in the broken village on 26 April was having an effect. He had commanded the Intelligence Branch at General Headquarters.

Hamilton had found an ingenious solution to his communications woes—he had organised a private telephone company to assist his landings. A cable ship, SS *Levante*, carrying drums containing kilometres of copper cabling, waited offshore. Rubber-coated submarine telephone cabling was laid on the ocean floor by *Levante* on 29 April. Telephones now connected Bernard Issac on Tenedos with Sir Aylmer and his headquarters dug in above W Beach. A cable office in a gully was manned by suited employees of the Eastern Telegraph Company. Even by today's standards this is impressive. It took a week for my telco to connect me, and there were no shells exploding in my suburban street. But this unavoidable delay of four days meant that Bernard could not speak with Sir Aylmer's staff just when he was needed. From 2 May a web of undersea cables connected *Arcadian* (Hamilton's new headquarters ship anchored offshore) to Birdie at Anzac Cove and Sir Aylmer at Cape Helles. It is incredible that there is no record of how many of these civilian contractors were killed. Perhaps their names are listed in gold lettering on a board somewhere in the United Kingdom.

Sir Aylmer's staff were keen for information and a stream of prisoners of war provided a window into the enemy's mind. Captured Turkish soldiers were escorted to the Divisional Headquarters for interrogation, to be met by a kindly Turkish-speaking Intelligence Officer. In the pocket of a dead Turkish officer was his diary listing his orders, to the point of his death. This and the results of oral interrogation were summarised in a printed pamphlet. This intelligence identified where Turkish units deployed from and the order of battle, but not the actual location of Turkish trenches. These were identified by Charles' observers and recorded by Bernard on his master map. But this information was not in a form that could be easily sent from Tenedos as it required printing on overlays by lithographic presses on the *Arcadian* (which by then was moored in Kephalo Bay). This fractured the reporting methodology available before the landing. As a result of this unavoidable delay, Sir Aylmer lost his situational awareness.

Until the telephone was connected there was no opportunity to fold Bernard's priceless information into Sir Aylmer's orders for the First Battle of Krithia. Instead of enemy locations, objectives were defined by dotted phase lines on a map. Bernard had the Turkish trenches marked on the map hanging from the pole of his tent. Instead of using Bernard's map, a cyclist company was sent out to draw sketches. These had little value in the ensuing battle. Company commanders did not know where to find the enemy. The artillery did not know where to explode its shrapnel. The loss of situational awareness experienced by the British was *in extremis.*

Without accurate location of Turkish gun batteries, British and French artillery were unable to bring effective counter-battery fire to assist the advancing infantry. At 8 am on 28 April, British and French soldiers began skirmishing forward in long lines. They walked across the onion fields, jumped an occasional stone wall, then moved into the open. Trenches dug in front of Krithia and the lower slopes of Achi Baba (not described in orders) poured a murderous fire into the ranks of the 87th Brigade on the left, the 88th Brigade in the centre and the French 1st Division on the far right flank. Unmolested by counter-battery fire, Turkish gunners fused their 75 mm shrapnel shells with precision. The toy-like figures fell. Officers waved the remaining men forward, pointing vaguely at the middle distance, still unsure where the fire was coming from.

It was artillery heaven. A Turkish forward observer stood in a trench on the slopes of Achi Baba and corrected the fall of shot over his telephone. In the late afternoon, a Turkish 9th Division counterattack drove out the 29th Division men who had captured a number of skirmishing trenches in the morning. The British stumbled back to their own trenches, grateful for some cover. Ultimately Sir Aylmer's plan was a complete and bloody fiasco with 2000 British and 1000 French dead and dying.

Unlike Birdie, Sir Aylmer did not organise for aeroplanes to silence Turkish gun batteries during the assault. The Turkish batteries remained active, exploding shrapnel and killing hundreds of soldiers as they slowly walked across the fields. Charles' flight records reveal that no aeroplanes were flying at the time the infantry climbed out of their safe positions and advanced in the open. A reconnaissance flight was flown from 5.45 to 7.45 am followed by a spotting flight for *Prince George* from 9.40 to 11.40 am. Despite a mere 20-minute transit from Tenedos, there was no aeroplane overhead from 7.20 to 10 am just as British and French troops were skirmishing forward over open ground.

Instead, Charles' squadron supported the afternoon assaults in coordination with naval warships. The air service on Tenedos used the naval radio net. Bernard reported directly to de Robeck on *Queen Elizabeth* via naval radio and picket boat. Two spotting missions were flown in coordination with the navy, spotting onto Turkish troops assembling for the afternoon counterattack south of Kereves Dere. Now it was time for the Turkish infantry to suffer. Five reconnaissance flights reported three field batteries limbered and redeploying in the open, with over 2000 Turkish troops forming up at various times for the afternoon counterattack. The warships out to sea fired down the bearing and were given corrections by Charles' observers. Horses died in their traces, the guns were dragged under cover. Soldiers scattered, their ears ringing with the high percussion of naval shells. If they survived, they were brutalised, fear gnawing at the edges of their minds. The bursts—air or ground—of naval shells were too much for flesh to cope with. These shells were designed to

punch through steel at 20 kilometres. What it did to a man
was indescribable.

Turkish gunners usually covered their guns with brushwood to conceal their positions from aerial observation. But
these were newly arrived reinforcements and they were slow
to learn. They were seen and targeted with 20lb bombs; more
importantly, however, they were drawn on Bernard's map. At
11.09 am, in his fury, Charles dropped three 100lb bombs
on a four-gun battery. It had pulled up alongside the road,
its 75 mm guns sending shells above the lines of advancing
troops. Charles could see a bursting black cloud, then a line
of fallen men. The enemy gunners were new to the peninsula. They were not aware of the threat lurking overhead:

> I dropped a bomb alongside. A great explosion. I saw a
> wheel spinning into the air. Then my next hit a wagon,
> filled with shells. This too went up!

Charles could clearly see enemy trenches snaking across
the battlefield. The trenches were lined with brown-clad
Turkish soldiers. The British could not see them; they
walked slowly forward until a Turkish officer gave the order
to fire. It was factory murder—corpses were created as if on
a production line. First, take one innocent 19-year-old boy,
dress him in a khaki uniform and order him to walk vaguely
forward . . .

After the battle, Charles' aviators flew missions over
the Turkish rear echelon, their logistic and supply areas.
A picture developed of Turkish plans. Fifteen missions
were flown on 30 April, one a dedicated military reconnaissance with Captain David Jenkins as observer, while
five were combined reconnaissance and bomb attacks
against major concentrations of Turkish reserves:

> ... a long reconnaissance to beyond Bulair to locate
> enemy reserves and movement of troops ... the long
> reconnaissance to Bulair was successful and troops and
> camps were located.

Large transport columns were seen moving towards Krithia, including one of more than 200 pack animals. Six 100lb and nine 20lb bombs were dropped with 'good results', sending camels scattering in panic. Then Charles saw over 7000 Turkish infantry on the march. Reports from *Ark Royal* and *Manica* of transports through the Narrows during the previous days were also in Hamilton's possession but had eluded Sir Aylmer. The telephone was now in operation. All Bernard heard when he rang through was the engaged tone.

On the evening of his triumphant defence of Krithia, General Otto Liman von Sanders formed a Southern Group under Colonel von Sodernstern, instructing him to make a decisive assault against the remnant force at Cape Helles. The failure of the Allied push provided an opportunity for his new reserves to drive the weakened invaders back into the sea. The German colonel had more imagination than Sir Aylmer; he proposed a night attack with the newly arrived 3rd, 7th and 11th infantry divisions. These men had disembarked from steamers, marched down the roads and were bivouacked in camps around Krithia. The newly erected camps were cherries to Charles' aviators. Their occupants had not had time for, nor knew the importance of, digging protective trenches but remained under the flimsy protection of canvas, proof against weather but not against bombs. The experienced Turkish 3 Corps had learnt in the weeks prior to the landing to protect themselves from aircraft raids by digging slit trenches and using camouflage. As fresh battalions arrived by steamer, they learnt this important lesson the hard way. Charles' air superiority had dire consequences for the Turkish 5th Army. It had to prosecute a daytime ground battle without a viable answer to hostile aircraft overhead.

But Colonel Eduard von Sodernstern knew enemy aeroplanes were restricted to daylight operations. His night attack coincided with moonset in the early hours of 2 May. Total surprise was achieved with an attack by 18 battalions forcing a limited breakthrough in the centre—but it was a momentary success. Even an imaginative attack could not cope with the reality of deep trenches. In the early dawn light, a British counterattack cut the enemy salient and by morning both sides were back in their original lines.

Charles and Bernard were learning that they could read the battlefield like an open book. At 6000 feet they could read the signs of future events. Colonel von Sodernstern's attack should have been cut down; it had lost the element of surprise. An engaged telephone was the difference between success and failure, a modern version of an old nursery rhyme:

> For want of a nail the shoe was lost.
> For want of a shoe the horse was lost.
> For want of a horse the rider was lost.
> For want of a rider the battle was lost.
> For want of a battle the kingdom was lost.
> And all for the want of a horseshoe nail.

To bridge the gap between Bernard and Sir Aylmer, Charles surveyed a forward aerodrome at Cape Helles. A flat stretch of earth was levelled ending at the Divisional Headquarters. Sir Aylmer's mole city became Hunter-Weston Redoubt, and in the first week of May three shuttle flights brought spares, oil, fuel and ground crew to service two airframes based at this forward aerodrome. By 5 May it was a working forward base. In cases where an observer saw something of urgency and it was too detailed to be relayed via a Morse keyed radio, the pilot could land, allowing his observer to dash into the bunker and provide a verbal report. In some cases written messages could be dropped to allow an important flight to continue.

The forward aerodrome came too late to inject aerial intelligence into Sir Aylmer's headquarters for the next daylight assault, the Second Battle of Krithia, which was launched on 4 May. Sir Aylmer was reinforced with a brigade from the Lancashire Division and the 2nd Australian Brigade and the New Zealand Infantry Brigade from ANZAC. They would suffer for their assistance. Bernard finally got through to the redoubt and received a request for a copy of his map. But this came on the first day of the battle, too late to be included in orders. In reply, Bernard put a folded map in the hands of an observer and sent him across the sea to the forward aerodrome, where he arrived early on 5 May, just as the second day of the battle began. The scale map fixed the elusive enemy front lines, supplying grid references for trenches and gun batteries. But once again it was too late for the poor bloody infantry. The pity of it was that another 1000 young men were cut to pieces.

On 4 May, the opening day of the battle, Turkish gun batteries on the Asiatic coast at In Tepe were targeted. The navy had its head on correctly: it ordered Charles' aviators to conduct four spotting flights and one photographic mission. The navy finally discovered the magic that aircraft kept the Asiatic gun batteries (on the opposite shore) from shelling the exposed beaches. Naval gunnery officers in their towers saw that aircraft flying over enemy batteries kept enemy gunners respectfully silent. Only two reconnaissance missions were flown from Tenedos to Krithia in support of the army, but no aeroplanes were sent aloft to support the infantry assault itself. As the battle dragged on with a pattern of murderous daylight assaults on 5, 6, 7 and 8 May, aeroplanes based on the exposed forward aerodrome corrected for naval gunfire support, then belatedly for army gun batteries.

With the rush to establish the aerodrome in support of the coming battle, no prior practice in radio communications was conducted between Charles' aeroplanes and the field brigade artillery designated to support the assault. Typically, this rendered air support ineffectual. Charles' observers tapped out corrections on their Morse key to the gunners serving the heavy artillery, but the military receiving stations could not pick up aeroplane signals as the army did not have the naval bandwidth. Only warships, which had this capability, were able to respond to spotting corrections. In order to overcome this frustrating breakdown with the army, pilots actually landed their aeroplanes at the forward aerodrome. David Jenkins, Reginald Marix and Charles Samson ran into Hunter-Weston Redoubt and placed their index fingers on the gunners' map. Then the chief gunner and the frustrated observer spotted the battery onto the target by firing a series of coloured flares. This caught the enemy's attention and they either dragged their guns to safety or the artillery fell silent.

The attacks by the New Zealand Infantry Brigade and the 2nd Brigade on 8 May went ahead without Charles' support. The ANZACs were subject to a poorly organised, last-minute issuing of orders by Sir Aylmer. It was 5 pm and the men were boiling their billies in a hidden gully, making their tea. Then the telephone rang. They were ordered to advance over 1000 yards of open ground, keeping the main road to Krithia on their right. The men were ripped apart by shrapnel while advancing across open fields to get to the forward trenches even before they could participate in the assault. The location of enemy trenches remained a mystery, despite four days of repeated assaults. Although Charles' aviators flew 13 supporting missions on the day, only one aeroplane was aloft in the late afternoon on spotting duties, and it returned to Tenedos at 5 pm. There were no aeroplanes to silence enemy gun batteries just as the Australian 2nd Brigade advanced from the safety of its gully. The ANZACs littered the ground. They died without knowing where the enemy was.

Two days after the end of the battle, a composite photographic trench map was passed to Sir Aylmer's planners. Henry Butler worked in a makeshift darkroom built from an aircraft packing case. The photographic mosaic was then reprinted and delivered in a shuttle flight. It was a work of wonder. It gave forward observers a point at which to aim and a chance to produce a range card. This was particularly valuable given the tight rationing of artillery shells.

Hauptmann Erich Serno's 1st Aircraft Company had one simple purpose: to destroy the enemy air service. Harry and Philip were their primary targets. Supplies eventually reached Channakale from their illegal overland route. Equipped with replacement propellers and tins of petrol, they embarked on a campaign to destroy the RNAS. Eight bombing attacks were launched against ships off Gaba Tepe, five against *Manica*, one against *Ark Royal*, with two against overloaded transports. Philip reported to the Admiralty that his ship had been attacked three times in four days by an aeroplane which, on one occasion, almost succeeded in hitting her. Likewise, Turkish gun batteries focused their

attention on Harry and Philip. Their goal was to poke
Birdie in the eyes:

> The Turks have taken a real dislike to this ship and yes-
> terday morning they picked her out from everything
> to fire 11 inch shells from the Narrows at us and jolly
> good shooting they made. If we hadn't got under way
> immediately after the first shell, they would have strad-
> dled us. The same thing happened on two occasions
> later in the day.

Hamilton's expeditionary force did not capture any of the
dominant ground. It spent its time looking uphill. But it
did have the perspective provided by the balloon allowing observation of Turkish logistic areas. The kite balloon
was aloft during daylight hours on 13 days from 26 April
to 17 May and was paired with a number of warships for
directing the guns onto Turkish supplies. Philip concentrated his efforts on starving the Turkish 5th Army. If you
can't kill them, make them thin and hungry.

Dawn on 27 April was clear. Philip climbed into the wicker
basket knowing that he had, at the end of his telephone,
the most powerful warship afloat. *Manica* slowly belayed the
kite balloon to its maximum height of 3000 feet. Philip had
a clear view over the high ground of Sari Bair at 971 feet
to the straits on the other side. Still tied alongside to the
jetty at Maidos was a steamer. Ant-like creatures were busy
unloading crates by hand. The steamer started belching coal
smoke; Philip could see that she was about to cut her bonds
and head for safety. Speaking clearly over the telephone,
he quoted the grid reference. *Queen Elizabeth* then fired a
single ranging shot. The sea erupted 100 yards beyond the
steamer's stern. Philip gave the correction: 'one hundred

yards over'. The next 15-inch shell landed on a shed just in front of the steamer: '30 yards under'. The third 15-inch shell passed through the decking and exploded in the bowels of the steamer. It simply ceased to exist. Philip had quietly 'walked' indirect fire over 17,000 yards. Birdie told his diggers of this event in an Army Corps Special Order, similar to the announcement that the Australian submarine *AE2* had passed through the Narrows. News was plastered onto billboards near the beach to tell his men that they were, at times, getting their own back on the enemy.

Over several days Philip continued to smash enemy supply movements. He directed attacks on enemy ports on 29 and 30 April and 2, 5 and 7 May. Buildings and sheds were left burning into the night and for several days after the shelling. Reginald Marix identified 20 Turkish transports off the port of Ak Bashi Liman at dusk on 10 May. Philip was up the next day sending naval shells into the docksides on the far side of the peninsula. On 17 May he directed *Triumph* onto ammunition stores stacked in the village of Boghali, setting the supplies and parts of the village on fire.

The Turks responded to this threat. *Manica* was under observation from the hills of Koja Chemen Tepe and from the garrison on Gaba Tepe. When they saw the balloon slowly rise, they telephoned the port on the other side of the peninsula. Warnings went out. Sea transport which was not of an urgent nature was conducted at night. The Turks played a cat and mouse game with the balloon; it could not be everywhere at once. Air reconnaissance revealed that the Turks continued to unload when they could.

Turkish vessels were consistently reported in the Dardanelles suggesting that Allied submarine 'successes' did not prevent use of the sea. The Turkish 5th Army was reinforced by steamers for all its attacks throughout May.

Steamers disembarking 1 Corps troops from Istanbul were also observed by Harry:

> 12/5 I made a flight with Joe Kilner at the request of Vice Admiral de Robeck to examine the whole Straits from Channakale to Gallipoli and report on shipping. It was a beautiful evening and a good flight. We could see the whole peninsula and right down beyond to Tenedos. We had a good look at the north end—I reported 2 Torpedo Boats besides the *Turgud Reis* and a large number of transports (19 above Nagara and all collecting about 4 miles above Nagara Point in the dusk)—so we warned them.

RNAS reconnaissance reports dating from May to December tell of over 14 craft, usually of small draft, unloading off the docks in daylight at any one time.

How the Turks were feeding their troops was a priority intelligence requirement. Interrogators focused on the amount of rations and ammunition reaching the front. A Turkish soldier's daily allowance of rations was quantified in detail, including the amount of bread, olives and beans and the number of cartridges issued. The disruption to Turkish supplies was manageable as prisoners reported having basic food and water, and being issued with between 100 and 150 cartridges. The Turkish Army had an efficient logistic service based on German principles established some years before the war and it was far closer to its source of supply than the Allied armies.

A close relationship developed between the air service and the submarines which waged an ongoing war. Submarines threatened the supply lines of both sides and exaggerated claims of German U boats were sent to Hamilton in early

May. A number of sources told of German submarines being assembled in Istanbul or numerous clandestine bases along the Aegean coast. Hidden among these were accurate reports from Malta on 11 May of the passage of a U boat into the Mediterranean. A small German coastal submarine, *UB8*, under *Kapitan* von Voigt, proceeded cautiously into the Aegean. The threat was circulated to ships' captains and onto the air service. From 15 May, *Ark Royal* was confined behind anti-torpedo nets in Kephalo Bay on Imbros, just out to sea from Anzac Cove. Owing to a prevailing north-east wind, Clarkee established a shore base for a seaplane station with a southerly aspect:

> I had been doing all the flying lately so the Skipper thought I would appreciate a rest. He gave 'Sloppy' Allsop and me the job of building a seaplane shed on the other side of the point, so that when the wind is blowing into Kephalo Bay we can get a machine off from there.

Harry and Sloppy scraped a land base at Aliki Bay under a protective cliff. They pulled down an old Ottoman stone fort and piled the stones into a sea wall to protect the seaplanes from the weather. A thin spit of sand divided Aliki Bay from a salt lake, enabling seaplanes to use either the lake, Aliki Bay or Kephalo Bay, depending on local climatic conditions. Harry declared the base operational on 17 May.

Three anti-submarine reconnaissance patrols were conducted along the western coast of the Gallipoli Peninsula by the remaining serviceable seaplanes at Imbros. No submarines were sighted. The faster, single-seater Sopwiths were ideal for this patrol work, as they had a wide radius of action and were able to carry four bombs (20lb) on under-wing racks. On 30 May *UB8* torpedoed the dummy warship *Tiger*, ending speculation as to whether submarines were present.

Hamilton had strategic plans for the air service. Following intelligence collected from prisoners of war, he identified a vulnerability in the Turkish defence of the peninsula. On 10 May he sent Vice Admiral de Robeck a formal request for a strategic attack on the sole Turkish gunpowder factory at Istanbul. Hamilton's rationale was sound, as he argued that this was the Turks' only cartridge factory and it was vulnerable to attack from the air. A successful bombing raid could have important results. In his request, Hamilton acknowledged the distance from Cape Helles and the potential risk to his few serviceable airframes. After discussions with de Robeck on 13 May, Hamilton suggested that, by establishing an aerodrome on Xeros Island, the RNAS would find the cartridge factory and other strategic targets within reach. Hamilton also argued that Charles could reach the port of Sharkeui, 'the enemy's principal supply depots and the railway junction at Uzun Keupri'. Hamilton believed that the destruction of Turkish supply infrastructure might prove of great importance.

In pursuit of these strategic aims, Reginald and Charles flew the Breguet, a long-range 'heavy' bomber, with its maximum payload, on an operational mission on 17 May to bomb Maidos. The Breguet was the only aeroplane with the range to attack Istanbul, but its engine was known to be unreliable. They tested its future use by bombing the large camps growing in the valleys behind Anzac. They set off before dawn, hoping to catch the enemy eating their breakfast. The camp cooking fires gave the camps away; hundreds of little lights twinkled in the valley below. To their surprise, Reginald and Charles identified two further divisions of reinforcements disembarking from steamers at

Maidos. The mission was a success and bombs fell among the unsuspecting reinforcements. The Breguet's engine ran rough and was stripped on its return, resulting in the postponement of Hamilton's plans. But the Turkish 5th Army lost the value of surprise for its massed assault on Anzac just as Hamilton and Sir Aylmer learnt the value of such reporting.

CHAPTER 5

The big Turkish attack of 19 May

Private Richard Bulkeley recorded the events of 18 and 19 May 1915 in his diary:

18 May: Off till 11 am when we went into the firing line digging trenches till 5 o'clock. Went into the firing line trenches at 6 pm. The enemy have been reinforced & an attack is expected tonight so every available man is in reserve even the cooks. On first observation with Newton. Very sleepy & tired. Just before midnight there was terrific rifle & machine gun fire all along the left but we were pretty quiet & steady waiting for our turn.

19 May: About an hour before dawn the attack started & the rifle & machine gun fire was terrific. Just at dawn the Turks were everywhere, but they hadn't a hope against our fire, it was terrible. Our boys were just great. They pulled the sand bags off the top of the trenches & fired over the top. The Turks would only

go a few yards & then roll over like rabbits. After it was over there were hundreds of dead & wounded lying in front of the trenches. Some of them got up to within a couple of yards of us. Things were pretty quiet about noon, when we came out & had a rest. Were in reserve all night. Self being on sentry half the time. Could not sleep even though I wanted it badly.

The Turkish Northern Group had attempted to overrun ANZAC on 19 May in a massive surprise attack. The assault was cut to pieces thanks to the timely warning provided by just two men, Charles and Reginald. The Turkish 5th Army was reinforced from Istanbul by two trained divisions from Turkish 1 Corps. These men were crowded onto the decks of steamers with the first relays disembarking at the port of Ak Bashi Liman on 12 May. All this was in preparation for a major offensive. These two divisions were attached to Esat Pasha's Northern Group battling ANZAC—their goal was to destroy ANZAC. On 17 May the recently arrived regimental commanders met in conference in Esat Pasha's tent on Mal Tepe. They were given clear orders for a surprise night attack. The Northern Group's two experienced 19th and 5th divisions and the newly arrived 2nd and 12th divisions would simply swamp ANZAC's two depleted divisions. They would swarm across the narrow gap between the trenches and rush downhill to the beach below. It was a simple plan based on numbers and surprise.

The discovery of Turkish infantry massing for the attack was not accidental. General Birdwood's request for aeroplane reconnaissance over the valleys behind the front line was timely. Birdie ordered Charles' aviators to fly over the villages of Kojadere, Boghali and Biyuk Anafarta which were staging areas for the enemy. Charles' squadron conducted five long-range reconnaissance flights behind Anzac Cove on 16, 17 and 18 May. Three flights were flown as far north as the Bulair Lines and observed the disembarkation of the 2nd and 12th divisions onto the piers of Ak Bashi Liman. They also saw several large encampments outside Maidos and along the road to Boghali. By 18 May the missions had only one objective: 'reconnaissance of Maidos area to observe disembarkation of Turkish troops'.

Bernard built an intelligence picture of an impending Turkish attack on an enormous scale. The preceding days' reports from Harry's seaplane flight and the kite balloon had described to Sir Ian Hamilton and Birdie transports disembarking large numbers of men. From his balloon Philip had observed four steamers transiting the straits and disembarking reinforcements at the docksides. All this information pointed to a decisive battle.

After first camping outside Maidos, Turkish reinforcements were ordered to move at night to the villages of Boghali and Kojadere because of the threat of observation by aircraft. Despite these precautions, and because of the novelty of this threat to the recently arrived troops, their fieldcraft and use of camouflage was sloppy. Reconnaissance missions confirmed the concentration of these reserves from their cooking fires in the early mornings. On 16, 17 and 18 May, the squadron flight journal recorded multiple military reconnaissance missions and bombing attacks after reporting and refuelling at the forward aerodrome at Cape Helles:

16 April: Richard [Peirse] and Major Hogg for 2 hrs 40 minutes, Lieutenant Osmond for 4 hours 30 minutes

17 April: Herb Collet for 4 hours 20 minutes, Reginald Marix and Charles Samson in the Breguet for 2 hours

18 May: Lieutenant Osmond for 3 hours, Richard
[Peirse] and Major Hogg for 4 hours 45 minutes

Reginald and Charles' flight in the Breguet represented
the tipping point. The propeller was swung and the heavy
biplane turned into the wind. It was 7.50 am, the sky was blue
and held the promise of a warm and sunny day. Reginald sat
in the front as pilot with Charles sitting behind as observer.
The machine carried its maximum payload and appeared
to waddle, its wings curtseying when the wheels found a
pothole. With its nose into the wind the Breguet ran at full
throttle. It was a pusher, its Clerget engine mounted at the
rear. Having clawed height, engine coughing and banging,
Reginald turned across the sea towards the ANZAC lines
at Gaba Tepe. The flight over the sea was 30 minutes in
duration. The coastline from Cape Helles to Gaba Tepe
was all cliff, although not as steep as the famous chalk cliffs
of Dover. Where men occupied the land, the earth showed
the scars of trenches and shell craters. Warships clustered
around each beachhead, but between the two points of hate
the fields at the southern end were deserted. The unreliable
engine coughed again; Reginald adjusted the throttle and
oxygen mix. The biplane slowly rose and had reached 5000
feet by the time he pointed its blunt nose over Anzac Cove.

The men below lived like puffins. They dug into the cliffs
and gullies for protection. Even at 5000 feet, both aviators
could smell the open latrines and the heavier sickly odour
of decayed flesh. The two opposing trenches were almost
indistinguishable at this height. The ANZACs appeared to
be holding onto the coastal fringe by their fingernails. One
strike with a hammer and they would slide into the sea.

The view was panoramic. The peninsula was defined as a
crooked finger. The Narrows were at their feet. With a pair

of strong binoculars Istanbul was a blur at the far side of the Marmara—except that the Breguet's engine vibration made this view impossible. In a minute Reginald and Charles had passed the broken villages of Kojadere and Boghali. The surrounding areas had been stripped of vegetation as soldiers scoured the bush for firewood. Tented camps rose like mushroom clusters. Vague attempts at camouflage appeared sporadically, but vegetation thrown across tents had to be changed daily lest the foliage fade to brown and betray the position. The camps were known to both aviators. What surprised them was the sight of four steamers tied to the jetty at the port of Ak Bashi Liman. It was unusual to find such targets so late in the morning.

Reginald expertly placed himself so that the sun was positioned to his rear. The craft had not been spotted. At this height, in the bright early morning, they would be difficult to see from the ground. Throttling back, Reginald pushed the control column forward and eased his foot off the left pedal. The Breguet sounded grateful for the respite, the propeller beating rhythmically behind. Reginald was careful to keep the machine at a 20 degree downward angle, no more. With the wings carrying a full payload of bombs in the under-wing racks, there was a risk that too much strain would cause the wooden struts to crack. Reginald had no bomb sight. Practice told him that the bomb would more or less follow the trajectory of his aeroplane. He pointed the blunt nose of the machine over a crowded base of the dock. Hundreds of brown-clad figures were unloading goods from the steamers. It was a massive target area.

On the ground, all was new and exciting. A drum and flute band played folk music. There was a sense of purpose. Having arrived at the front these men were ready to prove themselves. A whole class of young officer cadets from the military academy in Istanbul—most a mere 16 years of age—had volunteered to lead the departing regiments. There was a sense of inevitable victory. The sun was shining. They had crossed the Marmara without mishap. Then the ground turned liquid. It rolled in waves. The air turned to water—waves of compressed air could actually be seen. Then the noise. Then the screams.

Reginald had to look over the stretched canvas side to see his target. They had descended to 2000 feet and the nose of his aeroplane now covered the dockside. He pulled the first lever and the 100lb bomb was released. He corrected his descent; the Breguet jumped slightly as its load was lightened. He quickly pulled his right-side lever and seven 20lb bombs dropped from their wire cradles. Having not seen them curve towards the earth, Reginald pushed forward the throttle and gently pulled back on the control column, turning away from the land, his right foot pushing forward on the rudder bar. The Breguet climbed gracefully, obediently, in an upward right curve. Charles was all child-like enthusiasm, twisted in his wicker seat, his beard flattened by the racing wind. Looking over the right side he saw the first flash of orange. Bodies were flattened to the ground. He whooped with joy.

The remaining flight was bumpkin to him. The joy of hitting the target was replaced by the science of war. The map was drawn from a deep pocket and the large camps checked off. No new camps, but one or two had grown overnight. The largest, deep in the third valley east of Boghali, was over 1000 yards square. It held a division of 18,000 men. Reginald didn't have to lose height to send his remaining bombs on a trajectory. The camp was large enough to hit by simply pulling the left-hand lever on their second approach.

Seven light bombs fell into the crowded camp. The soldiers below were prepared; they had heard the sounds of detonations coming across the coastal plain. Several tents were flattened. Mules ran terrified.

Reginald and Charles mouthed a conversation. Reginald gathered that his commander was asking to be dropped off at Cape Helles aerodrome. He wanted to report those steamers. Reginald flew the length of the peninsula; it was ten minutes from the ANZAC lines to the British lines. As expected, the Turkish artillery attempted to snatch the biplane from the sky. Angry black air bursts followed their trail. The landing at Helles was tricky. They had no time for a circuit. It was straight to the ground, bleeding speed, and taxiing quickly to a protective earth berm before artillery explosions kicked up the dirt. They landed safely at the forward aerodrome at 9.10 am. Reginald climbed down to check the Clerget engine; the ground staff helpfully passed him an oil can. Charles clambered onto the lower wing and headed for the entrance to the divisional dugout. A smartly dressed, red-capped military policeman stiffly saluted the airman assuming him to be an officer. Once inside the subterranean room, Charles claimed an audience with Sir Aylmer. He was out. Charles reported his observations to an intelligence captain before returning to Tenedos where he recorded the flight, although he failed to mention the boring bit about talking to the army:

> On May 17th Reginald had his big Breguet ready for action. We carried no less than one 100lb and fourteen 20lb bombs, also a Lewis gun, a pretty formidable amount for those days. Off we set with the idea of giving Ak Bashi Liman a look-over. Arriving there, we found the place a scene of great activity. We let go all

our bombs and created a complete panic, and also did a lot of damage.

Later that afternoon, Charles and John de Robeck met in Bernard's operations tent and discussed the meaning of the new bivouacs partially hidden behind Anzac.

Esat Pasha's intentions as Northern Group Commander were correctly interpreted by Charles. Similar indicators had presaged the Turkish night attack at Cape Helles on 2 May. The next day a telephone call was made to Hamilton accommodated on *Arcadian*. Bernard was also able to verify over the telephone that an enemy bivouac measuring 1000 yards by 1000 yards was observed and attacked and that steamers were observed off the coast. At 5.15 pm Birdie was called to the phone and warned. He passed the warning to his two divisional commanders, telling them that an aeroplane had reported signs of an imminent Turkish attack. His two divisional commanders were warned to remain alert and to stand to arms:

Narrative Operations A & N. Z. A. C. 18/20 May 1915

18 May 15

5.15 pm. From ANZAC—Aeroplane reports troops and 4 small steam boats Dardanelles Shore. Section Commanders to be warned confidentially to be on alert for night attack and stand to arms early. Arrival of enemy reinforcements generally followed by activity at night.

6.26 pm. Each Brigade told to make preparations to repulse every attack.

6.50 pm. 2nd Infantry Brigade warned to detail 2 battalions as lying piquets.

7.07 pm. 1st Brigade reports very heavy shelling of trenches for nearly an hour. Trenches much knocked about.

9.45 pm. Instructions to 1st and 3rd Brigades to throw out loose barbed wire in front of trenches. Supports and reserves are properly placed and know their positions in case necessity for reinforcing firing trenches.

19 May 15

12.53 am. All battalions report heavy firing. All well.

3.43 am. 1st Battalion reports Turks attacking in force.

3.55 am. 3rd Battalion reports no enemy in front.

4.14 am. 1st Battalion reports enemy attack failed. Heavy losses inflicted on him. Holding our own easily.

4.15 am. Turks attacked 11th Battalion.

4.20 am. 4th Battalion reports enemy moving left to right.

4.27am. 1st Battalion reports enemy attacking in force. Attack failed. Heavy losses inflicted on enemy. Easily holding our own.

4.32 am. 4th Battalion reports Turks retiring rapidly over parapets into their trenches.

4.45 am. 3rd Battalion reports all well.

6.40 am. 3rd Brigade reports enemy retiring, our front well held; casualties light, enemy repulsed, but hanging onto dead ground 50 to 440 yards from our trenches.

11.26 am. Shell fire ceased since our aircraft being up.

Unlike Cape Helles, the trenches at Gaba Tepe defining the ANZAC and Turkish positions were extremely close, without an appreciable no man's land—the perfect setting for a surprise attack. However, ANZAC had no view of the Turkish communications area, except the vista from Russell's Top back along the beach to Gaba Tepe or northwards to Nibrunesi Point. They could not look into the valleys beyond the second ridgeline and could not observe Turkish movements until an attack in the forward trenches was in progress.

As a stretcher-bearer, Private Herbert Reynolds found himself making his way to and from the front lines collecting the wounded during the surprise Turkish assault:

> At about midnight the enemy launched a tremendous attack on our trenches, but despite numbers and the force with which they made the attack our lines did not give an inch. Our rifle and artillery fire was very intense, particularly the latter, and our machine guns spoke to some order as one of the enemy's crack regiments of Nizan infantry found to their dismay, for when day broke it revealed lines of them, lying in 'no man's land' where they had been mowed down by our Maxim gun fire, the slaughter was terrible and beyond description. These troops were brought from Constantinople

by Gen. Liman Von Sanders, and with them he boasted of the fact and evidently advertised it, that he was going to sweep us from our positions and drive us into the sea, but it resulted in a hideous slaughter of both his plans and troops.

As day broke the enemy commenced to bombard our whole position, with greater violence than he has ever before done. From 6am to 8am it reached its height for intensity and shells were exploding everywhere, they appeared to have it in their minds to wreak vengeance for the terrible failure of their infantry attack by shelling every inch of our positions. It was my section's night off duty and when the attack started we were instructed to be in readiness but it was not till 4.30am that we were needed, as our own casualties till then were so light they could easily be handled by the parties on duty. However then the enemy opened up with their artillery in earnest at dawn, our casualties became heavier and we had a very busy and extremely uncomfortable time. On one occasion we were forced to take shelter with a patient we were bringing down, behind a bit of a cliff opposite Dawkins Point, it sheltered us from extremely heavy shell fire from Kaba Tepe but gave us no protection to the shrapnel from directly up the gully but we were forced to make the best of it till the shelling from Kaba Tepe eased off a bit.

An infantry man after negotiating the stretch of beach between Clarke's and Victoria gullies took shelter with us, as it was hopeless to attempt to go on to the ASC depot as things were then. He was sent down for rifle oil for the trenches. Several shells fell close to us and made us a bit anxious when with a crash a high explosive hit the bank opposite. We had no time to discover if any of us were hit, when a second crashed nearby, nearly on top of us. The concussion flung us about a bit and we were relieved on getting up to find we were alright apart from being bruised a bit. The infantry lad was less fortunate as he received a severe wound beneath his right eye, after bandaging him up we found the enemy has lengthened his range and the shelling on our track has eased off considerably so we made the best of it and pushed on down to the Casualty Clearing Station.

Later in the morning we got mixed up in a pretty hot patch of shrapnel and H E Shells near the No 2 ASC depot in which we took shelter. Here to make things worse an enemy plane flew over and used the depot as his target for some of his bombs, however much to our relief they fell wide of the mark and exploded in the water at the edge of the beach doing nothing further than giving us a splash of salt water. About 10.30am the enemy's bombardment eased off considerably and for the rest of the day kept up only spasmodic fire. At 7.00pm we all turned out and cleared the casualties from all the dressing stations as they had been collecting all day and only those whose circumstances required to be removed to the C.C.S were brought down on account of our communications being so heavily shelled through the day, however our casualties were extremely light and out of all proportion to the enemy's enormous losses.

Bernard had carefully fitted the 'pieces' together on his map. Each aviator saw only a portion of the entire panorama; Bernard assembled the whole picture which now hung from the central wooden tent pole. Charles used this map to convince the generals that an attack was imminent. He later recorded some measure of personal success in his diary:

20 May. We have had good news. Last night Australians have repulsed an attack made by Turks at Gaba Tepe (these troops were reported by us in the afternoon). This morning there are 2,000 dead at our front. The Australian casualties only 200. Good news continues to come in from Headquarters.

ANZAC was well below its war establishment following casualties suffered in the first three days of fighting and losses sustained in the Second Battle of Krithia. The effective strength of the corps on 16 May 1915 was 17,406—down from 30,000. Against this, four Turkish divisions of the Northern Group launched 50,000 infantry, the divisions attacking abreast and simultaneously across a frontage of 3500 metres with the simple objective of eliminating the ANZAC beachhead. ANZAC's preparation for this Turkish attack offers an insight into the use of joint firepower to inflict maximum casualties, including the coordinated use of aircraft. Artillery batteries and the 2nd Naval Squadron were given designated areas to target, including assembly points and trenches, as part of defensive preparations. Further, a signal in the war diary also requested air support: 'An aeroplane has been asked for to be up at 5.30 a.m. tomorrow.'

Turkish casualty returns for 19 May totalled 9484 with 51 officers and 3369 soldiers killed. Although portions of the ANZAC front line were briefly occupied, no ground was taken. The losses marked a change from the German-inspired doctrine of the primacy of offensive operations. From now on, the Turkish 5th Army would concentrate on defence. In the aftermath of the attacks of 19 May, No. 439 Private John Fisher of 7th Battalion, 2nd Brigade, wrote in his diary:

Germany realises that once the Narrows are forced there is not much hope for her. So she put the flower of the Turkish Army against us one night with orders to drive us into the sea. But instead of doing so they asked for an eight hour armistice to bury their dead. The kangaroos are not to be played with.

Preparatory to the attack all was quietness. Every eye was strained for such silence denoted something unusual was to take place. Presently the white clad figure of a Turkish priest was seen to leap out of the earth, his white robes flying in the gentle breeze calling on his men to charge in the name of 'Allah God'. But he soon embraced the dust by a well-aimed bullet from one of our rifles. He was a brave man and rose twice only to go down each time. The Turk, enraged at such treatment, scaled their trenches to rush ours, when every rifle and machine gun of ours spoke as one. Still they came on only to be mowed down, like wheat before the scythe. But they were determined to have their revenge; they however found our lads just as determined to prevent them, for considerable decrease could be noticed in their lines.

On they came, getting closer and closer, their numbers smaller and smaller. The kangaroos, ever anxious to use that length of glistening steel, could not miss such an opportunity and when came that command 'Prepare to Charge' which stirs the very blood in your veins and makes you grip the rifle with an affectionate and determined grasp, the eye glistened and the features assume the appearance of a worn and tired warrior of old who knew his hopes were once more to be realised. Like the runner on his mark waiting for the pistol which is the signal to start, every nerve and ear strained to hear that word 'Charge'. The officer who is to give the word sees the opportunity he is waiting for, and his voice rings out loud and clear 'Charge Australians and show them what you are made of'.

With the agility of an athlete, every man is on the parapet of the trench, his voice giving vent to a wild 'Hurrah' which in places breaks into a curse and a threat. They start in a mad race which is to result in either victory or death. The enemy, not wishing to meet these bronzed giants of Australia who come on to them with such a rush, their bayonets shining in the faint light of the moon, turned and fled. Some did not get far before they felt the cold steel pierce their backs and very few indeed reached the safety of their trenches. They were a fine body of men opposing us, some reaching six feet in height, but the determination of our boys was too great for them and such was the result of their attack.

When daylight succeeded in chasing the blackness of night away, what a sight was revealed to our gaze. The ground before us was covered with the dead and the dying. Some had fallen on their dead comrades and were piled two and three high. Some died with a smile on their lips, others with distorted features, writhing in the agonies of death. It was when the stench from the decay from those bodies made the place unbearable that the armistice was asked of us, and readily given. It took them all day to finish the job, for the dead were estimated at 5,000 and that their casualties all told must have been 20,000.

The armistice had been carefully negotiated to clear the masses of rotting corpses that lay in no man's land after the 19 May attack, posing a lethal threat to the living from

disease and pestilence. Harry recorded the delicate negotiations over a ceasefire to bury the Turkish dead including
an incident featuring an Australian soldier that came close
to derailing the process. Several senior officers were sitting
around a table in the carefully orchestrated conference:

> while a pow wow was being held in a headquarters dug
> out [between] Turkish Headquarters staff and ours, sud-
> denly a head popped in, 'Say, have any of you F------ seen
> my bloody mess tin?'

It is a tribute to both parties that the negotiations recovered
and the armistice proceeded.

Birdie noted the important role of aerial intelligence
in blunting the 19 May assault, expressing his thanks to
Hamilton for the valuable work of his air services:

> The last big attack made by the enemy followed closely
> on the arrival of large reinforcements, and the warn-
> ing we got from aeroplane reconnaissance proved most
> valuable.

Hamilton, however, once again neglected to mention the
fact that he was gaining intelligence from his aviators.
His signal happily described the bombing inflicted on the
Turkish reinforcements, but omitted the significantly more
decisive role the air service played by informing ANZAC
Headquarters of the imminent attack:

> Aeroplanes yesterday dropped 15 100 pound bombs on
> Turkish reinforcements landing at AK BASHI LIMAN
> causing considerable loss to enemy. Turks made strong
> counter attack against A. & N. Z. Corps during the night

of May 18/19 and were driven back with loss not less than 7,000 casualties of which 2000 killed. Our casualties 500. Turks were dressed in light blue and belonged to 1 Army Corps recently arrived from Constantinople.

Hamilton's continued burying of air intelligence was causing concerns in London. The RFC in France was being commended for its performance of this essential role. Why was the RNAS failing the army in the Dardanelles?

CHAPTER 6

May, June and July: the fall of Charles' aviators

Training air force officers can be a little tricky. Army officers are trained from the basic building block of the soldier
upwards; the officer cadet's first lesson is how to clean
and fire a rifle. Then they are taught basic military skills:
launching an attack and fighting in defence. Eventually, the
budding officer is taught the skills of a platoon commander.
Training an air force officer is more abstract. Only one in a
hundred entrants trains to be a pilot. The rest exist to serve
the application of air power—this means keeping the pilot,
aircrew and machines battle ready.

After my two periods of service in Iraq in 2003 I was
posted as an instructor at the Air Force Officers' Training
School at Point Cook, Victoria. Our Commanding Officer
at the time was a leader with a strong vision for realistic
training. After all, our graduates were likely to deploy into
conflict soon after marching out.

We taught the basics of the air war in the classroom
while our army equivalents lay in a muddy ditch practising

ambushes. In the air force way, we first taught the ten principles of war. One of these principles is the element of surprise. According to modern warfare doctrine, 'Surprise can produce disproportionate results by taking the initiative away from the enemy, degrading decision-making and disrupting the enemy's decision cycle.'

While our cadets learnt the ten principles, we impressed upon them how aircraft change the nature of conflict. I used to show maps of historical battles and explain the concept of the 'fog of war'. Until aircraft flew over the battlefield, commanders were essentially blind. To illustrate how even rickety biplanes could change the face of battle I would guide them through the events of the last chapter.

The impact of aerial intelligence at Gallipoli was profound. The flight path of Reginald Marix and Charles Samson at 5000 feet robbed the Turkish Army of its success on 19 May. This mission, and many others like it, provided the conditions in which ANZAC could survive, clinging to the coastal fringe. The Allies now had the advantage, not in terms of terrain, but in the timely reporting of enemy intentions. It was the information that the aviators captured during missions, rather than their bombs, that proved most valuable in the hard months that followed.

Statistics can be dangerous. Adding up all the RNAS missions from 1 May to 30 July gives a mission total of 813. The monthly totals amounted to 303 in May, 239 in June, and 271 in July. The order of priority was clear: spotting 240, reconnaissance 207, photography 71, bombing 95, anti-submarine patrol 39 and anti-aircraft 15, while other missions inclusive of experimental and trial flights totalled 79 and transit flights between aerodromes 67. The danger is that these statistics may hide something. For Charles' aviators, a small coterie of pilots was flying a dwindling number of aeroplanes. Worse, Charles was flying the majority of missions himself. He and his friends Herb, Reginald and Richard Bell Davies flew to the point of collapse. Charles Samson was not the ideal commander.

The Turkish 5th Army had sustained significant casualties in the attacks of 19 May and its morale had suffered a heavy blow. The Allies now cast about for a means to maintain the momentum. The British and French embarked on a third major offensive against the village of Krithia beginning on 4 June. This time the planners knew where their enemy was located. Again, only minor advances were made towards deep Turkish trenches. Following the loss of Hamilton's reserves in this attack, the character of assaults changed to a series of minor trench raids prior to the August offensive.

The navy was also challenged in the summer months. The Naval Intelligence Department reporting of a second German U boat was confirmed when *U21* sank *Triumph* off Gaba Tepe on 25 May. Two days later *Majestic* was torpedoed off Cape Helles despite deploying protective netting. *Queen Elizabeth* was recalled and the flanks of the army were protected by destroyers until the arrival of specially built monitors. These were ungainly, almost ugly vessels; they had bubble sides to absorb torpedoes and a single gun on their Spartan flat decks. *Abercrombie* and *Roberts* with 14-inch guns and *Humber* with 6-inch guns served to replace the missing warships frightened off by the U boat menace. To avoid further losses, battleships were corralled at Mudros and only ventured out to support substantial attacks on the peninsula following the placing of anti-submarine netting, including 30 drift nets, across areas designated for naval gunfire work. Before a sortie by battleships the area of operations first had to be swept by aircraft to ensure that it was clear.

For the air service the summer months on the peninsula

presented ideal flying conditions. Pilots and observers all remarked on the clear air. Such conditions provided an opportunity for Charles' aviators to help crack the stalemate forced on the opposing armies. Spotting for the army's artillery in these clear conditions became paramount. Shells were tightly rationed, with the artillery restricted to firing five rounds per gun per day. Aerial corrections onto Turkish trenches and hidden gun batteries became mandatory; no shells could be wasted.

Meanwhile, Hamilton's silence on the work of the RNAS had caused consternation in London. The Air Department naturally believed that there was little or no cooperation between the RNAS and the army at Gallipoli. Oblivious to Hamilton's politicking, Charles and his squadron continued to support the army, flying from the forward aerodrome at Cape Helles. Bernard was also in telephone contact with the Intelligence Department in Army Headquarters, allowing an uninterrupted flow of information. However, *Ark Royal*'s isolation in Kephalo Bay meant that *Manica*'s balloon became the obvious presence off Anzac Cove.

Men and replacement airframes arrived intermittently by steamer. A 20-year-old pilot, Sub-Lieutenant Harold Spencer Kerby, joined Charles' team on 12 June, full of fight and promise. Harold, who arrived with two friends, lieutenants Barr and Dawson, had gained his 'wings' only a month earlier. He was born in Hamilton, Ontario, and is rightly claimed by Canadians as one of their aces. He completed his engineering degree before taking passage to England to join the air service. After serving at Gallipoli, he shot down nine enemy aeroplanes in France and rose to the rank of air vice marshal in the Royal Air Force (RAF). However, as an inexperienced pilot in the Dardanelles, he was not immediately employed on his first operation:

I am not down in orders. I have the day to myself. Had a splendid swim before lunch, really the beach and water is perfect. It doesn't look as if we newly joined up pilots will do much flying as we are hard up for some new machines.

Gallipoli was his first taste of war and it crushed him. Like most young men of his time, Harold kept a diary. His entries were candid and track his own decline and that of his troika of friends. Gallipoli was not a place for young men; it required stamina and a tough heart:

9 July 1915. I made my first flight here this evening when I went up with Commander Richard Davies to have the country and various positions and landing grounds pointed out to me. Never have I seen such clear atmosphere for air reconnaissance. It is really remarkable the distance you can see. We flew over the lines at first so I could get an idea of the position of our batteries and trenches. We then went up to ANZAC to where the Australians have landed. The whole south-ern end of the peninsula is one maze of trenches and concealed batteries; from above it looks like some huge puzzle laid out below you. It is apparently devoid of life; yet in those few square miles of earth below thousands of troops are hiding in their trenches and shelters.

Geographically it is the most impossible country for aeroplane work as there are only three possible landing places and of these two are very poor; in case of engine failure I guess it is a case of try and pancake the machine into the sea and pray a torpedo boat picks you up before the Turks blow you to pieces with their guns.

HMS *Hector*, carrying a new kite balloon section, arrived in theatre on 15 June. Philip Mackworth had written a detailed report listing a number of improvements which were rolled into *Hector*:

> The gain in efficiency from working the balloon off a ship has been very marked; instead of being least mobile of all units it becomes more mobile than infantry, and is free to choose the most suitable position for each job. Under good conditions the ship can change position with the balloon in the air, thus saving much time, and if fired upon, can move out of range without hauling down the balloon.

> The main work of the Kite Balloon has been found to consist in:
> (a) accurate control against distant targets
> (b) suppression of hostile batteries
> (c) location of forts and batteries
> (d) observation of movement of troops

> The main function of the kite balloon is to provide an observation platform at heights varying between 2,500 and 3,000 feet for the direction and control of artillery fire at long ranges. The kite balloon generally in use is about 80 feet in length, and has a capacity of about 28,000 feet. Two or three observers are taken aloft in it, and they communicate with the station below by telephone. Both in land and sea operations it is generally sent up four or five miles behind the firing line, and it is thus out of range of the enemy's guns. It has been found that the kite balloon renders valuable service in sea operations, and the Dardanelles fighting provided

an opportunity of which at first much was made. At the first instances, merchant ships were adapted to accommodate the kite balloon and gas making plant, together with the officers and men of the section.

Aboard *Hector* was the 2nd Kite Balloon Section ('Experimental' had finally been dropped from its title). This balloon was sent to supplement the newly arrived monitors. The kite balloon was regarded as an excellent platform for the Gallipoli campaign. The balloon's loiter times, sometimes up to eight hours, deterred the enemy gunners from firing their howitzers and field guns for most of the daylight hours. A Royal Naval Reserve officer, Captain David Preston, kept a diary of his adventures off the Gallipoli coast in the kite balloon. On 15 June he described practice ascents at Lemnos which preceded his first foray into active service on 2 July.

Harry's seaplane flight and Charles' squadron received replacement airframes to bring the total number of aircraft (including the two kite balloons) to 45 by the end of May. Charles' squadron was equipped with Voisin pusher biplanes which kept the squadron aloft, although attrition whittled his total to two airframes by the end of July. On 29 May a French escadrille, deployed in support of the French Corps and equipped with 12 airframes, arrived to base itself alongside Charles' aviators on Tenedos. Charles was amply supplied with bombs, both 20lb and 100lb in weight, delivered by monthly steamers. The aviators also began to experiment with a new type of homemade incendiary device. They had discovered that the Turkish gun batteries were so well dug in that only an (unlikely) direct hit would destroy the guns. This new devilment weighed 270lb and was constructed from petrol tanks retrieved from smashed aeroplanes.

Ben-my-Chree finally arrived in June with her torpedo-carrying seaplanes. Experiments were conducted launching the 700lb torpedoes slung between the floats of the Sunbeam seaplane in the hope that they could sink the bevy of steamers that always seemed to be anchored off Maidos. The pilots first had to learn how to conduct such an attack, having not attempted this prior to their arrival in the Aegean. *Ben-my-Chree* represented a significant increase in warfighting potential. She was a converted cross-channel steamer designed for the pre-war Isle of Wight run. With speeds in excess of 15 knots she had the ability to quickly transit the Aegean and replicated *Ark Royal*'s earlier freedom of movement. Since she was not purpose designed, her complement of four seaplanes was housed in an aft shelter. A 24-year-old pilot, George Bentley Dacre, arrived with her and was given responsibility for developing the aerial torpedo. Unlike Harold Kerby, George was an experienced aviator who had gained his wings in 1911 and joined the RNAS at the same time as Harry Strain had joined as an observer. He had undertaken the arduous pilot training that Harry had been loath to commit to, finally appointed lieutenant in December 1914. George also kept a diary, his entries providing a perfect window into his seaplane operations:

> Leaving Malta on June 11 the *Ben-my-Chree* shaped a course for Mitylene, passing many Greek islands well known from Biblical times. We commenced a busy week's practice before entering active service. I took up my machine, a 225hp Sunbeam Short but stripped the bottom of a float getting off. Tried a torpedo run alone but the torpedo fell off before I got off and I only did an imaginary shot at a practice target.

Considerable effort was devoted to conducting experimental flights to establish whether such an attack was indeed possible. The majority of flights were taken up with experiments in flying the heavily burdened seaplane and practising attack runs. The torpedo was held by a cradle below the fuselage, in between the twin floats. It was so heavy that it hung submerged in the sea. This caused significant drag and made it very difficult for the seaplane to rotate (take off) as water holds objects with considerable surface tension:

> Edwards and I did a practice dawn attack with torpedoes, carrying passengers as well. We found we couldn't get off with passengers. After dropping them off I was the only one able to get off with a torpedo and having done a circuit of the port made an attack on the BMC but didn't judge my height quite right. The torpedo dropped off at 1000 yards and passed 25 yards ahead of the ship. The gases from the engine CO_2 gave me a bad headache so I slept until breakfast. Our flying kit consists of flannel shorts, shirt, scarf, socks, shoes and white sun helmet. Clarke Hall, skipper of the *Ark Royal*, arrived and gave us an interesting lecture on the Dardanelles operation to date.

With *Ark Royal*'s confinement to Kephalo Bay due to the submarine threat, Harry's seaplanes suffered a drastic fall in capability. Their flight was hampered by local weather conditions, despite the alternative arrangements and, while managing some 63 missions in May, this sum fell to almost half in June and July, yielding a total of 131 missions for the three summer months. Reconnaissance missions also fell from a high of 24 in May to a rough average of five missions each per month for June and July, the majority of the effective missions split between spotting, maritime patrol and reconnaissance. The burden for reconnaissance and spotting at Anzac now fell to the aeroplanes and the two kite balloons. Harry was not at all happy with the 'blue funk' and being forced to abandon ANZAC:

> The arrival of enemy submarines at the end of May made a vast difference to the campaign. *Swiftsure* and *Vengeance* were attacked on the morning of the 25th May and our old friend *Triumph* sank off Gaba Tepe later in the day. Attacks became persistent and it soon became obvious that capital ships could no longer remain in position to support the troops with their fire. We were all put in Kephalo Bay on Imbros Island where we lay behind a flimsy indicator net which would have stopped neither a submarine nor even a torpedo.
>
> We made ourselves very unpopular. We had no fresh fish for a very long time and we thought we should seize the opportunity of being in harbour. We collected a quarter pound of dynamite charge and took it in a motor boat to a suitable sandy bay, the idea being to stun the fish, go overboard and chuck them in before they recovered. All went according to plan except that we were not proficient otters and only managed three or four grey mullet into the boat, they were so slippery. In coming back to the ship we noticed great activity among the signal staff of all ships. All had felt the concussion of our quarter pound charge and were enquiring of one another who had been torpedoed. We were duly had on the mat on our return.

Harry took the morning ferry service from K Beach at Imbros to Anzac Cove at least once a week to confer with

ANZAC Headquarters, dug into a gully at the entrance to Monash Valley. He was also keen to reassure the men clinging to the cliffs of his support. This close relationship blossomed and Harry remained a keen observer of the Australians he encountered, men who seemed to challenge every estimation of soldierly conduct:

> The Australians' idea of discipline and decorum was elementary; they not only referred to their General Officer Commanding General Birdwood as 'Birdie' but addressed him so to his face. They had every essential of a splendid fighting force and Birdwood and his staff understood them and had their confidence.
>
> There was, however, one member of the gilded British staff they did not understand; he was too precise and formal, always immaculately dressed and always with a gold rimmed monocle glued to his face. Of course they called him 'Tin Eye'.
>
> He had landed from *Queen Elizabeth* with some message at ANZAC jetty. The jetty had suffered from shell fire and a working party of Australians, dressed only in their slouch hats and identity discs were busy repairing the damage. When Tin Eye started to walk along it he made some criticism of their work which they did not like and then proceeded to mince his way along the footboards . . . Immediately, the Australians clambered onto the jetty behind him, stuck their identity discs in their eyes and, waggling their bottoms in imitation, marched up the footboards behind Tin Eye. Not good for discipline if allowed to pass!
>
> Tin Eye walked on, unconcerned, until he got ashore where he turned, adjusted his monocle and slowly ran his eyes over them from the toes upwards. Naked men

are apt to be sensitive with such a deliberate scrutiny. They shuffled mutinously and awaited what he had to say. Without moving a feature Tin Eye let his monocle drop into his hand, tossed it into the air, caught it in his eye and said, 'Now, you blighters, do that.'

When I was next ashore numbers of Australians had their identity discs off the string and were tossing them up, trying to catch them in their eye. Tin Eye was as popular afterwards as any member of the staff.

The daily tempo of Charles' squadron followed a predictable pattern. His aviators flew an average of eight missions per day, surging on days when they supported infantry assaults. A dawn reconnaissance patrol was flown (often with one 100lb bomb) followed by hourly missions designed to maintain an aeroplane over the front lines to reduce enemy artillery fire. Photographic missions became increasingly important following the publication of the first aerial map. A series of 1:8000 scale trench maps was drawn from aerial photographs produced by Henry Butler and delivered to the headquarters of the 29th Division on 20 May. This was given to the army well prior to the Third Battle of Krithia.

But Hamilton's reporting had sown the seeds of doubt in the Air Department in London. By early May the air units at the Dardanelles were considered in need of reorganisation and a substantial increase in numbers so as to effectively support military operations. While this was undoubtedly the case, Hamilton's agenda forced a course of action that would later cause considerable difficulties. The Air Department embarked on a radical solution: a memorandum was sent to the War Office on 25 May requesting the Army Council to lend Colonel Frederick Sykes to the navy so that he could report on air requirements at the Dardanelles. The selection of a veteran RFC officer over a suitably qualified RNAS officer inevitably caused jealousies.

Frederick Hugh Sykes was a prominent officer on the staff of Major General Henderson, first commander of the RFC. Apart from the fact that he was an army officer, Sykes was a good choice, having briefly led the RFC when General Henderson was posted to command the 1st Division in France from 22 November to 20 December 1914. During his brief period of command, Sykes reorganised the RFC into two wings of four squadrons just as the British Expeditionary Force was divided into two armies on 25 December 1914. Each wing was detailed to support an army, an arrangement that proved ideally suited to the situation, and Colonel Sykes was regarded as possessing key organisational skills following the implementation of this simple transition.

Sykes and his junior, 'Boom' Trenchard, also became involved in the evolution of aerial photography. The RFC, with encouragement from army corps, produced aerial photographs using a purpose-designed camera in March 1915. Imagery of Neuve Chapelle taken by the RFC had immediate value for First Army Headquarters, with a copy even arriving on the desk of Sir Douglas Haig. Sykes remained abreast of developments in photography including the almost weekly advances in technology, also managing the publication of photography onto 1:8000 scale trench mapping. Similar advances, on which he was fully briefed, included the adoption of the clock face method in artillery correction onto targets. Sykes appeared to be a solid candidate to investigate the efficacy of the RNAS.

In comparison to the close support the RFC provided the army in France in the first half of 1915, there were only rudimentary attempts at intra-service cooperation in the Dardanelles. There was no air service conference in a peaceful farmhouse behind the lines or meetings between the various commanders to harmonise the air war, as occurred with the RFC in France. Individual visits did occur in the Dardanelles, with Lieutenant 'Sloppy' Allsop visiting Tenedos aerodrome. But his visit concerned only the conduct of local training on the Canton Unne engine. Neither Charles nor Clarkee discussed unity of effort. Unlike the RFC, which was united under one commander with a supporting wing headquarters, the RNAS in the Dardanelles was scattered and reported separately to naval divisional commanders. Clarkee, Philip, Charles and, latterly, George Dacre were hampered by their punishing schedules and the separation of the two services.

On 30 May, John de Robeck, as the overall naval commander, rationalised Charles' squadron via an inclusion in the Standing Orders entitled 'Aircraft Organisation' in an attempt to codify air support for the British. *Ark Royal* and *Manica* were not included in this orders set as they were operating in support of ANZAC. No. 3 Squadron's tasks were defined in areas of responsibility. The squadron was ordered to conduct a reconnaissance flight each morning and to keep an aeroplane available to assist in artillery or naval gunfire support. Spotting duties were coordinated with the senior Royal Artillery officer at division and the senior naval officer based at Cape Helles. After each reconnaissance mission a verbal debrief was to be delivered direct to 29th Division Headquarters once the aeroplane landed at the forward aerodrome.

The Standing Orders of 30 May included a target list focused on the immediate concerns of the infantry. In a separate paragraph, a list of 'exceptionally favourite targets included batteries actually firing, camps of 500 soldiers, batteries on the move, and transports of at least 10 wagons or 100 pack horses'. The Standing Orders also regarded radio failure as a dominant issue. There was an onus of responsibility on both parties (the senior Royal Artillery officer and aircrew) to examine and report the reasons for these failures. Observers were ordered to test their radios and confirm that they were working before conducting spotting missions. The newly laid telephone cable allowed the observer at the aerodrome on Tenedos to speak to the artillery commander at 29th Division prior to the mission. The driving factor was the dawning realisation in the British Headquarters of the benefits of integrating aircraft with military operations. The squadron now followed a proscriptive daily cycle meeting the requirements of gunnery support to tactical infantry operations. The days of Charles' aviators conducting missions independently of 29th Division Headquarters were at an end.

Major Hogg, who was on loan from the RFC in Egypt as an observer, confirmed the close relationship between the squadron and the artillery, commenting that 'spotting has been a matter of daily routine. Gun ammunition here, as everywhere, is very valuable, and our guns never fire practically, without a machine to spot.' Charles' aviators contributed to the set-piece assaults of the Third Battle of Krithia and the Standing Orders were written into the artillery fire support plan.

Further to this, reconnaissance and photography provided a significant improvement in mapping during the planning of assaults. Henry and Bernard worked together to produce maps of trenches and gun batteries on overlays for the 1:40,000 scale maps. On 1 June they printed more detailed trench schematics on a 1:8000 scale map. Enemy trenches were colour-coded and named in series: J, F, G and H.

These trench maps were compiled from aerial photographs developed in a makeshift darkroom that had served to transport the useless Maurice Farman biplanes picked up in France. The maps detailed placement of barbed wire, roads, nullahs, ravines, olive groves, vineyards and scrub patches aiding identification of enemy trenches. Effectively, the RNAS had now caught up with the RFC in France.

The level of preparation for the Third Battle of Krithia was a significant improvement on that which had preceded the first two battles. But despite having knowledge of the enemy's positions, once again as on the European battlefields, the infantry could not make headway against entrenched opposition. The practical assistance of Charles' aeroplanes in the infantry's execution of Sir Aylmer's ambitious plans remained crucial as artillery shells were tightly rationed. Accurate placing of the limited allowance of high explosive shells on enemy trenches was vital. Furthermore the accurate fixing of enemy trenches onto artillery range cards improved the effectiveness of all preliminary bombardments. Once the bombardment had ceased and the infantry brigades were engaged, kite balloons, aeroplanes and Harry's seaplanes all corrected counter-battery fire to provide the advancing infantry some respite.

On the opening day of the battle Charles' aviators had eight ready airframes. Four aeroplanes were based at the forward aerodrome at Cape Helles. They prosecuted multiple reconnaissance and spotting missions with three aeroplanes flying missions lasting over five hours. Use of the forward aerodrome during the battle allowed multiple repeat missions with refuelling, maintenance and rearmament by ground crews outside Sir Aylmer's headquarters.

The forward aerodrome improved coordination with the army and aeroplane loiter time over the Turkish lines.

It eliminated flight over the sea, providing approximately 40 minutes of extra air time. Major Gillam, a transport officer working out of the Hunter-Weston Redoubt, was intrigued by the constant coming and going of aircraft during the battle:

> Aeroplanes are very active now. They go back to Tenedos each night, and come sailing over the sea back here after breakfast. It is too dangerous for the machines to remain on at the aerodrome here, on account of the shell fire.

The aerodrome was in turn targeted by Turkish artillery. Every time an aeroplane landed, explosions followed the machine to its hidden berm behind the redoubt. Its daily use was soon discontinued as, in one afternoon, the aerodrome (and the nearby headquarters) was struck by over 100 shells resulting in the destruction of two aeroplanes. The aerodrome was then used only for emergency landings or when time-sensitive information had to be directly relayed to artillery officers. In a sense the aerodrome had bridged the gap between the two services and its loss as a daily base was felt by both. Its absence gradually became less noticeable as the services became better at communication.

The new trench maps put together by Bernard were given to the air observer, and to the gunnery jack in the monitor's tower. Each now had a clearer idea of how best to lay an effective barrage during the attack:

> The attempt to advance from Helles on 5th and 6th June and the heavy counter attacks gave us plenty to do. My job was to spot for *Humber*, a funny flat iron boat with two, new pattern six-inch guns which made

excellent work, and for *Edgar*, both of which were enfilading the Turkish batteries around Krithia and Achi Baba. It was the first time I had seen the French 75mm in action and most impressive it was, the fire literally rippled up and down the Turkish trenches. Nevertheless we only advanced a few hundred yards but failed to hold even that as we had not enough support to make good the casualties and were practically driven back to our former lines when the Turks counter attacked a few days later. After that we more or less marked time until the Suvla landings.

Manica's balloon also spotted warships onto Turkish positions in front of Achi Baba during the battle, *Hector* having not yet arrived in theatre. Her role involved directing suppressive fire onto gun batteries once the British infantry had left the safety of their trenches and advanced into the open of no man's land, suggesting that the British had finally caught up with ANZAC in their use of the air. A combination of balloon, seaplane and multiple aeroplanes overhead at the critical moment when the infantry advanced towards the enemy front lines certainly saved lives.

Harold Kerby and his two friends arrived following the conclusion of the Third Battle of Krithia. His tent mate, Lieutenant Barr, was given the opportunity to visit the forward trenches as the squadron had more pilots than aeroplanes:

> Lieutenant Barr who came out with me has been over at Cape Helles for a couple of days and he returned last night laden down with enough Turkish rifles and bayonets to stock a museum. He says it is perfect hell on earth over there; the stench and flies are horrible.

At Krithia our front lines are untenable on account of the stench from rotting corpses. Barr says the whole southern end near Sedd el Bahr fort is one huge cemetery, not surprising when we have had 50,000 casualties already. I expect to visit next week.

The disappointing results of this battle, high casualty rates and loss of reserves forced Sir Aylmer and French General Henri Gouraud into a new pattern of small, localised advances. These assaults followed concentrated artillery fire aided by detailed knowledge of enemy saps and trenches. The ability to target a specific trench before an orchestrated rush was the result of trench mapping by Henry and Bernard. They then produced updated maps before each new attack. Small-scale attacks were conducted on 16 June, 21 June, 28 June and 12 July. New editions were published on 22 and 26 June 1915. Bernard was very busy indeed.

The squadron flight journal reveals a split in targeting during these smaller engagements. Spotting was effected by the kite balloon in close proximity to the advancing troops while bombing missions struck targets some distance behind the front lines. On 21 June, Charles, Herb, Reginald and Richard flew six bombing and two reconnaissance missions dropping six 100lb and four 20lb bombs in support of the attack on 28 June. A total of 17 flights were conducted with Charles and Herb flying a medley of reconnaissance, spotting and bombing missions behind the lines. Of the 12 missions flown by No. 3 Squadron on 12 July, Charles flew three missions, including spotting for counter-battery fire. On each occasion Philip's kite balloon was aloft and was the principal spotter guiding naval fire onto targets. The four most experienced pilots, Charles, Herb, Reginald and Richard, were flying the lion's share of missions. Fatigue was setting in.

Harold piloted Voisin 9 with Major Miles as observer in support of the 12 July attack. Target selection was made the day before with individual flight plans completed at the squadron level by Harold's flight commander, Richard Davies:

Sunday 11 July. Tomorrow we are making a big attack and we are besides spotting for all guns going on a raid. I am flying No. 9 Voisin with two bombs to drop on a Turkish bivouac at Sogun Dere. This is my first experience on a big expedition like this and I truly hope and pray that I make good; it will mean three hours' continuous flying at about 7,000 feet so I am going to bed at once as I will need all my energy for my trip tomorrow.

At three this morning the big attack commenced and the cannonade was terrible till about 7 am. Absolutely like nothing on earth. They then eased off to give the infantry a chance to advance and did not restart the fireworks till about 11 and since then it has been one continuous war. From daybreak to sunset we have always had at least one machine up spotting for our artillery batteries and sometimes more. I went up at 2.15 and was up till after 5, exhausted after such a long, trying flight.

My orders were to take up Major Miles as observer and two bombs which were to be dropped on Sogun Dere, so off we pushed and arrived off Cape Helles at about 8,000 feet thanks to a head wind and an engine running well. I flew over Krithia and then altered course to the right to get over my destination. Hardly had I done so when I noticed what looked to be a line up of carts going along the road towards Krithia. I called the Major's attention and through his glasses saw that they were a Turkish supply column coming up. So I got directly in line and when I thought it about right pulled the lever and plumb goes a bomb. I turned the machine so I could see the result but the nacelle insisted in getting in the way so I did not see it fall but the Major followed it all the way and said while not a direct hit it did do some damage as they scattered in all directions. I went on to Sogun Dere and saw a likely looking store house. I let off my other bomb which by good luck went right through the roof and blew the thing to bits. I only hope it was full of Turks.

We then went back to a position above our own lines and the Major signalled by our wireless we were ready to spot and for the next hour I kept going about in a big circle or figure of eight while the Major signalled to our battery on the ground whether their shells were hitting or falling short. We were fired at quite a bit while doing this job but I only saw one very close, and that certainly did give the machine a bump but it was only 20 yards under us.

I got very cold and my arms were aching from the heavy controls on the Voisin so I was glad indeed to turn about to Tenedos, as a flight that length under shell fire is certainly trying on you at first, so I am now turning in early.

If young Harold was feeling fatigue from his occasional flights then Charles Samson was suppressing exhaustion. It is unusual for a squadron commander to commit to daily flights and Charles did not have an executive officer to carry the administrative burden of the squadron for him. Certainly he was lagging behind in his reporting. While Clarkee produced daily, weekly and monthly summaries which he sent to Murray Sueter, the Director of the Air Department in London, Charles mustered only one semi-official handwritten letter. It was dated 27 June 1915 and was written in his schoolboy cursive:

Dear Commander Sueter,

Everything is going all right except for trouble with Canton Engines. It is the valve springs and valve stalks they are not up to the work. We crashed the Voisin on Rabbit Island (outside mouth Dardanelles) and just got there on the very edge of the sea. The engine always stops dead with a crash when the valve spring goes. We are trying to get the Breguet to Constantinople but the engine is very troublesome. We are going to get the ammunition factory there. The soldiers are very keen on it, the Admiral not so keen.

We got our first Taube [enemy aeroplane] with Captain Collet and Major Hogg in a Voisin. Hogg with a rifle fought him for 20 minutes and shot him in the engine. He came down and was destroyed by our artillery.

The Australian corps are awfully pleased with us as we have put the fear of god into the Turks opposite them. It is a good target up that way. One bomb hit their first line trench and killed a lot. The rest came out and the Australians shot them with a Maxim, it was a splendid bag.

Cape Helles is out of bounds for us nowadays as the Germans shell it like hell if an aeroplane stops there. 100 high explosive shells are the norm.

Our 100lb bombs are simply splendid and have an enormous moral and killing effect. I am sure the winter work will be a bit bad and the aerodrome a swamp.

I am your servant,
CR Samson.

Unlike Clarke Hall's factual reporting, there is no indication of the rate of effort or any of the squadron's achievements. Clearly, Charles preferred the cockpit over the desk. This style of leadership had dire consequences for his squadron; Murray Sueter had no idea what No. 3 Squadron had achieved over the past four months. Needless to say, the supply of spare parts and replacement engines was compromised by such poor reporting standards. There is evidence that victualling also suffered as Charles was more intent on the thrill of flying than submitting ration statements to the supply officers of the fleet.

But Charles did know something about bombing and, throughout the summer months, his aviators attacked the targets listed in the Standing Orders. The flight records (rather than Charles' flaky reporting) list the number of bombs dropped with a total of 304 bombs (193 bombs of 20lb, 110 of 100lb, and one of 250lb) over the three months. The Turkish Army was forced to protect its ports and supply bases with anti-aircraft batteries. This obliged the aviators to fly at ever-increasing heights (between 7000 and 8000 feet) which added to the burden of each flight. The cold and decreasing oxygen had a cumulative effect on their health. Harold began to record his fear of 'Archibald':

> The Turkish anti-aircraft fire is getting better and Lieutenant Gordon Thomson said that this morning the one near Krithia was within five yards of him several times in spite of the fact he was flying at 8,000 feet.

While the isolation of the aviators on Tenedos created a range of difficulties, it also had its benefits, including providing an opportunity to experiment with new forms of warfare away from the prying eyes of bureaucracy. Enemy gun batteries were often protected by deep emplacements and impervious to blast and shrapnel. In his search for a solution, Lieutenant Osmond, a former engineer, used his skills to draw up blueprints for an incendiary device. A 24 gallon fuel tank filled with a petrol/paraffin mix was welded to a 20lb bomb. Fins were added to give the large, barrel-shaped explosive ballistic qualities once released from the aeroplane. Its total weight was 275lb. The idea was to drop it close to the gun pit, sending flames over the gunners and burning them alive. Harold recorded this exciting trial:

> Squadron Commander Richard Davies took up one of our 300 lbs petrol bombs and endeavoured to drop it on 'Gallipoli [Beachy] Bill' but it fell short and hit their camp setting it afire.

Hamilton had not given up on his idea to bomb the lone cartridge factory outside Istanbul and Harold was fascinated with the concept of bombing the enemy capital: 'The engine on the Breguet is nearly finished and I think the Turks will be surprised when she reaches Constantinople and unships her load of bombs.'

Bernard was allocated the task of planning the best route. Charles was once again in the cockpit fulfilling a role that any one of his observers could now accomplish. The risk of losing him on the perilous flight to Istanbul does not seem to have crossed his mind. It was sheer madness, as Bernard noted:

> Busy with maps reference the journey to bomb factory of explosives ten miles this side of Constantinople. Make

225

out three routes distances etc. Commander is observer not me! Marix tests the Breguet but engine misses. Begin to doubt the engine. We are at dinner when mechanic rings to say engine all right. So Marix and Commander decide to start. We all say our goodbyes, it is a solemn occasion. At 1.45 am they get into Breguet and the engine sounds all right. We all go to see them off. They go up into the black sky and are soon out of our sight and hearing. We go to bed but in an hour's time we hear them coming back with engine missing badly. But they had dropped all their bombs at Gaba Tepe [this must have frightened the Turks with 14 20lb bombs]. The Breguet just reached the aerodrome.

The army remained practically focused on whittling the enemy's ability to fight by squeezing the flow of supplies onto the peninsula. *Manica* and *Hector* concentrated on the movement of food into ports and stockpiles in the villages behind the Turkish front lines. Considerable effort was expended in July with six days of heavy naval shelling of the ports, setting buildings on fire well into the night. The shelling began on 5 July with the balloon ascending to correct HMS *Venerable* onto the port of Gallipoli, setting the docks on fire. David Preston wrote: 'I think the balloon is going to prove very useful as it would be impossible for battleships to find the range unless the balloon was up.' This exercise was repeated on 16 July with the shelling of stores sheds outside Maidos. Then *Hector* and *Manica* spotted corrected gunnery onto Channakale on 20 July. Once again, on 29 July, Maidos was heavily bombarded by monitors with the balloons correcting the fall of shot.

Despite the fixation with severing the enemy's supply lines, only five bombing raids were conducted against the ports—two daylight and three night bombing raids. The two daylight attacks occurred following reports by early morning reconnaissance flights of large numbers of transports berthed at Maidos. Bernard flew on his first mission to bomb the warehouses and docksides at Maidos:

> Ships have been blazing away all night. Called by sentry at 5 am. Borrow a life vest from Newton-Claire, carry field glasses, pistol and map. Feel loaded up. Climb into Maurice Farman No. 1 with Richard Davies. Carry two 20 lbs bombs inside fuselage and one 100 lbs bomb in bomb dropping racks. We fly up Dardanelles at 5,500 feet and find barracks and proceed to drop bombs. A much more difficult proceeding than I thought. It was necessary to lean right out to avoid hitting control wires. When pin is removed it has to be swung outwards to avoid hitting lower wing. Both bombs went near enough to kill, one in a house and one ten yards away. The 100 lbs bomb made a terrific crash between barracks and houses. I was lucky enough to discover two hidden batteries. Returned safely. Signalled batteries to Vice Admiral for target.

At night Ak Bashi Liman was often lit with torches while goods were unloaded. This provided excellent points of aim. On 22 June, with the aid of the moon, four aeroplanes flown by Charles, Herb, Richard and Reginald bombed the dockside, completely disrupting the unloading of food. The aeroplanes set out at 20-minute intervals to ensure that work couldn't continue.

For his part, Harry's seaplane station at Aliki Bay was ordered to counter the submarine threat. A telephone cable was relayed from a purpose-built wooden shed which housed the *Ark Royal*'s seaplanes and a visual signalling station was established. Seaplanes conducted 17 anti-submarine patrols making this the greatest point of effort. Lieutenant Commander Charles Brodie, a submariner, was attached to the flight as a specialist observer to offer advice on this mission. Charles and his brother Theodore, also a submariner, were identical twins. Charles had developed a large pimple on his nose at 16 years of age and was consequently referred to as 'One Spot' Brodie, while his brother Theodore became 'No Spot' Brodie. On 23 May One Spot was an observer on a patrol attempting to locate a U boat reported off Cape Helles. On 25 May when *U21* sank *Triumph*, a seaplane was immediately despatched carrying One Spot in hot pursuit of the U boat, its task to bomb the submarine on the surface with a brace of 20lb bombs. After *Majestic* was sunk, One Spot was taken on a long patrol of the Aegean coast to identify possible landing places where a U boat could be refuelled. The Naval Intelligence Department reported that local potentates on the Aegean islands were providing support through a network of German spies. One Spot was taken on eight anti-submarine patrols in search of these elusive bases. None was found.

The air service continued reporting on changes to the Dardanelles defences. Regular flights over the Narrows kept a steady stream of intelligence flowing to the submarine flotilla. The Turks had suspended a net across the Narrows to stop the passage of submarines and senior naval officers with the submarine service were taken on flights to study the position of the nets. On 16 June, Lieutenant Commander Bruce was taken aloft to look at the Narrows, while Commander Nasmith and, later, Archibald Cochrane on 27 June, were both provided an opportunity to survey the Narrows from the air before navigating its confines in their submarines:

> *Ark Royal* at the time acted as a foster-mother ship to our submarines. Being an oil burner she could give them a bit of fuel, and perhaps most important of all, she had long fresh water baths wherein the officers could wallow. When in harbour the submarines usually lay alongside the *Ark* and their officers inhabited our wardroom.

Ark Royal and the submarine flotilla had plans for resupply once an Allied submarine had passed through the Narrows. The crew of submarine HMS *E11* had prearranged a rendezvous:

> Nasmith [*E11*], before he went, took petrol and spares for our seaplanes and made a rendezvous in the Marmara so that we could take him anything which he required. We flew him over the Narrows so that he could see the dispositions of the nets for himself, and then in he went.

On 24 May *E11*'s periscope was shot away so the seaplane flight was ordered to fly a replacement across the peninsula. Harry, as Intelligence Officer, noted the passage of *E11* and considered that 'taking a new periscope was a perilous undertaking and I was much relieved when the mission was called off as there was no suitable spare'.

Harry continued to visit Anzac Cove on the early morning ferry:

> I wonder what would have happened to ANZAC if it had not been for *Ark Royal's* petrol tins? Apart from

229

the men's water bottles no provision had been made to supply them with water, and with many of the posts held, water had to be hauled up the cliff by rope. We had some thousands of two gallon petrol tins which we washed out and continually filled with water. The forward posts had to rely on that alone for a while.

Meanwhile off the coast of Izmir near Mitylene, George Dacre on *Ben-my-Chree* continued his trial runs to establish weight and attack profiles for a torpedo attack. Finally, on 17 July, the concept was judged sufficiently mature to allow live warheads to be carried. George discovered, however, that his engine was not powerful enough to lift the 700lb torpedo above 600 feet once airborne. George's senior, Flight Commander Charles Edmonds, attempted the same with his Sunbeam:

> Later Charles Edmonds went out with a torpedo for practice and hit something and burst his float which swung the machine around towards us. He let go of his torpedo to lighten the machine, not knowing where he was aiming. It passed ten feet ahead of us and went under a small patrol boat just missing it. Then between a man's legs who was swimming. Great panic amongst the ships.

On 23 July *Ben-my-Chree* was ordered to Rabbit Island outside the mouth of the Dardanelles. From this point on George assisted the monitors firing on enemy gun batteries on the Asiatic shore. He was often paired with *Roberts* and the smaller 9.2-inch guns of *M19* while anchored in the lee of the island:

HMS *Ark Royal*, the world's first aircraft carrier, anchored off Anzac Cove on 17 February 1915.

A Short seaplane, lowered from the aircraft carrier *Ark Royal*, is about to conduct a mission over Turkish trenches before the landing on 25 April 1915.

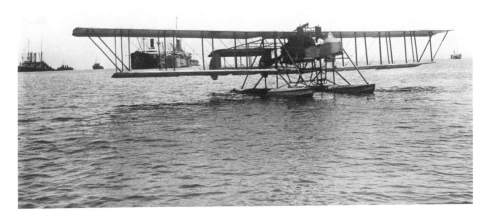

A Wight seaplane before a mission. Seaplanes located Turkish artillery batteries and trenches at Anzac Cove.

Harry Strain flew in a Short 184 seaplane over Anzac Cove on 25 April 1915.

A fast single-seater seaplane being lowered into the sea from *Ark Royal*.
This seaplane reported enemy troop movements behind Anzac Cove on
25 April.

Lieutenant Harry Strain flies over Anzac Cove on the morning of the
landing.

Aerial photography of Sedd El Bahr Fort at Cape Helles. British
soldiers landed here on 25 April 1915 and suffered horrendous
casualties, turning the sea red.

Balloon ships HMS *Manica*, *Hector* and *Canning* operated off the
Gallipoli coast from 17 April, correcting naval gunfire onto Turkish
camps, trenches and artillery batteries.

HMS *Hector* was the second balloon ship to support the ANZACs.

In May 1915 a seaplane base was constructed on the island of Imbros to allow flights over Anzac Cove.

The forts defending the Narrows were bombed by aircraft and shelled by balloon 'spotters' during the campaign.

Two gunnery officers were suspended 3000 feet above the Turkish coast, directing naval gunfire by telephone.

Charles Samson commanded No. 3 Squadron at Gallipoli from 27 March 1915. He was an aggressive pilot. More than 2000 combat missions were flown during the Gallipoli campaign.

A Voisin biplane of No. 3 Squadron about to bomb 'Gallipoli Bill' with a homemade incendiary device. The radio aerial, which was deployed in flight, is attached to the side of the cockpit.

Flight Commander Richard Bell Davies (left), who was awarded a Victoria Cross at Gallipoli, stands beside a 500lb bomb before flight.

The Turkish Air Service was engaged by Nieuport 11 biplanes over Gallipoli. A deadly air battle unfolded.

A homemade gun mount on the Tenedos aerodrome in June 1915. The aerodrome was regularly bombed by the Turkish Air Service.

The aerodrome at Imbros in September 1915, next to Sir Ian Hamilton's General Headquarters.

To raise flagging morale, mechanics formed 'Fezz Follies' to entertain No. 3 Wing in September 1915. The death of Captain Herb Collet was widely felt.

A blimp (submarine scout airship) operated over Gallipoli from September to December 1915. SSA No.7 conducted extensive anti-submarine patrols.

A blimp conducting anti-submarine patrols off the coast of Gallipoli. General William Birdwood, ANZAC, was taken on a reconnaissance flight.

The blimp returning after a mission scouting for German submarines that operated in the Aegean.

HMS *Ben-my-Chree*'s seaplanes launched the first aerial torpedo strike at Gallipoli in August 1915.

Colonel Frederick Sykes had plans for a seaplane to fly over the peninsula for a 'piggy back' ride on a submarine to bomb the ammunition factory in Istanbul. Cochrane's submarine (foreground) is practising surfacing under a seaplane.

31 July: I flew up the straits nearly to the Narrows and saw all the British and Turkish trenches at Cape Helles and the no man's land between. It struck me then what a very little piece of land at the tongue of the peninsula we were holding. Edwards spotted for HMS *Roberts* . . . I watched the *Roberts* from the masthead drop shells near the Asiatic batteries. War is too scientific nowadays. It is marvellous to hit a gun 11 miles away with a projectile weighing 2 tons from a ship hidden behind Rabbit Island and directed by seaplanes 1 mile above the target which wireless back the results.

Air support at Anzac continued throughout the summer, but at a reduced rate. The seaplane flight continued spotting operations in support of ANZAC with 12 missions spotting for monitors with some notable successes. On 15 June Joe Kilner and Harry flew over Anzac and guided a battery onto a heavy gun on 'W Hill' with accurate shooting. Similarly, three direct hits on enemy gun emplacements were achieved when a seaplane was twinned with *Humber* on 22 June. Either enemy gunners had become sloppy with their camouflage or the process of aerial photography was revealing the once-hidden gun batteries to closer scrutiny with a magnifying glass.

Private Herbert Reynolds, with his view out towards the Aegean from the first aid station, witnessed *Manica*'s balloon in action on Friday 25 June:

An aeroplane passed over here at about 11am but it was hard to distinguish who it belonged to. The distinguishing mark on our planes is a red, white and blue circle on each wing. The enemy is the same as the Germans, a black cross. At about 3pm the *Lord Nelson*

accompanied by a balloon ship, and escorted by T.B.Ds
[torpedo boat destroyers] took up position about midway between Imbros and Kaba Tepe point and from
there fired broadside after broadside at the enemy away
inland towards Maidos, the balloon from the balloon
ship directed her fire. The enemy field guns began firing at the battleship but she took no notice of them,
they could be seen flashing on the high ridge in front
of our right flank. At about 4.30pm when the *Lord
Nelson* and other boats steamed off, great columns of
dense smoke could be seen rising away to the south-
east towards Maidos. An enemy aeroplane flew over our
lines at about 5pm and set a bundle of papers loose but
the wind carried them all into enemy territory.

The kite balloons ranged off Anzac became increasingly
sophisticated in their coordination of naval gunnery. Philip
Mackworth in *Manica*'s balloon spotted for *Talbot* but, in
order to move closer to view the target, operated within
range of enemy artillery batteries and was subject to heavy
air bursts. To reduce this menace a seaplane was sent up
to spot *Humber* onto enemy artillery targeting the balloon.
The seaplane was flying a type of 'protective mission' for
a tethered kite balloon. This teamwork played out on four
occasions with the destruction of ammunition dumps in
the Biyuk Anafarta villages, Boghali and Kojadere. *Hector*
became an important addition to the order of battle as now
a balloon could serve each sector. David Preston described
the kite balloon as supporting the army at Anzac one day
and Cape Helles the next.

With Harry and the seaplane station at Aliki Bay focused
on the submarines, another ANZAC artillery officer,
Captain Keith Jopp, was detached to fly as an observer with

Charles' squadron for the duration of the campaign. His role was to act as the eyes over Anzac. Charles described his Australian observer in glowing terms:

> Keith Jopp, who was an Australian, was the observer whom I detailed to specialise on ANZAC; he had an eye like a hawk, and it wasn't long before he had discovered most of the guns that were causing trouble.

Keith flew his first mission on 18 July and completed a total of 14 missions prior to the August offensive. Just before his first flight, Keith had been given some disquieting advice in Bernard's tent:

> Commander Samson warns about Turkish atrocities. We are always to be armed. He hints that it would be best not to fire away our last cartridge. I hate thinking about these things.

The squadron continued with long-range reconnaissance and frequently dropped bombs against targets opposite ANZAC trenches. With Keith on board as observer, Charles was more confident bombing Turkish trenches on the 400 Plateau. Keith proved a welcome addition. Bernard was very pleased to have an ANZAC officer to help with map-making and to pin down the location of Turkish gun batteries.

Throughout the summer, reconnaissance remained Charles' priority. In an indication of the closer relationship between the army and the air service, senior staff officers now asked to be taken aloft. Brigadier General Hugh Simpson Baikie, the senior Artillery Staff Officer in British IX Corps, was the first staff officer to overfly Turkish lines when he was taken up on 18 June from the forward aerodrome on

Cape Helles. Simpson Baikie was keen to gain an understanding of the Turkish trench system.

Bernard continued to distribute post-mission reports and was sent on five missions as an observer to help with his orientation. His second flight suggests that the novelty was wearing thin:

> Get order to start at 1.45pm with Marix in Voisin No. 7 to drop two 100 lbs on gun emplacements. Commander explains at some length where it is (153 P G). We go over sea nearly as far as Imbros, then up Xeros looking for submarines; then cross peninsula and down narrows to Kum Kale. Could not get above 4000 feet. Machine would not climb with bombs. We went over emplacement and saw three howitzers. We were under fire for ½ an hour. Released first bomb too soon. Made 5 runs before setting line for second bomb attack from coast to target. Bomb fell in middle of emplacement. Large fire started. Somewhat tired and weary on return. Come to conclusion I am too old to indulge in the excitements and dangers entailed in flying over enemy and releasing bombs at 4,000 feet. Collet gets slightly squiffy at dinner.

While photography could not win the battle, it proved a vital enabler at Gallipoli. Henry Butler flew 57 photographic missions in three months. Even Charles, who preferred offensive work, confirmed the importance of this solitary and painstaking task: 'our photographs are always wanted by the General. We have mapped out, with photographs, all the vital country.' Henry's borrowed camera was fixed on the outside of the nacelle of his underpowered Maurice Farman which he flew solo. This produced better quality pictures than the hand-held civilian camera he had used in April and May. Major Hogg, one of Charles' observers, commented on the importance of photography in his reports to Army Headquarters in London:

> We have only one camera, private property, and a Naval Pilot (Lt Butler RNAS) has been taking photos with this. The first experiments were not satisfactory, but latterly excellent results have been obtained, and are of the greatest value. The photos, in addition to their value to the General Staff, correct the map and enable the observer to place the enemy's positions and trenches with greater accuracy. Developing and printing are done here by the owner of the camera. Photographic results have been very satisfactory. He places the photos together to form a map, which is sent to Army Corps Headquarters. Trench reconnaissance is done in this way exclusively.

Henry's work was brought to an end on 28 June. By this time the Maurice Farman could barely claw a height of 4000 feet above the enemy trenches he was photographing. Bernard wrote:

> Butler gets a rifle shot through the ankle, but by wonderful luck, landed all right. The bullet seems to have missed all the bones and passed through the floor of the machine and his foot. Doctor says if the wound is not septic, he will be better in ten days. His place (photography) is to be taken by Julian Newton-Claire.

Harold also followed Henry's fate closely. A sour note in his diary suggests that his morale was flagging. His inexperience kept him from the daily flight list despite the appalling workload of the four most experienced pilots:

> Flight Commander Butler who was shot in the foot about a month ago while flying over the lines, left for home much envied by all the rest of the squadron. This is a most awful place to while away the time, absolutely nothing to do. Today I have done absolutely nothing— lay about and read. No flying; not enough aircraft. Had a ripping swim though this afternoon, the big waves rushing in made it a top hole indeed.

The seaplane flight also conducted photographic missions in support of ANZAC with a captured German Aero camera sent out from France. Clarkee had requested assistance from the Air Department in the supply of photographic equipment. On 15 July two 'useful photographs' were taken over gun battery positions at Kum Dere and Harry mapped the olive grove behind Gaba Tepe by taking a photographic mosaic:

> 'Martha' Park and I undertook the making of what I believe to be the first map of enemy country from the air where there was no land survey in our possession with which to coordinate it. The part to be mapped was the olive grove and land behind Gaba Tepe on the ANZAC right front.
>
> We got the ships to measure the distance between two easily recognisable points as accurately as possible then took overlapping photographs. The map was a success and served its purpose.

On 28 July a seaplane fitted with the camera overturned

during take-off, destroying the camera. Undeterred, Harry and his observers used their own Kodak instead:

> Latterly we have taken to photography from the air and checking maps and gun positions and trenches. GHQ are very keen on them and they really have been of some use lately.

The skies over the peninsula were now contested as the Turkish Air Service became increasingly active. The first aerial engagement occurred with Herb Collet and Major Hogg bringing down an Albatros with 30 shots fired from Major Hogg's rifle. Herb and Major Hogg were up in a Voisin pusher correcting an artillery battery onto an enemy trench below Achi Baba. A shadow passed quickly overhead and they soon discovered this to be an Albatros, newly arrived from Germany. It was a two seater, the Turkish observer armed with a pistol.

Herb gave chase and cleverly flew under the enemy machine. This denied the pilot a turn of speed by loss of height and enabled Major Hogg to engage the unprotected 'underbelly' of the enemy aeroplane. Herb had to keep 'jinking' to stay in place as the Albatros was expertly flown. For over 20 minutes Major Hogg fired his Lee Enfield into the machine flying ten metres above. Contending with violent movements from the aeroplane and the turbulence of the slipstream, Hogg had to reload his rifle with clips at least five times. Eventually he hit the engine and the Albatros bled black smoke and oil. Herb broke away and followed the Albatros down until it landed close to the base at Achi Baba when heavy machine-gun fire forced him back up again. Noting that the enemy aeroplane was damaged, he flew onto the forward aerodrome for bombs to finish it off.

While he was on the ground he learnt that the artillery had smashed the enemy aeroplane. From this point on, both sides flew with machine-guns. The hate intensified.

It was now the turn of *Hauptmann* Erich Serno's 1st Aircraft Company to undergo significant organisational changes. In late June the company was transferred from Fortress Command at Channakale to under direction of the Turkish 5th Army. The aircraft company moved from its aerodrome at Channakale to a prepared coastal strip at Galatia, north of Maidos. Serno established his headquarters in Istanbul, placing the aircraft company under command of *Leutnant* Preussner with a young Turkish observer as his executive officer. The Turkish Air Service was significantly reinforced with several machines that flew over Bulgaria, completing a seven-hour trip. Three out of seven airframes were lost in the attempt. Fortress Command was rewarded with its own seaplane unit under command of *Kapitan Leutnant* Liebmann of the *Wasserfliegerabteilung*, comprising two Gotha seaplanes with 100hp engines. These had been smuggled across Bulgaria and reassembled in Istanbul. Two of these formidable airframes were flown to Channakale and housed in sheds astride the straits.

Harold Kerby described the Gotha seaplane as a twin seater, the observer armed with a swivel-mounted machine-gun. The seaplane was much more aggressively flown than the Albatros, with two intense aerial engagements occurring on 24 and 29 July. Harold witnessed the result of one of these unequal engagements:

> 29 July. A German aeroplane shoots and wounds French pilot and observer this morning. They were in a M.F. [Maurice Farman] with no weapons, but landed safely though in a state of collapse.

The Gotha seaplane courted aerial combat with the superiority of a mounted machine-gun over unarmed observers or, at best, those armed with a handheld rifle:

> There are some more Taubes out here, for Lieutenant Gordon Thomson went upstairs this evening and was attacked. It was a really nasty Taube too because he has a machine gun mounted, and as I have the early morning reconnaissance I will have to take the Lewis gun along on the old Voisin in case he appears again.

Tit-for-tat bombing raids on each other's aerodromes continued. On 5 July Charles led two aeroplanes in a 'bomb attack on Chanak aerodrome' to catch the seaplane in its shed. During the evening of 15 July, two aeroplanes again raided the seaplane sheds and also attacked the old aerodrome at Channakale with 100lb bombs. During the full moon on 25 July, Richard Bell Davies dropped two 100lb bombs on Channakale aerodrome from 1000 feet. The Turkish Air Service replied with its own series of raids. Their aeroplanes had survived undamaged.

In late May, Frederick Sykes was ordered to proceed to the Dardanelles. His duties were to consult with John de Robeck, Hamilton, Birdie and Charles before reporting on the role of aviation in the Gallipoli campaign. Sykes was ordered to investigate arrangements for reconnaissance and bombing attacks, and the number and type of machines most useful for operations. He arrived in the Dardanelles on 24 June and conducted a series of interviews, visiting Charles' squadron last of all. Underlying tensions between Sykes and Charles began to fester. Sykes stayed one or two days with the various air service units observing the part each played. He inspected the seaplane station at Aliki Bay and viewed naval gunfire support from *Manica*'s balloon. He reconnoitred a proposed site for an aerodrome on Cape Kephalo's finger-like promontory. It was relatively flat and clear of obstacles, albeit exposed and windblown. He pronounced the area fit for aeroplanes and for a future submarine scout base for airships to engage in anti-submarine patrols. Charles thought otherwise.

The proposal to establish an airship base came from Sykes' meeting with de Robeck during which the submarine threat was discussed at length. The airships were required for anti-submarine patrols in which submerged U boats would be attacked with sea mines dropped directly onto the boat by means of a cable. It is unclear whether the cable innovation was a Dardanelles invention because of its clear waters or a feature of anti-submarine warfare conducted in the North Sea. Surfaced boats could be attacked by bombing. In a private letter to Churchill, Sykes also revealed a plan to use the airships in strategic bombing raids on Istanbul. Hope was expressed that *Ben-my-Chree* and her more powerful seaplanes would carry torpedoes and strike Turkish shipping to fulfil her original role as discussed in the Air Department conference of 3 April.

On 9 July, following his deliberations, Sykes cabled an immediate request to the Admiralty for a major commitment of RNAS assets with a further 36 aeroplanes, six photographers with RFC cameras, and eight airships. He returned to the Air Department with a 26-page document describing the air requirements, deficiencies in the air services and the means to address these. He downplayed the achievements of the aviators in the Dardanelles which further exacerbated his uneasy relationship with Charles. His comments were galling considering the effort expended. Sykes wrote that many of the units had 'no experience of service away from

sheds and other conveniences and only a moderate measure of success had been obtained'. These were harsh words
from an RFC pilot who had been billeted in chateaux while
flying in France.

The 9 July report clearly points to aerial reconnaissance
as the primary role. In his covering letter Sykes expressed
the key point that 'the necessity for aerial reconnaissance
is very real and urgent'. This was logical as the enemy held
the dominant high ground and, without the use of the air,
headquarters was effectively blind. Surprisingly, in justifying
his substantial requests for matériel and his emphasis on the
importance of air reconnaissance, Sykes made no reference
to the detection and ultimate destruction of the Turkish
attack at Anzac Cove on 19 May. Once again, Hamilton had
clearly preferred to remain silent.

Difficulties in communication between the two services
remained. Addressing this problem, Sykes made a strong
case for centralising the air service on Cape Kephalo on
Imbros, juxtaposed with navy and army headquarters. He
argued that the scale of land operations had increased since
the landings and the need for extensive aeroplane reconnaissance and systematic cooperation had become more evident.
Centralising the air service on Imbros would reduce risky
over-water flight and group the service with its supporting
infrastructure in one place, promoting economy of effort
and improved efficiency.

Most important of all was a proposal to form an Air
Headquarters with supporting staff to manage the air services once the various units were concentrated in one place.
The Air Headquarters would command an expanded order
of battle with an aeroplane wing, a kite balloon squadron, a
submarine scout squadron and a mother ship. Sykes' plans
for the aeroplane wing included three aeroplane squadrons,

with three flights each, and a seaplane flight. The aeroplane wing would have a total of 38 aircraft with 18 airframes in reserve plus 18 spare engines. Not surprisingly, he recommended the despatch of two homogenous aircraft types: the BE2C and Maurice Farmans with 100hp engines. He proposed the establishment of a photographic section along the lines of the RFC in France with a camera section located next to General Headquarters. He advocated the creation of a training unit for observers using airframe types present in the Dardanelles but deemed unsuitable for warlike operations. His recommendations included eight submarine scout airships in two flights to support the navy in its battle against the German submarine menace. At the heart of his proposal was the adoption of recent organisational changes effected by the RFC. Sykes' simple justification for new airframes was that the air services in the Dardanelles should be equipped with the same number of aeroplanes flown by the RFC in its support for the British Expeditionary Force in France.

Sykes similarly expressed his belief in the separation of strategic and operational-level flying based on air support to corps and divisional headquarters. Strategic reconnaissance would be ordered by the newly established Air Headquarters while tactical-level reconnaissance would be directed by the two corps commanders. His argument for three separate squadrons was based on one dedicated squadron for strategic or theatre-wide intelligence requirements, with the flights of the remaining two squadrons dedicated to the requirements of the tactical divisional headquarters. Again he based his proposal on the system used in France.

Sykes' proposal to establish a submarine scout airship squadron was immediately approved and two blimps and supporting infrastructure were despatched to the Aegean.

They arrived in boxes on 9 August. The two airships were the first installment of his new system to arrive in theatre.

On his return to London, the Lords Commissioners of the Admiralty appointed Sykes temporary wing captain with command of all air service units in the Dardanelles. In many ways his appointment was inevitable as it can be assumed that he was quizzed on likely candidates for the position. His description of air support in his 9 July report stymied the candidacy of Charles Samson, who would otherwise have been the likely choice.

The response to Sykes' report was immediate. It met with Admiralty Board approval and No. 1 Squadron RNAS at Dunkirk was warned for immediate departure for the Dardanelles. A later series of unrealistic and overblown signals recorded a total of 45 additional machines listed for despatch with 33 due to arrive on 9 August. Inclusive of the airframes being sent out were heavier Maurice Farmans. In reality only a third of the airframes confidently described in initial telegrams were actually sent. The welcome news of a small tranche of replacement aeroplanes of improved type was relayed to No. 3 Squadron on 18 July just as the aviators were operating their last three serviceable aeroplanes.

While Frederick Sykes was in England preparing for his new command, the August offensive was reaching the final stages of preparation. This offensive would see the Mediterranean Expeditionary Force, reinforced with a second army corps (IX Corps under Lieutenant General Frederick Stopford), finally break its stalemate. Planning for the offensive included the requirement to extend air reconnaissance northwards to Suvla Bay. Charles' men were briefed on the coming attack and the preparations required to support it. Harold once again saw holes in the preparations:

With 60,000 more troops ready to land I look for a big change out here in the next three weeks. At any rate we are moving to our base on Imbros, to be closer to the operations as they advance. We have only three machines; really, if our new supplies don't arrive soon we will have to borrow some from the French.

The appointment of Frederick Sykes and plans to establish an effective air service were, in fact, out of step with the operational tempo. Just at the point of maximum effort and perceived breakthrough, Sykes was in London and the air service was at its lowest ebb. One or two members of Charles' squadron were beginning to suffer forms of mental collapse. Bernard recorded the strain displayed by Charles' own brother:

> Bill appears in limping condition and confides in me that he has considerable trouble in making his ankle appear bad enough to induce Patterson (Surgeon) to send him home.

Despite this, Sykes' concentration of Charles' squadron on Kephalo helped the squadron by reducing the long flight over the sea. But No. 3 Squadron was suffering a crisis in capability. It was barely able to conduct supporting operations let alone respond to a surge in activity. Allusions to this emerging problem were captured in Sykes' 9 July report but the breakdown in capability only increased following his return to London. On 15 July Harold recorded that the squadron had 11 pilots with only two serviceable aeroplanes:

> Another machine down this morning at Cape Helles. Really, if the Admiralty don't rush us some new

machines it will be a joke; we are forced to overwork what 2 machines we have left. Eleven pilots with only two machines is really too ridiculous for words.

16 July: Our big Maurice Farman smashed an aileron when landing this morning, so we have only one machine. I don't know what we will do for new machines if they don't arrive before the landing of the 80,000 troops we have waiting at Imbros. It is four days since I have done any flying.

The effects of an inadequate and monotonous diet and high operational tempo also placed stresses on Charles' core aviators and ground crew. Harry and George's aircrew billeted on the seaplane tenders were victualled at the naval rate and were the best fed of all. Charles' isolation on Tenedos and his lack of enthusiasm for reporting and logistics resulted in poor victualling for his aviators. The younger pilots seemed to suffer the most:

I wish we could get some decent grub, this bully beef is awful. I want a change from this Greek bread, bully beef and hard tack. Our mess is bad but heaven knows what the petty officers get to eat.

Harold wrote that the monotonous diet and poor conditions saw half the ship's company fall ill as a consequence. The young Harold noted his hunger and his slipping fitness to undertake missions. Poor diet, plagues of flies and the stresses of flight were beginning to affect morale. John de Robeck recognised the imminent collapse of the squadron and sent its two most senior pilots, Charles and Reginald, to Alexandria on two weeks' leave just before the August offensive. Either this was a miscalculation or evidence of the scale of exhaustion. Charles was absent just as his squadron embarked on the difficult move to Cape Kephalo and prepared itself for the big offensive.

Just as Sykes was on the cusp of instituting change, the air units finally reached their most parlous state. While the army had been invigorated by three new divisions and the establishment of a separate corps headquarters, Charles' squadron was teetering on irrelevance with its two most senior officers on leave. Harold uttered one last lament before the move to Imbros. Everyone was prepared for the big attack except the RNAS:

> 29 July: We are going to land 120,000 troops we have waiting at Imbros. Some at Gaba Tepe and some at the salt lake. I think we will simply rush them off their feet. Besides yesterday 200,000 rounds of lyddite shells arrived so our artillery have plenty of ammunition for a continuous bombardment of over two weeks. I do hope our machines get here before the big push.

CHAPTER 7

Looking down on the August offensive

Most Australians have some understanding of the August offensive thanks to Mel Gibson's role in the movie *Gallipoli*. The offensive has become synonymous with poor planning and the futile charge of the Light Horse at The Nek. While the movie correctly demonstrates the futility of infantry attacks against prepared defences, it doesn't touch on the broader events of the campaign. The aviators, of course, are ghosts in the narrative.

The August offensive was an attempt by Sir Ian Hamilton's expeditionary force to capture key ground, defeating the Turkish Army before the onset of winter. The idea of a major offensive was first discussed by the War Council in London as early as 14 May. Hamilton was eventually told that he would be given three New Army divisions for an assault in mid-July. This was later increased to five with the inclusion of two territorial divisions to ensure a decisive result. The reinforcements were part of the newly formed IX Corps under command of the bumbling and inexperienced Major

General Frederick Stopford. While the army was bolstered by the arrival of over 100 transports stuffed full of troops, the air service, by contrast, was in tatters.

The arrival of Stopford's corps saw a marked deterioration in the ability of the air service to provide assistance. As Frederick Sykes had explained in his report, the air service in the Dardanelles was well below parity with the RFC in France where each division was supported by a squadron of aeroplanes. With the arrival of Stopford's five new infantry divisions the air service was at least 80 aeroplanes short.

Hamilton committed his reinforcements to a plan for an ANZAC breakout devised by General Birdwood and his ANZAC staff. Birdie's evolving plan expanded (with the addition of IX Corps) to three overall objectives: to cut Turkish Army land routes; to gain a commanding position so that Allied artillery could smash Turkish port facilities; and to secure Suvla Bay as a winter base. All the assaults were based on the use of surprise—that critically important factor in warfare. The assaults would take the form of silent night attacks commencing on the night of 7 August with a breakout from the left of Anzac to seize Koja Chemen Tepe on the Sari Bair Range. At the same time, an amphibious assault was planned to secure Suvla Bay. Both attacks were synchronised with the setting of the moon to achieve tactical surprise.

The plan was complex, involving reinforcements hidden at Anzac in the days prior to the offensive. Simultaneously, British soldiers accommodated on transports in Mudros Harbour would steam to Suvla, land from purpose-built barges, and quickly advance across the plain to seize vital high ground and the northern Anafarta villages. The road down the spine of the peninsula would be cut. The ANZAC seizure of Sari Bair would allow Allied gunners uninterrupted views of Maidos; they could squeeze Turkish supplies and choke the enemy.

To create the optimum conditions for the plan's success, a series of heavy feints would be executed to draw enemy troops from Sari Bair and Suvla. An evening assault on the ANZAC right flank at Lone Pine and a major daylight attack at Cape Helles the day before would effectively engage all the enemy's reserves. A landing of irregular Cretan troops on Xeros Island was also included to engage enemy troops bivouacked north of Suvla. The aviators were tasked to provide intelligence on enemy positions; this was vital to secure success in the first perilous hours.

Of course the August offensive failed, achieving few of its objectives. It was also the last offensive operation of the Allied army on the Gallipoli Peninsula. Despite the parlous state of the air services, Charles Samson, Philip Mackworth, Harry Strain and George Dacre provided critical intelligence support—they got it right. They did a sterling job and it is time their story—with all its frustrations—was told.

The plan for a breakout from Anzac was originally conceived in late May after scouts discovered that the terrain north of the Fisherman's Hut and Outpost No. 1 was clear of enemy forces. Initially, intelligence was based on prisoner-of-war debriefs, primarily deserters who had made their way along the beach to the ANZAC lines to surrender. Birdie and his staff in ANZAC Headquarters then confirmed this with scouting patrols to build a picture of Turkish positions on the left flank. This was an ANZAC-inspired plan. Birdie's work coincided with the War Council's decision to despatch large numbers of troops to force a solution at Gallipoli. Birdie soon told Hamilton of the open left flank.

On 5 July General Sir Alexander Godley, General Officer Commanding the New Zealand and Australian Division, sent directives for patrols to scout beyond the far left of the front-line trenches. These patrols were tasked with assessing whether a column of infantry could navigate its way at night across the broken ground inland to Hill 971 on the Sari Bair Range:

MEMORANDUM

Please have reconnaissances made in the next ten days of the following, which are placed in order of importance. References are to accompany map.

Obstacles to movement.

Front of which troops can march without check.

Estimated rate of march on a moonless night.

Possibility of ascending in extended order the south slopes of Hill 971.

Whether the 971 Ridge stands out clearly against the skyline, or if not, what feature obstructs it.

The nature of the country, as affecting the movement of infantry.

It is desirable that reconnoitring parties should consist of selected officers, and 2 or 3 intelligent men, who could be utilised as guides for night operations.

Care must be taken not to send patrols out too frequently, as it is essential that the enemy's suspicions should NOT be aroused.

Reports should be in at Divisional Headquarters by
15th July without fail.

This request for information was answered with detailed
observations. The scouting parties were able to describe the
approaches but not the defences on the ridge of Sari Bair
itself.

The air service flew a total of 257 missions in August in
support of the offensive. There were fewer bombing missions: 63 reconnaissance, 115 spotting, 19 photographic,
5 bombing (including three successful aerial torpedo strikes),
5 anti-aircraft patrolling, 19 other and 26 cross-sea transit
flights. With a significant decline in capability, concentration
of effort was on reconnaissance prior to the assaults and spotting once the troops were in contact with the enemy. With
dwindling aircraft numbers and, at times, inclement weather,
tasks were apportioned carefully. The weather in the second
week of August was particularly 'unpropitious for air work'
for the seaplane flight and likewise affected Charles Samson's
aviators on the exposed promontory on Cape Kephalo.

Estimates given to Frederick Stopford on 22 July were
based on aerial intelligence and told of three Turkish battalions, approximately 2000 troops, in the Anafarta villages.
Two battalions were spread across the dominant high
ground surrounding Suvla Bay with an outpost on a small
hill called Lala Baba screening the seaward approaches:

Instructions for G.O.C. 9th Army Corps.

Reference Sheet Anafarta Sagir Gallipoli Map 1/20,000.

Small numbers of Turkish mounted troops and
Gendarmerie have been reported in the country north

of Anzac, and three guns with limbers, each drawn by six oxen, have been seen moving into Anafarta Sagir. An aeroplane photograph has also disclosed the presence of a few trenches on Lala Baba. A sketch of these trenches, which have apparently been constructed for some months, is attached. It is believed that the channel connecting the Salt Lake with Suvla Bay is now dry.

Your landing will begin on the night 6th/7th August. Your primary objective will be to secure Suvla Bay as a base for all the forces operating in the northern zone. Owing to the difficult nature of the terrain, it is possible that the attainment of this objective will, in the first instance, require the use of the whole of the troops at your disposal.

Essentially, the terrain was lightly defended, allowing a landing with at least a 9:1 majority in troop numbers. This intelligence information was distributed to IX Corps Headquarters.

Senior officer Richard Bell Davies (Charles Samson and Reginald Marix were on leave) organised a surge in reconnaissance flights during the preparation phase and photographs of the Suvla region were taken in the last days of July. Turkish positions were located and key terrain identified which noted the absence of Turkish defensive works around the salt lake and the two inland villages of Anafarta. By the end of July observers were answering specific questions from ANZAC on potential overland routes to the high ground of Hill 971 (Chunuk Bair) and any enemy defences likely to be encountered. Bernard telegraphed critical information to Sir Alexander Godley:

Copy of Telegram No. Dated 27/7/15

From: Aeroplane Tenedos

To: Australian Divisional Artillery

In accordance with your signal STOP D9 bed quite possible and appears even STOP Exit from gully on to ridge very steep but possible and appears accessible STOP Slope is broken and covered with scrub STOP Trench (about 20 rifles) across ridge at 80 K 2 intercepts advance on Chunuk Bair appears difficult approach bed narrow with frequent washaways sides of gully are chalk cliffs and very steep slope STOP The slope up the hill is commanded by seven small trenches at 80 F 3 total about 30 rifles STOP At 81 A four gun emplacements facing south STOP At 81 G 1 there are dugouts possible one hundred men STOP

It was this quality of information that was missing from scouting reports on the lower slopes. Aerial photographs of the actual approaches were sent to Godley to supplement Bernard's telegram. His military appreciation on 23 June used this aerial photography for the inland advance on Hill 971. Godley learnt from aerial photography that Turkish trenches on the ridge did not extend further north than Chunuk Bair. The description of a total defending force of 130 Turkish soldiers represented vital information. If the ANZACs could get to the top of Sari Bair in darkness, then they had every chance of seizing this ground.

The aviators were careful not to alert the Turkish 5th Army command to Allied intentions. The squadron was instructed to fly at a high altitude (7000 feet) and ordered not to loiter over Sari Bair or Suvla. Photographs of inland positions were taken by Gordon Thomson and Julian

Newton-Claire while coastal defences were photographed by Harry. These were distributed to Hamilton and sent on to Stopford to supplement orders.

The ANZAC diversionary attack on Lone Pine the day before the main landings on Suvla and the assault on Sari Bair was assisted by extensive photography of the existing network of Turkish trenches on the 400 Plateau carefully drawn onto mapping on 12 July. The ANZAC trench diagram No. II, 'The Plateau 400 Position 1 inch=70 yards', named each enemy trench using nomenclature similar to that used at Cape Helles, with the front enemy trenches named P, Q, R and S. Again on 20 July, while still on Tenedos, the squadron flew a total of only three missions, two of which were 'Flight with Camera' flown by Gordon Thomson. He took particularly clear photographs of Lone Pine which provided evidence that the enemy trenches were covered in logs. These photographs were developed in the makeshift darkroom on Tenedos and copies were sent to ANZAC Headquarters for closer examination.

Then Hamilton did something quite extraordinary: he flew on a reconnaissance flight on 27 July to see the ground for himself. He called at the aerodrome on Tenedos, first visiting Bernard and receiving a briefing on the latest intelligence on Turkish defences. Then he boarded a Maurice Farman with Herb Collet.

Herb was one of the first naval aviators—the first pilot, in fact—to 'loop the loop'. He was a wise choice for a risky flight, having been awarded the Distinguished Service Order for his extraordinary raid on the zeppelin sheds at Düsseldorf in 1914. Herb took Hamilton on a long overland flight from Anzac Cove to Suvla Bay. The Commander-in-Chief was taking a most extraordinary risk. His flight also ended idle debate on the role of intelligence during the campaign. Hugh Simpson Baikie, Hamilton's chief gunner, had previously overflown enemy trenches and gun batteries to check their positions for himself. Now Hamilton was following his lead. He saw that the salt lake emptying into Suvla Bay was dry; he looked down on Turkish soldiers on Lala Baba and the empty trenches scraped into the crest on Chocolate Hill. Herb's flight path also took him over the Sari Bair Range to confirm that only a few enemy soldiers held the crest. It was perhaps the first time a general had flown over the battlefield before committing his forces. While Hamilton forgot to enter his flight into his personal diary, Bernard recorded this historic event:

> Collet takes Hamilton as far as Gallipoli to look for troops, transports etc. It appears possible that the three new divisions might land on some of the beaches up there.

The squadron record simply states:

> Bomb attack and reconnaissance Gallipoli from 10.15 a.m. to 12.35 p.m. in Maurice Farman carrying a payload of two 20 lbs bombs.

In an attempt to maintain secrecy, air service units were briefed later on 29 July by the navy on their roles in the coming assault. Of course rumours had spread of the approaching offensive. Hamilton's appearance at the aerodrome two days earlier had added to the mill.

> Richard Davies is called to see Vice Admiral [and] comes back in evening with great news. We are to go over to Imbros for five days during which time there is

to be a great attack and new landings where we hope to walk through the peninsula and attack at Gaba Tepe and cut off the Turks. He brings us news that Colonel Sykes, who was here on 29 June, is to come and take command of all flying units. What will happen to our squadron is hard to imagine.

This gave the squadron little time to organise the move to Kephalo and to prepare for the new assault. The passage of information was also hindered by the absence of the squadron's two senior officers. Had he been present, Charles Samson would almost certainly have called on Hamilton or arranged a meeting, as had occurred in April.

Harry's seaplanes were tasked with gathering intelligence on the latest changes at Suvla. Low-level flights by seaplanes were the norm, so a low-level coastal flight could be attempted by a seaplane without raising suspicion:

29 July No. 307. Short 161

Pilot: Captain Joe Kilner; Observer: Lieutenant Harry Strain

Ordered to photograph the entrance to the Salt Lake, and if required, Spot Monitor 32 on to Maidos. Took the photographs with two different cameras, and subsequently spotted M. 32 on to Maidos, which was set afire. Time: 1 hour 40 minutes.

30 July No. 308. Short No. 161

Pilot: Captain Joe Kilner; Observer: Lieutenant Harry Strain

Again sent to entrance of Salt Lake, the former photos not sufficiently distinct and if necessary spot for M 32. Obtained two good photos with a different camera. Reported shipping in Narrows and trenches and emplacements on and to north of Suvla Point. Time: 1 hour 17 minutes.

The day after receiving rather vague orders from the navy, Bernard was on Tenedos juggling a removal to Imbros while preparing for a significant phase of operations:

30 July. We begin packing up petrol, oil, spares, and stores. Whittaker goes to Imbros in advance. Lieutenant Whittaker has talked Richard Davies over and tried to get my job during the next two important weeks. In any case he is to go over to Imbros in advance and act as 'go between' with us and the army. As if a go between were necessary! Richard Davies is weak. A pity the Commander is away just now.

The squadron was still out of the information loop because of the emphasis on maintaining secrecy. Hamilton had given Stopford his orders on 22 July; Bernard, however, remained unaware of the detail of the coming offensive, relying on naval orders and the rumour mill. Clearly, he had not read the orders for Stopford's landing:

31 July. Hear that the landing is to be made above ANZAC, probably at Suvla Bay on the flats near Salt Lake. Orders and maps coming along. A busy day.

In the nick of time Charles' aviators were supplemented on 1 August with crated aeroplanes on transports. Large wooden boxes contained the more powerful type of Henri Farman (100hp engines) demanded by Frederick Sykes before his departure for London. Harold Kerby reported sick from a 'bilious attack' and watched the frenzied activity from under his tent flap:

> This morning our ships with new machines arrived off the island and we have been busy as bees getting the cases ashore in spite of a heavy sea running. The men will be at work night and day as we must have at least a couple of new machines assembled before the big attack this week.

No. 3 Squadron was not well situated and personal diaries tell of mass confusion. The ground crew was busy erecting machines and testing engines while others packed stores. Harold wrote:

> 2 August. It is fairly raining aeroplanes for us now although we won't be able to have more than a couple assembled by Wednesday when the big attack is going to take place, still, every little bit helps. Barr isn't back yet [from hospital] so we have only six pilots. I can see an awful lot of flying ahead for me in the next couple of weeks.

In the 'down time' the mechanics packed spares for the overseas transit to Imbros. Disruption and chaos reigned supreme. Bernard picks up the narrative and the level of chaos becomes clear:

> 3 August. We do not pull away from Tenedos in our trawler until 3 pm. Very interesting trip past all ships

firing onto the peninsula. Get to Kephalo point on Imbros at 7.30. Landed my 33 men. Williams and David Jenkins [observers] with me. Lieutenant Whittaker has made no arrangements whatever, and it was only by me signalling to *Ark Royal* that we were able to get boats to leave the trawler. We had to dump all our stores on the wharf, and march up to the new aerodrome. There is no way of getting the stores up or feeding the men. No water. So we work most of the night. Keith Jopp and I get hold of a trolley and push some food up from the quay. Men all sulky. I then have a row with Whittaker. We sleep on the ground. Whittaker sleeps on *Ark Royal*.

Squadrons often move from one aerodrome to another, but such a move before an attack on the scale of the Suvla landing was a nightmare. Just before the commencement of hostilities in Iraq we moved to a forward base in the desert. Like Bernard, I had to move my large maps (stuck to a wooden easel) and my computers, hard drives and files. An advance party had already pitched tents and pre-positioned supplies for the rest of the detachment. Our key concern was disruption to the work routine of our valuable maintainers and the potential fatigue of our aircrew. It is fatigue (and the following litany of small errors) that is the biggest killer in aviation, not bullets or missiles.

The next day four aeroplanes made the overseas flight to the new aerodrome while Bernard erected his bell tent and updated his mapping. Harold flew the first aeroplane across:

Was up with the larks this morning and left for Kephalo in Voisin No. 10 about 6 am and arrived there about an hour later. Of all the places to expect an aeroplane to land this is the worst I have ever dreamt of. It is on a long high peninsula with high cliffs on either side. So if you overdo your landing, splash into the sea you go. And the ground itself is simply a succession of sand dunes and ridges. We have a bunch of Turkish prisoners working on it which should make it a little smoother.

As General Headquarters is just adjoining us we have to sneak in just scraping their tents if we are going to land. I see where Ian Hamilton slumbers in the early morning. It is likely he is going to be disturbed.

We were roughing it at Tenedos. But here we are worse than roughing it, we are merely existing. But I don't mind if we smash the Turks.

During the day six further missions were flown from Tenedos including reconnaissance, spotting and photographic missions. The squadron was now split between the two island aerodromes.

Bernard made contact with the army staff and delivered a brief on enemy defences around Suvla. It is unclear why Hamilton did not attend the briefing instead of inspecting another regiment of troops. Perhaps he was more concerned with the appearance, form and dignity of command than the necessity for information-gathering. After all, Bernard's tent was a five-minute walk from his own. This behaviour, this reluctance to interfere with a subordinate's role, would cost him the campaign. Bernard recorded his busy day including the fact that a submarine captain was quite at ease learning as much he could before his mission:

Busy all day with reconnaissances for the landing. Army General Headquarters say there will be no trenches on their walk through to the Dardanelles. Tomorrow the landing is to begin. Captain Clarke Hall is going to captain one of the motor dhows [specialist landing craft, also called 'beetles']. These have never been used before in warfare. The monitors are firing along the coast and an attack is in progress on Krithia front. Commander Nasmith VC comes to tea again. Richard Davies takes him over the Narrows to Nagara Point. He is going through again tonight in his E Class submarine.

The arrival of new aeroplanes disassembled in boxes was a boon, but out of kilter with the new assault. The crates split the ground crew teams, some of whom were taken to Kephalo while others remained behind to work on the new batch of Henri Farmans. Harold flew six shuttle missions between the two aerodromes further stymieing economy of effort. He was told on 2 August of a temporary two-week move across to Imbros to support the next phase of military operations. The French escadrille was ordered to take over spotting work at Cape Helles while Harold and his squadron were to conduct support work for the new landings.

No. 3 Squadron was still perilously underequipped. In order to remain operational they were forced to borrow an airframe from the French escadrille. The total of ready airframes for the air service fluctuated between 11 and 15 through the first three weeks of August. No. 3 Squadron had two or three, the seaplanes eight to ten, while the two kite balloon sections remained effective throughout the entire period. The submarine scout airships arrived on Imbros on 9 August and air service personnel began the long process of constructing the hangars and silicol hydrogen plant. The airship was not inflated until September and played no part in the offensive. Likewise, No. 2 Wing's machines, following Sykes' recommendations, arrived crated in Kephalo Bay on 14 August but, like the airships, played no direct role in the August offensive.

The plans drawn up by British VIII Corps Headquarters on Cape Helles showed they had learnt the benefit of coordinating air support. Sir Aylmer broke down and was repatriated to England in late July. Fortunately, Hugh Simpson Baikie, the chief gunner, remained behind and wrote the artillery fire plan. Over the first week of August, *Hector* targeted a series of gun batteries, designated D and E batteries, in front of Achi Baba that were poised to cut down the advance of British troops during the feint attacks. The kite balloons were aloft during the entire period of operations, spotting warships and gun batteries on Turkish artillery positions. In the preparation period on 2 August, Captain David Preston and *Hector* were in action again:

> August 2: Batteries were clearly visible from balloon and *Theseus* was quickly on target, firing was most accurate and very effective. Ten salvos falling on and between batteries, believed to have put all their guns out of action [six field guns in all].

For the infantry, both at Anzac and at Cape Helles, the balloons were a welcome sight. For Turkish gunners, the balloons had become a curse. David Preston was proud of his bizarre hybrid balloon-ship:

> I have been informed on two different occasions by army lieutenants that when soldiers in the trenches see the *Hector* coming along they send up a rousing cheer. And when the balloon commences her ascent they send up three cheers, so *Hector* must be proving herself very useful.

Hector and *Manica* were stationed off the coast to smash enemy artillery leading up to the big push in the south. David recorded the engagement on 3 August:

> Spotting for *Theseus* on battery at base of Achi Baba. Nine projectiles fell in very close proximity to battery, but it is doubtful whether battery was put out of action. *Theseus* was quickly on second target and her firing was very effective owing to the rapid succession of salvos. Projectiles were seen to fall in and around the battery which was completely put out of action. Hostile aeroplane sighted coming in our direction, our forward guns fire on him. We see him stagger apparently hit, but machine under control, he turned back hotly pursued by our shells.

On 4 August Gordon Thomson flew a reconnaissance inland and located trenches and gun emplacements:

> [Conducted] a reconnaissance over the area, in the vicinity of the proposed landings, discovered all the existing trenches and gun emplacements between the two Anafarta villages and the sea. A sketch was submitted to GHQ.

The next day Julian Newton-Claire took photographs of the unmanned scrapes on Chocolate Hill. On the same day, a reconnaissance mission over the Suvla zone showed that all the prepared emplacements were unoccupied and no troops were visible. This information told army intelligence that, despite the build-up in Allied numbers, the critical element of surprise could yet be achieved. In early August, Army Headquarters had received accurate information on

Turkish positions. The problem remained that army officers were content to wait for the typed air intelligence reports rather than walk along the beach, duck under a tent flap and speak directly to Bernard or his observers. Perhaps this was a product of inter-service rivalry. The army probably considered it poor 'form' to go behind John de Robeck's back and speak to the RNAS directly. Too often the character of the commander is emulated by subordinates.

De Robeck's naval squadron was divided into three divisions to support the various stages of the offensive. *Hector* accompanied 33 warships from the First Division to assist the feint on Krithia. The Second Division supported ANZAC in its feints on the ANZAC right on the 400 Plateau (at Lone Pine) and its *coup de main* on Sari Bair with support from No. 3 Squadron. The Third Division was to support the Suvla landing with *Manica* spotting for warships off Suvla Bay and the added support of No. 3 Squadron. *Ark Royal*'s seaplanes were on anti-submarine patrolling, providing security for the movement of the Third Division from the various Aegean islands to Suvla Bay. George Dacre on *Ben-my-Chree* was part of a small flotilla with orders to smash Turkish troop movements southwards from Bulair.

Stopford's five infantry divisions arrived on transports and it proved impossible to quickly familiarise the new arrivals with the importance of aircraft. Practice in artillery correction was out of the question. The guns were in holds. Radios were packed away. Lord Kitchener's army still equated aircraft with showground novelty. They had no idea of the importance of 'eyes in the sky'. This condemned Stopford to repeat Sir Aylmer's mistakes during his landing in April. As Bernard noted, Richard Davies had sent Flight Lieutenant Whittaker to act as a go-between with the army prior to the move. He proved unable to make any headway with the army and was sacked from his new position. Perhaps this proved Frederick Sykes correct—the air service was in need of an Air Headquarters which was ultimately established far too late. Sykes was in London. Charles Samson was in Cairo.

On 6 August the air service conducted a total of 15 missions in support of the various feints. Spotting was the main effort with six missions, followed by four reconnaissance missions, and three flown in transit between Tenedos and Imbros.

Dawn reconnaissance patrols flew over the main roads with three missions reporting on the movement of Turkish troops along the Maidos Road. The most effective tactic was the pairing of the two kite balloons with warships to suppress enemy artillery during the infantry assaults, with *Hector* correcting shelling onto gun batteries on the ridge of Achi Baba. The kite balloons with their long loiter times had a measureable impact on Turkish artillery.

Four divisions of infantry from the British VIII Corps conducted a significant feint at Cape Helles against 1200 yards of fortified trenches in the centre. On the British right the French Corps attempted similar assaults. Instead of a feint, enthusiasm had unwisely exaggerated the assault into an attempt to break through to Krithia. This frontal infantry attack was fought around 'the vineyard', a small terrain feature marked on the working 1:10,000 scale trench mapping.

Harry Strain and George Dacre's seaplanes from *Ark Royal* and *Ben-my-Chree* supported the overblown assault towards Krithia before contributing to the latter stages of the offensive at Suvla and Anzac. They played a role in correcting naval gunfire, bursting large calibre naval shells over enemy guns and scattering enemy troops. Observers were tasked to destroy or interrupt the fire of individual Turkish gun batteries resulting in deadly accuracy. This led to the invention of an established correction system for the seaplane flight. The observers first took photographs, both vertically and at an angle to the battery. A scale of distance on the ground was then overlaid onto the photograph with the observer able to read off the error in range and deflection while circling in the seaplane above the target. This system, while requiring a few days of careful preparation, produced exceptional results. Post-mission reports tell of enemy guns hurled into the air and explosive shells shattering enemy trenches:

No. 320 Short No. 162

Pilot: Lieutenant Edward Dunning; Observer: Lieutenant Harry Strain

Ordered to spot the Edgar [monitor] onto S Group and silence them during the infantry attack. D2 permanently silenced. D3 silenced for a time, but subsequently reopened fire when Edgar's fire was directed elsewhere. Fire was then directed to A Battery which was silenced, and afterwards onto a heavy gun in the scrub which continued to fire in spite of good shooting. The Edgar was given a hot time by field guns near the shore. Height 4,500 feet. Time: 1 hour 50 minutes.

While little had been learnt from previous infantry assaults, the gunners were maximising the effectiveness of aerial spotting. Hugh Simpson Baikie's guns were effectively coordinated by David Preston and No. 2 Kite Balloon on *Hector*:

6 August. Left in company with thirty three warships— looks like being a big day today. Achi Baba bombarded

from land and sea. I cannot describe the unearthly din; it needs anyone who has not seen warfare to read *Dante's Inferno* to give them an idea of what it has been like today. The ships we spotted for did excellent work. Seven batteries at the crest of Achi Baba silenced. Our troops were clearly seen advancing under cover of big guns. Shrapnel and high explosive shells bursting all over the place. After a while nothing could be seen except the flashes of the guns owing to the thick smoke and sand in the air. Battle abated somewhat about 5.30 pm after five hours' severe fighting.

Although the stated aim was a feint to draw Turkish troops southwards, repeated attempts to take a series of saps and trenches became an aggressive attempt to advance into the enemy's supporting trenches. Some ground was later gained only to be lost in Turkish counterattacks on the night of 12 August. This diversionary feint, which turned into an assault, cost 3500 casualties. No Turkish reserves moved southwards to Cape Helles.

In the late afternoon of 6 August the ANZAC diversionary attack against Lone Pine was launched. This was also designed to attract Turkish troops to the ANZAC right flank in the hope of stripping them from the left. The assault was a frontal attack by the 1st Australian Brigade reinforced by the 7th and 12th battalions over 220 yards of the heavily trenched southern lobe of the 400 Plateau. The fighting was desperate, with seven Victoria Crosses awarded in this action. The 1st Australian Division suffered 2200 casualties. The first three enemy trenches were captured and held despite repeated Turkish counterattacks. Private Richard Bulkeley was one of the first to leave the trenches. He wrote a letter to his family the next morning from his bed in a hospital ship:

Dear All,

We all knew that the authorities did not want a winter campaign in Gallipoli, & as Achi Baba was proving such a tough nut to crack, the original idea of moving up the peninsula could not come off for some time, we would have to shift. As early as the 1st August we knew that we would be advancing in a week or so & that our brigade, the 1st, would go first.

On the morning of the 5th we came out of the firing line & the 5th Battalion relieved us, we were told definitely that we would attack next day & let know as many details as was advisable then we were allowed to rest all day & go down to the beach & have a swim. The rest of the day we spent writing letters, seeing that our wills were o.k., putting our equipment in order etc. As I was looking after the tucker for my platoon, No. 9, the morning of the 6th was pretty busy, as every man (40) had to have what is called a bag of iron rations; a small calico bag, containing biscuits for 24 hours, a 1lb tin of bully beef & a small tin containing tea, sugar & two cubes of Oxo.

During the morning we had our bayonets sharpened & piled our packs with all our belongings in a heap. I hadn't seen the boys in such good spirits for I don't know how long, especially the old hands, who had gone through the mill. One of them had a mouth organ & this was the accompaniment to all the old songs we have known since childhood and all the raggiest ragtime. We left our scabbards behind & about two o'clock moved round to the second Battalion's lines & went out through the tunnel & into the sap, marked on the map, 'we charged from here'. This sap was really a tunnel running parallel to the firing line, with every few yards a couple of yards of the roof cut right through & what we call a posy where 4 to 6 men could get in. No dirt was thrown out on top it had all been taken out through the tunnel & dumped behind the firing line. It must have been half past three by the time we got settled here & we weren't going to charge till 5.30. From 4.30 to 5.30 our artillery were going to bombard all the Turkish trenches they knew. Our platoon was the first line & I was to be first man out of our posy, so I put in the time making steps so we could get out easily, putting the finishing touches on my rifle & equipment & writing my diary up to that moment in case it should be necessary that it should be sent back to you. At 4.30 the bombardment started & no mistake they did tear it in. Mostly big howitzers & they shook the ground like young earthquakes, & I was hoping all the time that the gunners wouldn't drop one short. Then along came the order; all bayonets fixed & stand by; when the bombardment stopped three blasts of a whistle was to be the signal to charge. I don't mind telling you frankly that those few minutes there crouched ready with your rifle in your hand, wondering if each shell as it exploded would be the last, were about the longest minutes I have seen go by.

At last there was a pause in the bombardment, I heard a whistle blow, & we were out & going for our lives. I saw men go down on either side of me, bullets whistled past my ears & chopped up the ground all around me, but in no time I was with a mob of others at the first line of trenches & blazing away at the Turks in them & they at us. When they were all dead or had cleared out we jumped over the first line or ran over the overhead cover, if there was any, & on to the second line & the same thing went on there. All this time the Turks in the trenches on our left across Owens Gully were putting a hail of bullets on us from machine guns & rifles & about this time the Turkish artillery a mile away on our left began to pour shrapnel on us like hail. I was blazing away over a heap of dirt at the enemy running away down the trenches when I felt as if something had hit my left hand, I looked at it & it was cut right across the palm & bleeding & when I got hold of my rifle to try & fire again it felt numb & useless, but not painful. So I sat down & got out my field dressing & started to tie it up, a chap alongside me finished tying it up & just as he did he got a bullet through his foot, I then started to take his boot off & while I was at this he fell back & I saw a bullet had hit him on the side of the head so I turned my attention to that & tied a pad over it.

By this time one of our machine guns had set up alongside us & was chattering away. As the shrapnel was coming very thick I slid down into the trench & pulled my wounded mate after me, just as I did a shell burst where we had been laying, knocking the machine gun out & killing three of the men working on it. I dragged my mate under some overhead cover & tried to make him a bit comfortable, but there were dozens of other wounded & dying & other men treading about. He asked to open his haversack & get out a card from his mother. I did so & got him what looked like a Christmas card, which he put in his shirt & seemed pretty content.

All this time our boys had occupied a line of trenches; connected up with the other battalions on our right & left & were hard at it making the bank at the back of the trench into a front so as to beat off the counter attack which invariably follows an attack such as we had made. As each man carried two sand bags with him, things began to look a bit ship shape, & all the time our supports kept dribbling in, that is those who got through the hail of shells they put on us. I could not use my rifle but could do my bit by collecting ammunition from dead & wounded men's pouches & taking it down the firing line where it was then wanted, & by tying up the wounded. Every man carries a field dressing. I bound up lots of wounds that evening that would ordinarily make you sick to look at, with all the indifference of a hardened doctor, less the skill. By jove the wounded are great, their grit & optimism is beyond belief. They were lying everywhere & when it got dark the reinforcements coming in would not see them & often tread on them & it was cruel, & one felt so helpless & could do so little.

In the early part of the evening they [the Turks] gave us a lot of trouble with hand grenades & bombs, but as our reinforcements came along with supplies of bombs we gradually got the upper hand. About half past ten we were well established & had plenty of men & ammunition & as all wounded who could walk were ordered to go back to our lines I went across. I saw a lot of dead & wounded lying between the trenches & though there wasn't very much risk I couldn't stop, & I knew the stretcher bearers would soon be there. I went to the first dressing station I could find & they were crowded & sent me down to the beach. I went to the dressing station there & had my wound fixed up. No one could be more gentle than the Red Cross chaps. I found here six chaps out of C Company & we all went out with a barge load of wounded on to the hospital ship Cisilia.

The advance we made in the afternoon was the beginning of a general movement along our line & we had not been on board long when we could hear a tremendous volume of rifle & machine gun fire on the left & knew we were advancing. Though we were comfortable & away from it all I would have given all I possessed to be all right & back with the boys on the ridge. Heavy rifle fire is a very stirring sound & makes you feel that you want to be in the thick of it. I hadn't had any sleep the night before & was dog tired & they gave us each a comfortable mattress & soft pillows & I had a great sleep that afternoon. Just about sun down we left for Mudros, the chief port of Lemnos which is our main base. When I woke up next morning we were laying in the harbour.

Harold Kerby was now in a windblown tent on Kephalo. He had forgotten his mosquito net and was busy swatting flies when he wrote his entry for the day:

ANZAC and Helles have been making a most terrific bombardment ever since morning, the din being really terrible. The big landing and attack is taking place at night and the following morning. It is terrible to think of the thousands of fellows who will be killed in the landing. But such is always the fate of the attacking side.

The next two days are the crisis and will decide the war for us. We all hope and pray for success and No. 3 Squadron will certainly do their utmost. We are the eyes of the army and ours is an important role indeed.

We are flying from dawn to dark tomorrow and I expect we will see some interesting things. I am up at 7.40 am and 4 pm for long reconnaissance trips.

Just metres away, Sir Ian Hamilton was standing on K Beach along Kephalo Bay. Once again he watched as the second amphibious attack of the Gallipoli campaign steamed silently to its place out to sea:

Saw the whole flotilla glide away and disappear ghost-like to the Northwards. The empty harbour frightens me. Nothing in legend stranger or more terrible than the silent departure of this silent Army, K.'s new Corps, every mother's son of them, face to face with their fate.

Capital news from the aeroplanes. Samson has sent in photographs taken yesterday, showing the Suvla Bay area. Not more than 100 to 150 yards of trenches in all; half a dozen gun emplacements and, the attached report adds, no Turks anywhere on the move.

At Anzac, the most formidable entrenchment of the Turks, 'Lone Pine,' was stormed yesterday evening by the Australian 1st Brigade; a desperate fine feat. At midnight Birdie cabled, 'All going on well on right where men confident of repelling counter-attack now evidently being prepared: on left have taken Old No. 3 Post and first ridge of Walden Point, capturing machine gun: progress satisfactory, though appallingly difficult: casualties uncertain but on right about 100 killed; 400 wounded.

At Helles a temporary success was scored, but, during the early part of the night, counter-attacks have brought us back to 'as you were.' Fighting is going on and we ought to be pinning the enemy to the South which is the main thing.

A little known sideshow to the August offensive was the landing of the corps of Cretan irregulars from *Minerva* and *Jed* in the Gulf of Xeros on the night of 6 August. The plan was to stage a northern diversion by landing the troops in darkness in order to destroy the bridge and wreak havoc. The intent was to give the impression that a serious landing had been made, which would prompt the Turkish Army to divert reinforcements away from Suvla. The landing was a near fiasco with the irregulars at first refusing to disembark from the boats because of rifle fire. The report recommended that no such undertaking using irregulars ever be attempted again. A seaplane from *Ark Royal* was placed aboard *Minerva* to support the landing but the Cretans fled back to the boats and the safety of the warships before dawn.

The night amphibious assault on Suvla was virtually unopposed. Some 25,000 British troops faced the enemy's Anafarta Detachment of 1500. On the morning of 7 August, the 11th Division took the small Turkish outposts on Lala Baba and Nibrunesi Point but not Hill 10. More troops landed on A Beach and attempted to secure the high ground of Kiritich Tepe in the north, but confusion meant this dominant feature was not taken that morning, and the opportunity was lost. The empty high ground was seen by observers from No. 3 Squadron.

On 7 August, the day of the main thrust, 15 air missions were conducted with seven reconnaissance missions at Anzac and Suvla, six spotting and two anti-submarine or maritime patrols:

> 6 a.m. A hostile aeroplane which was approaching Suvla was engaged by one of our aeroplanes and chased back to its aerodrome.

At 7.30 a 4 gun battery was located, 300 yards NE of Scimitar Hill: this battery was firing at the beaches. The ships were called up by wireless [radio] and spotting corrections sent.

At 9 a.m. A field battery, probably the same one, was discovered on the road close to Anafarta village. On the roads through Anafarta Sagir and Bayuk Anafarta the enemy were seen retiring through these villages. Evidently from this reconnaissance the Turks were retreating.

At 5.30 pm 2000 infantry were seen on the southern slopes of Green Hill. The aeroplane descended to low altitude and dropped a message bag on the beach; this bag was seen to be picked up.

Critically, in the afternoon, poor weather closed in, severely reducing visibility. The air service was unable to keep an aircraft over the front lines throughout the late afternoon to reduce the effects of enemy artillery. Despite this reduced effort, aircrew returned from missions with important news that:

There was little or no resistance at first if we had pushed through the day we landed. All aeroplane reconnaissances reported this and Hill 971 was undefended. The problem was this information was lost once again in the heat of the battle.

Harold Kerby recorded his flight in his Voisin over Cape Helles. Later he trotted over to Bernard's tent to ask for news of events at Suvla. Now that the aerodrome was sited next to the staff tent he was also able, in general conversation, to find out what army staff officers thought of the progress ashore. Harold observed a difference of opinion. He learnt more about the developing crisis at Suvla from examining Bernard's map than Hamilton did from relying on Stopford's infrequent and vague situation reports. Stopford had yet to advance from the coastal fringe. Harold wrote:

> Well the landing is done and we have one whole division ashore with surprisingly few casualties. ANZAC has extended their left line immensely and the newly landed troops are still advancing and even the latest reconnaissance to-night shows no digging which is a very good sign for us.
>
> I was up at 7.40 this morning for 2½ hours but my orders were to go down to the southern end of the peninsula and help in the attack there. They are making an enormous effort to keep the Turks there so they cannot draw back to oppose the new landing.
>
> Several ships were helping bombard and really from above you wonder how a single Turk came out alive from it. Shells bursting absolutely everywhere and the whole ground perforated like Swiss cheese. A trip as long as this morning in such a terrific bombardment is very tiring indeed. The commander 'washed out' my second trip because of low clouds, much to my relief.

Why Hamilton did not walk along the beach and duck under Bernard's tent flap is one of the unknowns of the campaign. The staff really had no idea of the stalled situation at Suvla. They were unaware that Stopford had yet to advance to the commanding ridge east of Biyuk Anafarta.

This lack of awareness in General Headquarters had serious consequences for the success of the campaign.

Despite the central placement of Bernard's tent there was little information-sharing. Both Harold's and Bernard's diary entries reveal that the aerial intelligence brought back from these flights was ignored. Bernard wrote:

> General Headquarters really know very little on our exact position [after] the new landing but from what we can piece together we are doing very well, but still have not succeeded in getting the commanding ridge east of Biyuk Anafarta.

Hamilton's actions appear somewhat bizarre. He was desperate for information as Stopford was not keeping him informed. Bernard's tent was five minutes' walk away. Aeroplanes were constantly roaring overhead. Hamilton recorded in his diary his growing concerns over Stopford's silence:

> From Suvla we have no direct news since the 'All landings successful' cable. I have caused this cable to be sent to Stopford:—
>
> 4.20 p.m. G.H.Q. to 9th Corps. Have only received one telegram from you. Chief glad to hear enemy opposition weakening and knows you will take advantage of this to push on rapidly.

By the end of the first day confusion and intermingled units stymied any attempt at concerted advance to the dominant hills regarded by Stopford as key to his lodgement. Clarkee, who was now in command of one of the armoured landing craft, was equally perplexed by events:

A number of motor lighters with protective ramps which can be let down to form a gangway, and each capable of carrying 500 troops protected from shrapnel fire, will beach themselves in the actual landing. A large army, 'Kitchener's' had been collected at Mudros and Kephalo, and on several successive nights had practised landings from the lighters.

So far as the actual landing at Suvla went, it was very well managed, and only cost 14 killed and forty wounded, but afterwards the muddle began. And we lost heavily. Secrecy had been carried to such a degree that the regimental officers did not know the plan of the campaign, and were left to themselves, and did not know what to do. There was practically no opposition, only two battalion of Gendarmes being in front of them. Nevertheless, after having advanced only a short distance, they were ordered to dig themselves in, and there they remained within half a mile of the beach, which is shelled in just the same way as ANZAC Cove, while the Turks have hurried up reinforcements and we are losing 2000 men a day.

The Sari Bair assault began in the evening following the heavy feint at Lone Pine. Two columns under the direction of Sir Alexander Godley commenced an advance into the twisted terrain north of Anzac assisted by General Herbert Vaughan Cox's 29th Indian Brigade. The wildness of the terrain spoilt the timetable, exhausted the men and destroyed the element of surprise. The right column established positions on Rhododendron Spur (a feature below the heights of Chunuk Bair), Hill Q and Koja Chemen Tepe.

The charge of the Light Horse Brigade on the morning of 7 August across Russell's Top onto The Nek was timed to assist the assault on Sari Bair. It was a wasted effort as

Godley's men were lost in the scrub below their objectives. At the cessation of a preliminary naval and artillery bombardment, several waves of dismounted troopers climbed out of their trenches in an attempt to dash across a spur approximately 180 yards across. The pre-dawn bombardment meant that the air service was not able to correct naval shelling onto targets.

The attack was scheduled to commence at 4.30 am on 7 August. The 8th and 10th Light Horse regiments were to advance on a front 80 metres wide in a total of four waves of 150 men each, two waves per regiment. Each wave was to advance at two-minute intervals. The plan required a simultaneous attack from the rear of Baby 700, creating a hammer and anvil effect on the Turkish trenches caught in the middle. Because Godley's advance was held up and failed to reach Chunuk Bair until the next morning, the enemy had no distraction when firing to their front.

The artillery bombardment appeared to end prematurely—the result of a simple failure in watch synchronisation. At 4.37 am the first wave of 150 men from the 8th Light Horse Regiment went over the top. They were met by withering machine-gun and rifle fire and, within 30 seconds, all of the men had been gunned down. The second wave of 150 followed the first two minutes later and met the same fate. The Commander of the 10th Light Horse Regiment attempted to have the third wave cancelled. It proceeded and, by 4.45 am, the ridge was covered with fresh dead and wounded Australian soldiers. Turkish guns then belched exploding shrapnel over the living and the dead.

Keith Jopp flew in support of this early morning attack taking off at first light at 5.15 am and arriving over the ANZAC lines ten minutes later—too late to assist. Some 4000 feet overhead, Keith spotted warships onto enemy guns that were bursting shrapnel over The Nek. He returned to Imbros at 6.30 am. He left no record of what he felt looking down on that tiny battlefield. He flew a second reconnaissance mission in the afternoon to capture the progress of Godley's lost columns.

On 8 August Godley again ordered both columns to advance and assault the dominant high ground with the 29th Indian Brigade to attack newly arrived Turkish reinforcements dug into scrapes on Hill Q and Koja Chemen Tepe. For a brief moment companies of the Wellington Battalion (New Zealand Infantry Brigade) held onto the edge of Chunuk Bair. Air intelligence reported to GHQ:

> At 2 pm 3000 Turkish infantry were seen moving towards ANZAC and appeared to be massing behind Sari Bair.

Repeated assaults on the heights by determined Turkish counterattacks (they also recognised the importance of this dominant terrain) denied any chance of success. Air reconnaissance reported the enemy digging trenches on the dominant ridge with Bernard despairing of any success in taking the heights. The next morning Harold flew over Suvla Bay and watched the unfolding battle:

> I was up over the new landing ground this morning and inland as far north as Bulair. The atmosphere was remarkably clear, we could see Constantinople over 100 miles away. There doesn't appear to be a lot of shelling going on about the new front so that it must all be done with the rifle. The Turks have not yet got any guns into position. Our exact line is impossible to say but we are well across the dry salt lake.

Had a sleep after I returned as the strain of the past week is telling on me. But in the afternoon had to go up again and practically cover the same ground. I dropped two bombs on Turkish reserves behind the village and the other I was rather proud of as it was a dandy shot and blew a warehouse in the town of Bayuk Anafarta to little bits.

Things don't look too good out here today as our advance seems to be held up. But more troops are landing tonight so perhaps things will look better tomorrow.

We will all be nervous wrecks soon if we have to keep this pace up much longer. Six pilots for as big a proposition as this is, is absolutely ridiculous. I suppose the authorities at home will realise we need more men. General Headquarters are demanding more work every day. They will probably send more pilots out when it is too late.

By 8 August Hamilton had become suspicious of Frederick Stopford's silence. Stopford had remained on his yacht, *Jonquil*, so Hamilton sent two senior staff officers to investigate the progress of the landings. Hamilton personally sought information on the progress of the assault by visiting Bernard's tent, a day too late:

8 August, Progress very slow. General Headquarters anxious. Sir Ian Hamilton is here. Saw attack on 971 Hill. Seems (even if we get it) impossible to hold without enormous losses.

Hamilton had received only one telegram from Stopford. His suspicions were aroused. Bernard was able to tell him that the objectives of the first day remained untouched. Stopford had not advanced and the high ground that surrounded the bay remained unoccupied by either side. General Headquarters was caught between Stopford's intermittent radio reports and air reports which challenged these vague assessments. Now that he had found Bernard, Hamilton was on the warpath:

> These extra [Turkish] reinforcements may arrive to-morrow . . . [in] the Anafartas; but, for at least another twenty four hours, they will not be able to get round to the high ridge near the Anafarta villages. So far as can be seen by aeroplane scouting, this ridge is still unoc-cupied; certainly it is unentrenched.

Hamilton was now aware of the stalled nature of Stopford's landing and the temporary weakness of the Turkish defences. He personally visited Stopford on his yacht that evening armed with information which clearly showed that the enemy had not yet dragged their guns forward. Given his late arrival at Suvla that evening, Hamilton pressed for a night advance, demanding action. There was still some hope as the Turks were not yet in a solid defensive position:

> I told them . . . it was imperative, absolutely imperative, we should occupy the heights before the enemy brought back the guns and before they received the reinforce-ments which were marching at that very moment to their aid. This was no guess: it was so. Our aeroplanes had spotted Turks marching upon us from the North. We might be too late now; anyway our margin was of the narrowest.

A general attack was ordered on 9 August with the ridge-lines of Kiritich Tepe and Tekke Tepe as the objectives.

The British were beaten to the high ground by two hours. Meanwhile, on Kephalo aerodrome, and with his access to mapping showing newly dug Turkish positions, Bernard speculated on whether the attack would result in a catastrophe. He was correct:

> 9 August: General Headquarters not satisfied. This new landing is growing into another failure worse than any before. General Headquarters and naval transport people are appallingly inefficient and incompetent.

The general attack failed, following the deployment of Turkish soldiers by forced march through the night. These men had been observed by the squadron at Bulair the day before. Now Hamilton was out of touch as he had made his base on the destroyer *Triad* anchored in Suvla Bay. He was separated from air intelligence reporting as telegraphic cables had not yet been laid and communications were maintained between Imbros and Suvla through an unreliable naval radio net:

> No. 1. *Date*, Aug. 9. *Time*, 4 p.m. *Place*, Suvla Bay.
>
> To:
> Dear Sir Ian,
>
> I . . . have not been able to advance to-day, but the Turks have been counter-attacking all day and he [Divisional Commander] has had to put in one of the Territorial Brigades to prevent being driven back.
>
> I quite realise the importance of holding the high ground East of Suvla Bay, but as the Turks advance

through the gap between the two Anafartas where all the roads are . . . if I were to seize the high ground without securing this gap, I might find myself holding the heights and the Turks pouring down to the harbour behind me. I will bear what you say in mind, and if I get an opportunity with fresh troops of taking the heights whilst holding on tight to my right flank I will do so . . .

I am, Sir,
Yours sincerely,
Fred W. Stopford.

The aviators were alert to the fact that the Suvla landing was fast becoming a catastrophe. By flying over the battle-field they could see events unfolding; the problem was that no-one was taking their advice seriously. Information was not getting to the right people. Diaries now filled with lamentations of failure. Clarkee's eyewitness account and entry in *Ark Royal*'s log are revealing:

They have made a mess of it. At Suvla the landing went off splendidly—there were practically no casualties. They advanced inland but a brigadier made the first mess as he delayed the advance until the morning, there being no opposition, but by later that morning the enemy had massed against them. Kitchener's Army was not good enough, they were driven back, and some broke badly. One hears stories of panic, of 50 men bringing back one wounded, but the thing that troubles them most is thirst—they are not used to the dry heat and when given enough water for 48 hours, instead of conserving it, drank it all. Men say that Australians with that chance would have driven straight across in the first rush. Now they have dug themselves in a mile to ½ from the coast and are heavily shelled. The Indians [Cox's Brigade] joined up with the Australians and have done very well but lost heavily. They hiked up ANZAC's left flank and advanced nearly to the top of 971, but were bombed out of it.

By 10 August Bernard was fed up with the gap between the squadron's knowledge of the battle and an overly optimistic military assessment by staff on K Beach:

10 August. General Headquarters staff has quite mistaken idea of our front. After a careful reconnaissance we put them right and they reluctantly altered it on their maps. This would seem hardly credible.

It looks like delay and mismanagement have resulted in the losing of another opportunity. The Turks are coming up fast digging trenches and bringing guns to the emplacements on all the ridges. There was little resistance at first if we pushed through the day we landed. All aeroplane reconnaissance reported this and Hill 971 was undefended. Anyway, it must be somebody's fault that we did not take the ridges behind Suvla and 971—certainly not the Turks!

The battle for control of the Suvla plain was over, with the Allies once again confined to the coastal fringe. Hamilton returned to K Beach after a short meeting with Birdie at Anzac Cove:

10 August. Imbros. Had to remain at G.H.Q. all day—the worst of all days. My visit to Anzac yesterday had infected me with the hopes of Godley and Birdwood

and made me feel that we would recover what we had missed at Suvla, and more, if, working from the pivot of Chunuk Bair, we got hold of the rest of Sari Bair.

They believed they would bring this off and then the victory would have been definite. Now—Chunuk Bair has gone!

The New Zealand and New Army troops holding the knoll were relieved by two New Army Battalions and, at daylight this morning, the Turks simply ran amok among them with a Division in mass formation. Trenches badly sited, they say, and Turks able to form close by in dead ground. Many reasons no doubt and lack of swift pressure from Suvla.

The Turks have lost their fear of Stopford and concentrated full force against the ANZACs. By Birdie's message, it looks as if the heavy fighting was at an end—an end which leaves us with a fine gain of ground though minus the vital crests. Next time we will get them. We are close up to the summit instead of having five or six hundred feet to climb.

The loss of the high ground at Suvla and on Sari Bair hemmed the two corps into the undulating scrubland of the lower plains. There they were under observation by accurate Turkish artillery. After supporting the feint at Helles for three days, *Hector* was ordered to support *Manica* targeting Turkish batteries that were shelling the open ground and killing Stopford's men. The presence of two kite balloons in Suvla Bay was a tempting target. A U boat attacked *Manica* on 14 August despite warships and transports in the immediate vicinity. The torpedo went under the balloon ship without detonating.

Aviator morale had plummeted. Harold Kerby was relieved of flight duties on 8 and 9 August; he spent the day reading on his camp bed. A feeling of hopelessness was affecting him and the small cadre of pilots with whom he messed. Regardless, Harold was soon back in the air:

> I have had two long trips today. We went over the peninsula to Maidos looking for Turkish reserves, came round by the port of Ak Bashi Liman and saw a number of Turkish transports. Dropped a bomb on advancing Turks with good effect. HMS *Chatham* was shelling Byuk Anafarta which was burning merrily.
>
> In the afternoon was up again doing the same thing. From what we see from our aeroplanes the brilliant generals on the other side have made a pretty mess of our new landing and advance. At present we seem to be pretty well hung up as far as our advance is concerned.
>
> My tent mate Lieutenant Dawson collapsed after his trip this morning. Surgeon says that is simply a case of nerves brought on by too much flying. He must be relieved from flying duties for some days so that means just that much more work for the rest of us pilots.

Charles Samson and Reginald Marix returned to Imbros from their leave on the night of 10 August to find the squadron on the point of collapse. Pessimism was rife. Charles inspected Sykes' placement of the aerodrome and considered it unsuitable, relocating the squadron to another site at K Beach. Once again the squadron moved in the midst of operations. Harold wrote:

> Only once aloft today, Could see very little as there was no firing whatever along our new front. I don't think we are advancing much. I observed several large Turkish transports in Ak Bashi Liman so I presume they are

bringing up troops to throw against our advance along our new front.

We are shifting all our hangars and equipment from Tenedos to our new first class aerodrome at K Beach to use as a permanent base. The food is really awful and I don't eat anything hardly at all. Sometimes it seems as if this war were never going to end.

Herb Collet sent Harold up to observe the movement of enemy troops. The Turks were reinforcing with vast numbers of troops while the British remained stationary. The rapidly tiring Harold provides a unique window into those stressful days:

12 August. Only one trip today. On our reconnaissance saw any number of Turkish transports coming up. I certainly am of the opinion that some of our generals have made a fearful mess. It just makes me sick.

13 August. Rested in morning and went aloft in afternoon. Spotting on enemy D2 battery. If our batteries always shot as well as they did this afternoon I wouldn't be so bored on these spotting trips.

Well Lieutenant Dawson is being sent home. This is a pretty poor place for a fellow suffering from nerves to convalesce in. I wouldn't mind going home with him. We did learn today that . . . Commander Longmore's . . . Squadron [is] on [its] way out here.

Commander Samson went over the Salt Lake landing today by motor boat to have a look at things. He came back very pessimistic. We are absolutely held up now

LOOKING DOWN ON THE AUGUST OFFENSIVE

and this whole new landing is a failure. We had our
chance the first day but our generals failed to grasp it.
The Turks dug in and fortified. The new front and Hill
971 which were taken by noon the first day of the landing is a second Gibraltar.

It is positively sickening the mess up out here. It now
appears that the horrors of a winter campaign [will be
upon us] with the Turks getting stronger all the time.

The Suvla campaign ended in tatters. Reputations were
destroyed. A single telegram from Stopford to Hamilton
illustrates this with awful clarity:

Priority

GHQ 13 August

General Officer Commanding 53 Division just reported
his division is exhausted and incapable of any defence.
This makes situation in my centre most serious in case
of attack. The Turks are showing distinct signs of offensive along a long frontage. Have no troops but 54th to
replace 53rd which are in danger and may bolt at any
moment. It is my duty to inform Commander in Chief
at once.

The kite balloons hovered over the collapsing Kitchener
Army. Their view of the battlefield, at 3000 feet, was the
only high ground. The Turks also recognised this and targeted *Manica* and *Hector* with a series of submarine and air
attacks. David Preston wrote:

14 August. Went out early morning spotting at Suvla Bay. Shortly after balloon ascended periscope of a submarine was observed fifty feet away from us. He immediately disappeared and about one minute afterwards he fired a torpedo at the *Manica* who had just lowered her balloon. Several shots were fired at torpedo but all missed. Torpedo went right under *Manica* doing no injury to her. The opinion is that the U boat intended to torpedo her first and us afterwards as we still had our balloon up. So we could not steam away.

15 August. Went out early again to spot off Suvla Bay, but sun was too strong for spotting so balloon was sent up with two dummies to represent men. The idea of the ruse to stop enemy's guns firing on our troops for fear of being located. We could see fighting going on with our troops ashore with the naked eye. I had been watching the fighting ashore all afternoon. Spotted later that morning on enemy positions. It was terrible seeing groups of men at a time blown to atoms. It seemed to me more like murder than warfare. I saw two Turkish guns with horses and men advancing on the road when a couple of shells burst right on them. When the smoke cleared there was nothing left of the guns, horses or men and that is an example of what was taking place all the afternoon.

Transports were seen unloading reinforcements in Ak Bashi Liman. George Dacre's seaplanes operating from *Ben-my-Chree* also reported numerous large steamers moving southwards throughout the daylight hours. George's boss, Flight Commander Charles Edmonds, sent a memorandum to John de Robeck warning of the possibility of a torpedo attack. The attack profile was limited to a flight duration of less than one hour because of the unreliability of the Sunbeam engine. He requested that *Ben-my-Chree* operate off the neck of Bulair to allow a shorter overland flight. De Robeck approved this plan and *Ben-my-Chree* was ordered to join a small flotilla of warships sent to sink Turkish shipping. On 11 August:

> We pushed off northwards to the Gulf of Xeros at the neck of the peninsula. Here Banks-Price went forth on a fast single seater Schneider seaplane over Bulair to see what ships there were in the Marmara for us to try tomorrow. He returned with a favourable account of a large ship off the coast five miles above the port of Gallipoli. This we intend to torpedo tomorrow if weather permits.

A much vaunted 'world first' occurred with the first aerial torpedo attack on a ship. This was prosecuted by George Dacre's boss Edmonds striking a large steamer the next day:

> At 4 a.m. I climbed to 1500 feet and crossed the Isthmus over the low land one mile to the north of Bulair. I arrived over the Sea of Marmara and shaped course along the coast to the north east. The steamer to be attacked was lying just to the north of Injeh Burnu. There were a number of smaller craft, about twelve in all.
>
> I glided down and fired my torpedo at the steamer from about a height of 15 feet and range of some 300 yards. I climbed and noticed flashes from a Tug, which was firing at me. Looking back I observed the track of the torpedo which struck the ship abreast the main mast,

starboard side. The explosion sent up a column of water and large fragments of the ship about as high as her masthead. The ship was of about 5,000 tons displacement, painted black, with one funnel and four masts. The force of the explosion was such that it is impossible for her to be of much use to the enemy.

One cannot help looking on this operation as being the forerunner of a line of development which will revolutionise warfare.

Charles Edmonds and George Dacre made a second attempt on 17 August. Edmonds torpedoed a transport, burning the cargo and superstructure, while George suffered engine trouble once he was across. He was forced to taxi on the Sea of Marmara, coming across an enemy tug and torpedoing it while still on the water. With his seaplane sufficiently lightened he managed to fly back over the neck of the peninsula to *Ben-my-Chree*.

The report of the torpedo attacks was sent to the Air Department in London. *Ben-my-Chree*'s captain sent a detailed technical report with recommendations that the ship be recalled to England. He wrote that another attack could not be replicated on account of local weather conditions and that it required further development to be truly effective. Nevertheless, the news of the success reinvigorated hopes within the Intelligence Department.

The newly appointed Wing Captain Frederick Sykes returned to Imbros on 18 August and found support for his reorganisation within the navy. Clarkee recorded his arrival at Cape Kephalo:

Colonel Sykes has arrived from England, and took up his abode in *Ark Royal*. He was a cavalry Captain who joined the RFC in its early days, and had been responsible to a considerable extent for its organisation. Lieutenant Harry Strain was commandeered to run the Intelligence and Operations Departments at RNAS Headquarters.

Two days after Sykes' arrival No. 3 Squadron suffered its blackest day. It marked the death of Captain Herb Collet, DSO, Charles Samson's long-time friend and Harold Kerby's flight commander, followed by the mental collapse of Harold. Herb was killed in a crash at the edge of the aerodrome—the first death of an aviator at Gallipoli. More would follow. The circumstances of Herb's death were dramatic. He stalled his machine while attempting to return to the aerodrome with a misfiring engine. The Voisin pancaked just outside Hamilton's tent and exploded in flames. Two mechanics pulled Herb's burning body from the wreckage in front of a horrified crowd. Harold wrote:

> I am heartbroken. Dear old Captain Collet was killed today. I will never forget his many kindnesses. It is hard to have to stand by helpless and see a friend's life ebb away in agony as his did. I am all unnerved tonight and feel just as if I never want to fly again. I was speaking to him not two minutes before it happened. It was hard for me to keep control of myself.
>
> Commander Samson, with Captain Keith Jopp as observer, started away this morning on early reconnaissance and over Suvla the machine was struck by an anti-aircraft shell and Jopp was wounded. They managed to get down safely, landing on the Salt Lake, but the machine was destroyed by Turkish shelling. Keith Jopp is in a hospital ship. The Commander got back just at dinner time on a destroyer. He knew nothing

about Collet's death. He and Collet were like broth-
ers and have fought side by side since the first days of
the war. He never shows his feelings but I know he is
heartbroken.

Surgeon Patterson has just been to see me. He told
me to go off to *Ark Royal* for a few days' rest. I feel so
blue and fed up tonight that really I don't care what
happens to me. I went across—the first thing I had
was a real bath complete with bath tub. I changed my
clothes, then sat down to a real dinner and went to bed
between clean sheets.

Sir Ian Hamilton was drawn out of his tent by the noise of
the pancaked landing. Herb's Voisin had missed Hamilton's
tent by several metres, clearly suggesting the proximity of
Army Headquarters and all its attendant military staff to the
aerodrome:

A shocking aeroplane smash up within a few yards of us.
A brilliant young Officer (Captain Collet of the R.F.C.)
killed outright and three men badly hurt.

Harold joined Sykes for a few days on *Ark Royal*. At the end
of the week Harold was repatriated to England following
a nervous collapse. He recovered, rediscovered his joy of
flying and became an ace over France. There is no record
of Sykes and Harold ever meeting, although it is likely that
they dined together in the wardroom. Perhaps Harold's
story helped Sykes make the changes so desperately needed.

John de Robeck published orders on 26 August supporting Sykes' vision. The newly established Air Headquarters
was tasked with commanding two wings of aeroplanes (two
squadrons each), two kite balloon sections, a submarine

scout airship flight, *Ben-my-Chree* with a seaplane flight, and *Ark Royal* as a parent ship. This establishment, even on paper, was below Sykes' initial recommendations. The wings were given specific tasks which followed the RFC model in France. The Admiralty gave new numbers to the RNAS order of battle: No. 3 Squadron was reorganised as No. 3 Wing while Wing Commander Arthur Longmore's squadron was named as No. 2 Wing, part of which had already arrived in theatre. Flight Lieutenant Scarlett was given command of the airship station, which had set up camp on Imbros on 9 August.

Sykes' demands were only partially met by the Air Department, and their partial fulfilment came too late to support the military in the key event of the campaign. Sykes was challenged by the eclectic mix of airframe and engine types that comprised No. 2 Wing. Only two airships were sent out to form the submarine scout airship flight. Adding to Sykes' difficulties as the new commander was the resentment felt by naval air services officers at his appointment. This enmity was public and widely known. Even the steady Harry Strain recorded 'that there could have been no more ill-conceived appointment'.

Harry was aware of Charles Samson's feelings of resentment at having Sykes, who was his junior, placed in overall command. These feelings were echoed by Arthur Longmore, who commanded the newly arrived 2 Wing. Most aviation officers were sceptical of Sykes' ability to command. De Robeck reprimanded Flight Lieutenant Scarlett for being 'subversive' following his criticism of Sykes in official reporting.

Despite the clash of egos the establishment of an Air Headquarters was an important event in flight operations in the Dardanelles. The evolution from separate air units reporting to the senior naval officer to a headquarters commanding and coordinating missions was profound as it demonstrated a first faltering step in the evolution of air power. Direct command of the various assets was taken from a naval commander and placed in the hands of a military airman who would support both services.

Hamilton relieved Stopford of command and replaced him with Major General Beauvoir de Lisle. Even with a more vigorous commander, little momentum was achieved. The final phase of the offensive began on 21 August with assaults on W Hill and the ANZAC assault on Hill 60. Both faltered in the face of previously unseen but strongly entrenched opposition. The attempt to gain a dominant position failed although the beachhead was significantly extended. A link-up was made between Suvla and Anzac following the capture of the lower seaward side of Hill 60 at the end of August. The ANZAC position extended to Suvla across the Table Top and Rhododendron Hill. North Beach was significantly enlarged and new piers, including Embarkation Pier, were built to ease the congestion at the cove.

Air service support for the final stages of the August offensive collapsed. On the days before the assault on Hill 60 the newly designated wing flew an average of only three missions per day. All of these were reconnaissance in preparation for a series of infantry assaults involving over 20,000 soldiers. No aircraft were patrolling over enemy guns to reduce fire during the assault itself. In the final days of August, Charles Samson's wing simply collapsed through attrition of available aeroplanes, fatigue and declining morale.

The aviators were aware of the magnitude of the August offensive's failure. The sacking of senior officers told a simple story. It was at this low point that the air service was first challenged, then invigorated by the arrival of Frederick Sykes with his ambitious plans.

In the end, Hamilton reported that the intelligence he had received concerning enemy positions at Suvla was accurate. Unfortunately, he did not attribute this to the air service, preferring to bury it once again:

> All that can be said at present is that my Intelligence Department were wonderfully exact in their figures as a rule and that, in the case in question, events, the reports made by prisoners, etc., etc., seem to show that the forecast was correct.
>
> Reliable information indicated the strength of the enemy about Suvla Bay to be one regiment, one squadron and some Gendarmerie with at most twelve guns, and events have shown that this estimate was correct.

CHAPTER 8
Stalemate and survival

Quicunque Vult or 'Unofficial Prayer'

Whosoever will be decorated, before all things it is
necessary that he hold the Mediterranean faith.
Which faith that except everyone do keep whole and
   undefiled,
without doubt he shall be stellenbosched everlastingly,
and the Mediterranean faith is this, that we worship
one GOC in Trinity, a Trinity in Unity.
Both confounding the Generals and damning their
   commands.

For there is one General of Egypt, another of the
Expeditionary Force; and another of the Levant Base.
But the Authority of Egypt, of the Expeditionary Force,
   and
of the Levant Base is all one, the Glory equal,
the majesty co-eternal.
Such as Egypt is, such is the Expeditionary Force; and
   such is

the Levant Base.

Egypt separate, the Expeditionary Force separate, and
the Levant Base separate.

Egypt incomprehensible, the Expeditionary Force
incomprehensible,

and the Levant Base incomprehensible . . .

And they that have done this well shall go into
the Honours List everlastingly and they that
have done evil into everlasting retirement.
This is the Mediterranean Faith; which except a
man believe faithfully he cannot be promoted.
Glory be to Egypt, and the Expeditionary Force,
and to the Levant base:
as it was in the beginning, is now, and ever
shall be;
Chaos without end.

This spoof catechism was written on the back of a manila
folder stuffed with secret air intelligence reports. Harry
Strain was the author but, probably for his own protection,
he did not sign his name. After the failure of the big push,
the military returned to the monotony of trench warfare and
endured worsening weather through the autumn months.

The men waited for the inevitable storms to roll in from
the sea. A weary, heavy stalemate cast its shadow across both
armies. Both were unable (or unwilling) to commit to offensive action. Sir Ian Hamilton lamented the whittling of his
army from disease and lack of replacements:

That the Dardanelles Committee should complacently
send me a message to say we 'quite understand that you
are adopting only a purely defensive attitude at present'

is staggering when put side by side with the carbon of this, the very last cable I have sent them. 'I think you should know immediately that the numbers of sick evacuated in the IXth Corps during the first three days of October were 500 men on the 1st instant; 735 men on the 2nd instant and 607 men on the 3rd instant. Were this rate kept up it would come to 45 per cent of our strength evacuated in one month.'

Three quarters of this sickness is due to inaction—and now the Dardanelles Committee 'quite understand' I am 'adopting only a purely defensive action at present.' I have never adopted a defensive attitude. They have forced us to sit idle and go sick because—at the very last moment—they have permitted the French offensive to take precedence of ours, although, on the face of it, there was no violent urgency in France as there is here.

The exception to this enforced stalemate was the escalating air war. Flying above the weary infantry, Harry, Charles Samson, George Dacre and the newly arrived Arthur Longmore found themselves at the 'point of the spear'. Frederick Sykes' air service grasped the opportunity to demonstrate its offensive capabilities while Sykes expounded his vision. Unlike the army struggling on the coastal fringes, he was full of fighting spirit. He centralised all wings, squadrons and flights under his command and pursued a number of innovations. The level of organisation he achieved, despite his disappointment with London's inability to meet his demands for numbers and aircraft types, confirmed his bold vision. Sykes was in his element. He was an organiser, and that was just what was needed.

Three new air service units arrived in theatre and were introduced into operations during this period: Arthur

Longmore's No. 2 Wing, the Submarine Scout Airship (SSA) Squadron and HMT *Canning* with 7 Kite Balloon Section. Arthur's wing broadly reflected the activity of Charles' wing but at a lower tempo owing to its underperforming aeroplanes. But it had a secret: the wing had an infusion of enthusiastic Australian pilots. After initial flight tests the SSA No. 7 (SS7) conducted a significant number of anti-submarine missions which freed Harry's seaplanes at Aliki Bay and George's seaplanes on *Ben-my-Chree* for devilry. *Canning* arrived with a replacement balloon for *Hector*, as the previous one's fabric was wearing thin from overuse. *Manica* was sent to assist with the British incursion at Salonika, her reassuring presence replaced by *Canning*.

Mission totals for the autumn amounted to: 214 missions in September, 226 for October and 195 for November. The majority of missions comprised reconnaissance, followed by spotting, bombing, photography, and maritime and anti-aircraft patrols. There was a plan: missions were pursued with vigour as Sykes' headquarters focused on intelligence-gathering. Bulgaria's entry into the war on the side of Germany and Turkey forced a concentrated bombing campaign in November with one of Charles' aviators awarded the Victoria Cross.

Sykes' Air Headquarters controlled concentrated effort on specific targets. For the first week of its operation his small cadre of officers was accommodated on *Ark Royal* to take advantage of the ship's communications system. Harry was recruited to head the operations and intelligence section. Sykes had made an excellent choice. Harry, apart from having direct operational and intelligence experience, was also able to ride the political maelstrom of his boss' appointment:

Two more squadrons have arrived, also some dirigibles with airplane fuselages—Sykes in command of all. About 60 machines. We have one new machine No. 163 Short and now lack floats. Sykes asked me to join his staff and take charge of Intelligence and Operations Department. Things were in a pretty mess to begin with. Sykes an army captain and a temporary Lieutenant Colonel has been given a position as Wing Captain and shoved over the heads of Samson and Arthur Longmore. It was natural that he should be met with apathy if not active obstruction and it says a good deal of these two that they fell in line as quickly and as well as they did. I had to take the brunt of it, issuing their orders, collecting information and organising attacks. I then had to disseminate it all to the proper authorities. After a time I got it all organised so a child could do it.

No. 2 Wing's commander, Arthur Longmore, was born in Manly in 1885 to an English couple, Charles and Janet Longmore. The family lived in Sydney for a further five years before returning to England. Young Arthur was commissioned into the Royal Navy in 1904. He passed his Aero Club certificate in 1912 and then pursued a path similar to Charles Samson, although he was several years behind Charles in his training. While Charles was the first to fly an aeroplane off a ship, Arthur beat him as the first to land an aeroplane on the sea with improvised air bags. Junior to Charles in seniority before the war, he quickly caught up due to his ability to adapt to the skills required of a squadron (and later wing) commander. Arthur brought with him another Australian pilot, Charles Gilmore. Tasmanian-born Gilmore headed off to England at 23 years of age to be commissioned in the RNAS and undertake flight training. Gilmore was proud of his Australian heritage, stitching a kangaroo and emu above the flap on his canvas tent.

Later in August, Sykes pitched his tents behind Hamilton's half-built hut on K Beach. Engineers were constructing more permanent buildings to cope with the colder weather. Sykes' first action took the form of an administrative tussle with London and the Air Department to procure the aircraft he deemed necessary to win the air battle. He then turned his immediate operational focus to intelligence-gathering. Harry was the key to this role. The files he initiated were incredibly detailed; there are over 300 individual mission reports and daily intelligence summaries in the archives in London:

> I was in constant touch with the intelligence branch at General Headquarters. And sometimes with the Holy of Holies—there I liked General Braithwaite and I'm sorry he was suspended with Sir Ian Hamilton. I found there Pollen, Ian Hamilton's brother in law and a man who I have considered to be a prize ass. They are a crowd!

Harry now directed the bombing effort as he was double-hatted as Operations Officer. He had the joy of dumping bombs on targets of his choosing. This double role was unusual. It was far more common to have an Operations Officer (usually a pilot) plotting the routes and ensuring aircraft were allocated to task, while the Intelligence Officer provided the aircrew with details of the target. Combining both jobs gave Harry freedom of action. Such a combined role was impossible in Iraq with as many as 10,000 individual mission legs in the airspace. The Operations Officer and I sat side by side and worked together. The 'Ops' role was far more complicated with a heavy emphasis on the deconfliction of missions. The probability of a mid-air collision at night was always uppermost in our minds. Fortunately for Harry, there were only two or three aircraft over Gallipoli at any one time.

Harry's old seaplane flight received a trickle of replacement aircraft. Ultimately, even improved engines and airframe types were no match for deteriorating sea states and heavy weather. *Ark Royal*'s seaplanes based at Aliki Bay continued to support Anzac and Suvla before her flight evolutions were halted. On the other hand, George in *Ben-my-Chree* had freedom of movement owing to the ship's speed and ability to find a lee in which to launch a seaplane.

Aircraft numbers remained steady through the autumn months of 1915. A bitter paper war concerning the disparity between the Air Department's accounting of aircraft numbers and those actually in theatre matched the actual air war in intensity. Bean-counters in London asserted themselves in a series of telegrams arguing over aircraft totals. By 20 November the Director of the Air Department had sent a fifth telegram arguing that Sykes had a total of 89 aeroplanes, 19 seaplanes (with four in transit), 3 SSA, and 3 kite balloons. It seems incredible that the RNAS accountants did not know what they had sent to the Mediterranean.

Arguments with supply officers are common—even today. We were waiting (camping somewhere on pink desert sand) in early 2003 for the Iraq War to start. Typically, we were far removed from any danger and oversupplied with chicken dinners by our allies. Nevertheless, we had to explain to a bean-counter in Australia (sweltering in a heatwave) that the desert was cold at night. It was only when a polite email was sent suggesting that Jesus was born in a manger because it was cold, that we received a response. We then had warm clothing issued. Sykes relied on typed reports sent via Malta on a steamer. It must have been extraordinarily frustrating for him.

According to Sykes' reckoning, combat-ready airframes comprised 10 per cent of his total. The war between accountants in safe billets and the soldier at the front raged on. Sykes appears to have been thoroughly modern—and particularly relentless. Again he demanded a similar scale of effort to the RFC supporting the British Army in France. Sykes sought the help of John de Robeck in his battles, arguing succinctly that the British in France consisted of 13 divisions and were supplied a total of 168 aircraft. The RNAS in the Dardanelles had a fraction of this proportion. Sykes and his aviators were supporting VIII Corps Headquarters (three divisions at Helles), IX Corps (six divisions at Suvla) and ANZAC (three divisions) and offering assistance to the French Corps Expeditionaire d'Orient (two divisions) plus assisting the navy suffering a submarine curse. In his second argumentative report to London he plugged for a minimum of four wings, two seaplane flights and six airships totalling 120 aircraft. Against this projected establishment, he had a quarter of this number. Little wonder he was an angry man.

Sykes also argued for three specific aircraft types. He divided his types into fighting, scouting and reconnaissance machines. Fighting machines had to be two-seater pusher biplanes equipped with two machine-guns, a radio and a payload of 200lb bombs. Reconnaissance machines could only be two seaters with 'tractor' engines with good climbing ability and able to reach speeds of 95mph. The scouts must be single seaters with speeds of 120mph in order to engage and kill Erich Serno's elusive Turkish pilots.

Only five replacement Maurice Farman 110hp pushers met these requirements. They were allocated to Charles' wing. Arthur's aeroplanes did not possess any of these characteristics. The aeroplanes in No. 2 Wing's order of battle were completely unsuitable and comprised mixed airframe types. Maintenance problems escalated. Over the weeks and months replacement aeroplanes were sent but these, more or less, only made up for losses. Nieuport biplanes were eventually sent out to make up for the losses of Voisins and the underpowered Henri Farman pushers.

At any one time the total aircraft in the Eastern Mediterranean was a mere 60 machines with only 12 airframes battle-ready at any point. Sykes was bitterly disappointed at the lack of support (and penny-pinching) by bureaucrats. His two 'wings' were, in reality, the equivalent of two flights with six 'ready' aeroplanes each. Arthur's menagerie of 22 aeroplanes consisted of six Morane Parasol monoplanes with rotary engines (often breaking down because of the dust), six underpowered but effective BE2C two-seater biplanes, six Caudron biplanes (not used for active service because of a poor power-to-weight ratio) and four Bristol single-seater scouts. Along with the machinery came an establishment of 200 personnel. These low numbers of 'ready' airframes account for the decline in total monthly flights, despite the arrival of Arthur's second wing.

The SSA Squadron was established on the flattened finger-like plateau of Cape Kephalo, relatively close to the two aeroplane wings sited on the beach below. A large canvas shed or Bessenau hangar was erected to house the SS7 and a silicol plant was installed for the production of hydrogen. Only SS7 was inflated because of slow hydrogen production and SS8 was kept as a spare. SS7 was not ready to undertake immediate patrolling on arrival because hydrogen production was slow and, obviously, a dangerous process.

As hydrogen trickled into the slowly expanding bag, *U14* entered the Aegean. She torpedoed the troopship *Royal Edward* with the loss of 900 lives on 13 August and on 2 September struck the *Southland* which carried 1460 ANZAC troops from the 6th Brigade, AIF. In response to calls of distress from the sinking vessel, *Ben-my-Chree*—as one of the fastest ships at Imbros—raced to the rescue. Reaching 26 knots she arrived in time to take aboard 815 Aussie troops. *Ben-my-Chree*'s speed and her ready response saved many lives, although 70 men including the Brigade Commander, Colonel Linton, drowned before she arrived. *Ben-my-Chree* was cheered into Mudros Harbour with her rescued diggers crowding her upper decks.

SS7 rose into the air ten days after the torpedoing of the *Southland*. A series of tests was conducted to see how she could be used at Gallipoli. David Preston on *Hector* watched the blimp coast over Imbros and Kephalo Bay:

> Our new air ship is making her trial trip around the harbour. She is cigar shaped with a cage underneath same as an aeroplane. Seems very easy to handle and imagine after the war wealthy people will use them for pleasure, as there is hardly any danger being up in one of them. This one is to be used as a submarine scout.

The Turkish Air Service quickly signalled its interest in this innovation, promptly bombing the large hangar hoping to set it aflame. This became the natural pattern:

Thursday 16 September

Wind N by E 5–10 MPH

7.45 am Three hostile aeroplanes dropped 7 bombs and many darts. Nearest bomb about 350 yards from shed. 3.15 pm Ship left shed. Two trips. Total time in air 50 minutes. 4.20 pm Returned. Sub-Lieutenant Thomas, pilot, took Vice Admiral de Robeck for flight lasting 15 minutes. Commenced digging dug outs for all hands.

SS7 was a thing of beauty. The long, cylindrical balloon was over 40 metres in length and painted a metallic silver. Suspended below the balloon was the body of a wingless aeroplane. Two men sat in the cockpit with the engine 'pulling' in the front. The aviators steered the balloon by operating the flight controls of the de-winged aeroplane which had elevators and a rudder at the tail. It was an extraordinary amalgam of balloon and aeroplane. Flight characteristics allowed long loiter times and cross-ocean patrols, but reduced height and speed. A big minus was that her hydrogen gas was explosive. Smoking was discouraged.

The stately SS7 conducted maritime patrols when weather permitted, with a mission tempo of one flying day in every two or three days. Multiple flights were conducted each flying day to change the crew and broaden their experience. On 18 September SS7 conducted three daylight anti-submarine patrols, taking General Birdwood as a passenger on its last patrol. Harry wrote of Birdie's flight:

18 September. Birdwood came over for a couple of days: I took him and gave him a flight in the 'Blimp'

> our little airship, then a hate began at ANZAC and one
> could see he was anxious, so I took him to 3 Wing and
> got Samson to take him over to ANZAC to see what
> was going on: it quietened down when he got there.

Birdie's flight over Anzac Cove is still relatively unknown.
His view of Sari Bair and the difficult terrain his men had
fought over must have caused him to reflect on recent
events. From 4000 feet what seemed to be an important
objective, even Sari Bair itself, appeared as just one summit
among many. Birdie flew as a passenger in the more powerful pusher Maurice Farman which afforded excellent views
over the front and sides of the gondola: 'Maurice Farman
25. Commander Samson. General Birdwood. 5.20–6.10 pm.
Flight to ANZAC on 18 September.' The perspective from
the air reduces the topography; Birdie would have seen the
Maidos plain and the Kilid Bair Plateau stretching beyond.
It may have occurred to him that, by seizing Sari Bair, he
had only just put his foot in the door. Charles recorded this
important event:

> September 18th was a red letter day, as General
> Birdwood came over to the aerodrome and said he
> would like a trip in the air. I took him up in a Maurice
> Farman, intending to do a local flight; but he told me
> to fly over the Turks at ANZAC. Off we went, and he
> made me go as far as Maidos, and fairly low down, so
> that he could see well. We got a proper reception from
> 'Archie' and I felt very anxious carrying such a distin-
> guished passenger.

The blimp's first operational mission was a night flight
along the peninsula. From this flight it was evident that

SS7 was highly visible from the ground and vulnerable to anti-aircraft fire. She could not be flown over enemy-held terrain:

25 September Saturday

Wind Noon N by E 15–20 MPH

8.00 pm E by S 0–5 MPH

8.30 pm Ship left for night spotting in neighbourhood of Suvla. Spotting was almost impossible owing to difficulty to see targets or burst of shells. W/T broke down. Bright moonlight night with ship working at 3800 feet about a quarter of a mile out to sea. Landed 10.32 pm.

The Turkish 1st Aircraft Company's response to this outrage took the form of an Albatros dropping bombs on the shed over the next two days. The bombs detonated a mere 175 yards from the volatile hybrid. Captain Scarlett of the SSA Squadron wrote candidly to Sykes and John de Robeck of the danger:

In my opinion should further stations be projected, experience points to the fact that no more sheds should be erected at Imbros. The distance from the enemy aerodrome is so small that it requires neither effort nor forethought to fly over and drop bombs on the shed, attempts have been made nearly every day since inflation.

Winter weather effectively grounded SS7 flight operations in late November. Strong winds first tore at the Bessenau hangar. Then rents in the SS7's gas bag caused deflation and put an end to flight operations. Continued attacks by Turkish aeroplanes precipitated a wise relocation of blimp operations further out to Mudros Island.

Kite balloon operations were also facing hot opposition, the balloons forced out to sea by accurate Turkish gunnery. This considerably hampered observation. A combination of shrapnel and Turkish pilots made balloon operations difficult. Sykes attempted to meet this threat head-on by pairing kite balloons with an escort warship with its own spotting seaplane. David Preston of *Hector* recorded the pattern of events:

> 14 September. *Hector* with *Theseus* and *Scorpion* for Achi Baba. Seaplane is spotting for *Scorpion* who is to fire on any batteries who open on us.

The combination of warship and circling seaplane silenced enemy guns, allowing the balloon to approach the shore.

Sykes and his Air Headquarters made immediate improvements to service life. Wood and cement were ordered for the construction of huts before the onset of cold weather. Almost immediately a better standard of messing was achieved. Soon mess chits were printed on a lithographic press. Officers' wardrooms and senior sailors' messes were established with proper victualling standards. Members of the officers' wardroom were charged 2 shillings per day with access to a wine account. A further 10 shillings per month was added per member for the Mess Servants' Fund which paid for local cooks and waiting staff. Officers were encouraged to bring a servant to Gallipoli, although these servants soon acquired the unfortunate habit of being in the wrong place at the wrong time. Harold Kerby's servant drowned a few days after arriving on Tenedos, suffering a fit while swimming. Harold ensured he was buried with full military honours. Likewise, Charles' servant was killed in an enemy bombing raid at the aerodrome. Statistically, it was more dangerous ironing shirts than flying aeroplanes.

Sykes was superb at flying a desk. He did not fly an aeroplane; he was too busy fighting an organisational battle. He imposed a level of coordination over the once-scattered air units. He met with each unit commander and established reporting systems. His files provide a wonderful window into the air war: individual mission reports, daily air intelligence bulletins and weekly bulletins were collated into thick manila folders. Sykes arranged for an army officer to be permanently attached to Air Headquarters and cooperation between the two services improved in a week. Harry wrote of his new boss, 'Sykes was a hard worker, excellent for writing reports and anticipating requirements in aircraft and stores.'

But Sykes was Charles' opposite. They did not attract. Again, Harry described the longstanding enmity between the two:

> Samson, who was senior to Sykes, had stated sometime before that he thought nothing of Sykes and would refuse to work with, much less under him, and this letter had, for some unknown reason, been published by the Admiralty. Sykes believed that they were waiting for him to make the slightest slip in order to try and get him removed. It was a strained atmosphere until I had a heart to heart meeting with Samson who was too keen on getting the job done to nurse his resentment at the expense of the service.

Courage in an aviator is a wonderful trait, and Charles was awarded several decorations for his remarkable skill and courage in the air in the early days of the war. But promotion attracts other responsibilities and, inevitably, a clear assessment was made of Charles' inability to 'fly a desk'. With his steady rise came the paper mountain. Charles' organisational leadership was not equal to his flying skills. His personal naval file describes him as 'second to none in gallantry, zeal and initiative and technical knowledge of his work, but wants tact. Efforts to circumvent orders of superior officers, narrow outlook, have marred his otherwise admirable efforts.' He was also later passed over for promotion to wing captain owing to his lack of the necessary qualities for successful administration.

Bernard Isaac also thought a great deal of Charles as a pilot, although he was not so fulsome in his praise for his administrative skills:

> 1 October. Marix begins a general 'strafe'. The wires on machines were rusty. Marix calls many Petty Officers before Commander Samson. It appears 18 are sick and no notice has been given. There is no organisation anywhere.

> 2 November. While at breakfast a fire broke out in stores where all the flares, several bombs, oxygen cylinders, etc. All the fire extinguishers had been taken by Warrant Officers for use as fly sprays in their cabins. The explosions were terrific. At 12 pm there was nothing left, spare engines, and all aeroplane stores were burnt. Sykes came over also the Admiral. They got terribly in Commander's way and were called down by him, and made fools of themselves. Warner ran away out of range in opposite direction instead of standing by Commander.

14 November. Blowing a gale and raining. No fly-
ing possible. Commander Samson recommends
Bill Samson [his younger brother] for Mention in
Despatches to Admiral. This makes everyone very
angry. The Commander is astonishing, perhaps mad.
Feel depressed and not well all day.

Sykes was desperately needed to manage the administrative
web spun by six air service units. He was the right per-
son for the task. The army in the Dardanelles had grown
dependent on its eyes in the air. Sykes also chose wisely in
selecting Harry to work in operations as he was the perfect
go-between among the competing factions. In his civilian
life, Harry was a lawyer. He was also a reservist, which kept
him somewhat isolated from the politics of career officers
and he was able to remain focused on his tasks. His diary
presents valuable descriptions of the evolution in bombing operations from the Turkish 5th Army Headquarters to
the flour mills at Gallipoli and finally the railway lines on the
Bulgarian border:

> We were examining a prisoner who said that Limon
> von Sanders Headquarters camp was behind a little
> wood not very far from Ak Bashi Liman. I sent out a
> machine to reconnoitre and located it all right. I then
> told Samson and suggested a return call. The next thing
> I knew 6 machines were in the air all loaded with bombs
> and they gave that camp a rotten time. I think we first
> got on terms [Harry and Samson] through hunting
> enemy H.Q. It was shifted hurriedly. Again and again
> we discovered where H.Q. had been hidden and each
> time we gave them a dose.

At the same time, Harry was also keen to increase the lethal effect of naval gunfire. He observed that the monitors followed a strict 'shelling' timetable. Obviously this limited their use as Turkish gunners learnt to seek cover at the same time each day. Bent on finding a solution, Harry visited VIII Corps Headquarters at Cape Helles and persuaded the artillery staff to change this pattern:

> I also had a trip to Helles to interview the Powers that Be to stop the useless waste of ammunition and flying time. The monitors were sent in each day to fire 25 rounds at specified gun batteries—what occurs is that the Turks see her coming and say, 'Hello here are the monitors, who is she going to fire at today?' They all go to earth and she begins. When they find out it is not their battery they come out and watch the fun. And when the monitors fire 25 rounds they know it is all over for the day.

Harry and Sykes worked well together. While Harry worked on more immediate problems, Sykes expounded his views on the power of the bomb. He was an innovator, but technology had not quite caught up with his schemes—he was undeniably ahead of his time. He communicated his personal views to the Air Department, no doubt justifying his pleas for more capable airframes:

> ... to carry out a strong aerial offensive, especially as regards bomb dropping. Local conditions which govern the enemy's operations in the Peninsula offer exceptional advantages for such an offensive. His local bases of supply, his harbours and landing stages and his shipping are contained in easy reach of Imbros. He has

neither the anti-aircraft artillery nor the air service to protect him from this form of attack.

In early September, Sykes and Harry turned their attention from bombing enemy headquarters to starving the enemy off the peninsula. Harry recorded that the 'principal objective is the destruction of the flour mills. The position and description is to be obtained from the observer of *Ben-my-Chree* before sailing.' Once the mills had been identified from the air, Harry gained approval from John de Robeck for a seaplane to be piggybacked aboard the monitor *Raglan* to destroy this important target:

I got an idea that the Flour Mills at Gallipoli which supply 75,000 to 80,000 loaves a day to Turkish troops, required serious attention. The only way to do it was for one of the big monitors to take a seaplane aboard and make a job of it. I gave the job to *Ark Royal* and got the Vice Admiral's approval. I considered myself justified in going. I then set off in *Raglan* with a very cheery crowd and a lunatic skipper, who was very good to me and gave me his cabin and bathroom. We sailed during the night, arriving off the enemy coast in the morning. Meanwhile the Vice Admiral had altered my plan, ordering an aeroplane to come and spot *Raglan* onto the mills while I kept an eye on *Raglan*. The aeroplane spotted over the target but the corrections were not bold enough. Both Pulford and I were getting terribly wet and cold when our engine started playing monkey tricks, just when I had seen a lot of transports coming along the road. We got down and were picked up without damage. It was unsatisfactory as the job was not finished.

A following reconnaissance assessment found the mills and bakeries to have remained in operation, still serving the army its daily bread. A further attempt was made on 2 October. This time *Hector*'s balloon was paired with the monitor M16. The flour mills and bakeries were bracketed by shells but not destroyed. They were protected by high ridgelines which made shelling from out to sea particularly difficult.

Then, a few days later, Bulgaria entered the war on the side of Germany and Turkey. The Turkish 5th Army on the peninsula now had access to the Ferejik railway with links to Istanbul. From this the Dede Agach railway line branched towards the base of the Gallipoli Peninsula. This branch line brought Turkish supplies and reinforcements much closer to the battle. It was immediately targeted by Sykes and Harry.

For the Allies worsening weather was an omen. Storms lashed the piers and sent barges crashing onto rocks. Trenches filled with water and the men began to suffer frostbite and trench foot. Hamilton was in command of an army in decline. The Turks, on the other hand, had a railway from the front line to their capital. Harry agonised in his diary:

> Are the High Gods bringing our new Iliad to grief in a spirit of wanton mischief? At whose door will history leave the blame for the helpless, hopeless fix we are left in—rotting with disease and told to take it easy?

Then Bulgaria overran Serbia. The Berlin to Istanbul railway (over occupied Serbia) now allowed transport of munitions and heavy siege guns from German factories direct to the Turkish 5th Army. There was still hope; the route was vulnerable at a point south of Kuleli Burgas, in Bulgaria, where the railway crossed the Maritza River.

This bridge was just within range of aircraft operating from Imbros.

Flying reports in November describe this concentration of effort. The attacks on the northern railway systems consumed much of Air Headquarters' interest with coordination of missions from the two wings and seaplanes from *Ben-my-Chree*. The first attack on the railway bridge over the Maritza River was conducted on 8 November with one aeroplane from Imbros and two seaplanes from *Ben-my-Chree*. Relatively accurate bombing was achieved by Charles flying at 800 feet with two 100lb bombs detonating five yards south of the bridge. The seaplane attacks were less successful with two 112lb bombs striking the embankment.

To extend the range of his aeroplanes Charles installed long-range petrol tanks which saw Keith Jopp conducting mid-air refuelling using a rubber hose and a petrol tin. Having inflicted no damage on a second raid on 10 November, a third attack was ordered four days later by two aeroplanes from Charles' No. 3 Wing, with Keith as observer. They discovered that anti-aircraft guns were now concentrated around the bridge, forcing them to make high-level attacks. This increased the inaccuracy of bombing as it was conducted without the aid of optical sights.

To surprise enemy gunners a night raid was prosecuted by George's friend on *Ben-my-Chree*, Flight Commander Smyth-Piggot. He had attacked the bridge in the morning which had given him an appreciation of the terrain and a likely approach. He flew over at midnight and saw the Maritza River glistening below in the moonlight. To make a silent approach he cut his engine and glided down to 300 feet over the bridge before releasing his bombs. He restarted his engine and immediately pulled back on the flight controls just above the treetops. He flew away without a shot being fired at him, finally completing the mission in four and a half hours. Sykes wrote to John de Robeck of Flight Lieutenant Smyth-Piggot's efforts: 'The flight was probably the longest night flight undertaken during the war and I think constitutes a record night flight.'

Eight multi-aeroplane bombing raids were launched in November against the bridge and railway sidings. This was a significant concentration of resources and accounted for over 60 per cent of the bombs dropped during autumn. Despite spectacular displays of airmanship, little damage was caused to the tracks and the trains continued to steam towards the front carrying ammunition and supplies.

The attack on the railway became famous with Richard Davies awarded the Victoria Cross on 19 November. Three aeroplanes from Charles' wing attacked Ferejik station, a mission recorded by Bernard in his diary:

> Late for breakfast. Slept better, Raids were again made on Ferejik Station by Samson, Barnarto, Smylie, Davies, and Heriot. Extraordinary aerial feats were performed by Davies and Smylie. The latter was shot down by machinegun fire, damaging machine (engine and planes). Smylie glided over station being at the time only 500 feet, let go two 100 lbs bombs and one 20 lb in station setting it on fire. Then he glided to marshes and landed safely one mile away. Bulgarians were now running towards him. He set machine on fire and ran to woods nearby. He then saw Davies in Nieuport coming to his rescue, but, there was a 20 lbs bomb on burning machine just where Davies would land. So he went back to machine and fired his automatic into bomb which

exploded. Davies landed and brought him back here safe and sound. Looks like VC gained.

Bernard then typed Richard's post-mission flying report with his usual brevity:

Nieuport 1 Sqn Comd Davies 1025–1225 19 Nov 15

Dropped 3—20 lbs bombs at Northern Station, 1st burst short. 2nd burst on edge of line opposite train of coaches. 3rd burst over. No movement observed in or near town. One locomotive steaming north from Ferejik. Returning saw H5 burning in marshes. Picked up pilot.

Fortunately, Richard's Victoria Cross citation was a little more descriptive:

The KING has been graciously pleased to approve of the grant of the Victoria Cross to Squadron-Commander Richard Bell Davies, D.S.O., R.N., and of the Distinguished Service Cross to Flight Sub-Lieutenant Gilbert Formby Smylie, R.N., in recognition of their behaviour in the following circumstances:—

On 19 November these two officers carried out an air attack on Ferrijik Junction. Flight Sub-Lieutenant Smylie's machine received very heavy fire and was brought down. The pilot planed down over the station, releasing all his bombs except one, which failed to drop, simultane-ously at the station from a very low altitude. Thence he continued his descent into the marsh. On alighting he saw the one unexploded bomb, and set fire to his machine, knowing that the bomb would ensure its destruction. He then proceeded towards Turkish territory.

At this moment he perceived Squadron-Commander Davies descending, and fearing that he would come down near the burning machine and thus risk destruction from the bomb, Flight Sub-Lieutenant Smylie ran back and from a short distance exploded the bomb by means of a pistol bullet. Squadron-Commander Davies descended at a safe distance from the burning machine, took up Sub-Lieutenant Smylie, in spite of the near approach of a party of the enemy, and returned to the aerodrome, a feat of airmanship that can seldom have been equalled for skill and gallantry.

The Nieuport 11 Richard was flying was a single-seat model. When Richard picked him up under rifle fire, Gilbert Smylie dived head first into the cockpit and wriggled past Richard's feet (past the rudder bar) into the foot well below. Smylie was so thoroughly wedged among the control wires that it took two hours to free him on their return to Imbros.

Despite the excitement and the effort expended against the railways there was little disruption to the enemy's overland route. Sykes' own Summary of Information reports record the effort throughout November without any obvious destruction or reduction in rail movements.

At the higher strategic level, Sykes maintained his intent to bomb Istanbul, devising a number of concurrent plans. The first was a rendezvous between a seaplane and submarine in the Sea of Marmara with the sub piggybacking the seaplane. The submarine in question was Lieutenant Commander Archibald Cochrane's *E7*:

> It was this submarine that came alongside the *Ben-my-Chree* a few days ago, so that we could fit a seaplane on its deck for trial purposes. It was proposed when the *E7*

was in the Sea of Marmara that one of us should fly over
the Bulair Lines with bombs, land at an appointed spot
in 'Marmara' and get a lift on the back of the submarine
to within 30 or 40 miles of Constantinople; drop bombs
and fly back to Xeros over the Bulair Lines. And in case of
engine failure sink the machine and get in the submarine.

On 3 September Cochrane brought his submarine alongside *Ben-my-Chree* in Mudros Harbour prior to his second
patrol. The submarine practised balancing a seaplane on its
slowly emerging hull. Once lifted off the sea, the subma-
riners were able to refuel the seaplane from tins of petrol.
Following this trial and prior to the *E7*'s attempt the next
morning, Cochrane was taken on a reconnaissance flight
by Richard across the Dardanelles to allow him a bird's-eye
view of the mission area. This careful preparation came to
naught, however, as the Nagara nets caught the submarine,
forcing Cochrane to surface and scuttle his vessel. This loss
aborted any attempt at a rendezvous.

Sykes formed a committee to find ways to destroy the anti-
submarine net at Nagara. On 5 September Sykes, George's
boss on *Ben-my-Chree*, Flight Commander Edmonds, and
Commander Nasmith of *E11* met and discussed ways to
destroy the net. The first suggestion involved a seaplane dropping a small parachute mine upstream to drift downstream
with the current and into the net. Other suggestions included
a torpedo dropped by seaplane and a gun mounted in an aeroplane which would shoot from the floats. The committee
endorsed the first proposal and, on 18 November, Lieutenant
Commander Murphy of Arthur's No. 2 Wing was ordered
to design a parachute bomb with canisters rigged to explode
at depth, cutting the stays that kept the steel net high in the
water. Harry described the unusual nature of this bomb:

Clarkee devised a parachute bomb with a lump of sugar as its safety gadget. It floated down the current to the nets when the sugar would have melted and the bomb became alive. He insisted on flying over and dropping it.

The second idea involved resurrection of the long-range bombing plan from 18 May. Sykes encouraged Charles to outline his plan to John de Robeck. The idea progressed in September with a flight plan describing an aeroplane flown solo by Reginald Marix with ten 20lb bombs. De Robeck initially decided against the proposal because of the risk of losing a pilot. A 'think again' letter was boomeranged back to Charles. Sykes later gave his permission for a joint British and French scheme. This revised idea hinged on Reginald flying the Breguet in concert with Captain Cesari of the French squadron flying a long-range Henri Farman. An attempt in the pre-dawn darkness of 27 September was cancelled when the French aeroplane on Tenedos was grounded following engine trouble. Meanwhile, Reginald was recalled to London to train budding aviators. Bernard recorded the last-minute rush:

> 3 October. Marix goes to see Sykes and gets permission to stay till tomorrow in order to do the Constantinople trip. He then flies to Tenedos to consult with Cesari as to possibility of going tonight, his last chance. Cesari's machine is not ready to do the trip. So it cannot take place so far as Marix is concerned.

Sykes corresponded with Churchill, writing an eight-page 'unofficial' letter on 4 November describing his plans to bomb Istanbul. He proposed two schemes, the first involving SS7 waddling to Istanbul; but this long journey was considered too dangerous by the airship squadron. So Sykes developed another plan which depended on the prevailing winds:

> Will tell you of another scheme we have, one for a continuous bombing scheme over Constantinople . . . a constant succession of winds blowing alternatively for several days at a time, from the N.E. and S.W. The idea is that if we could arrange for a ship as a seaplane tender in the Black Sea so the seaplanes might take advantage of these winds to fly to and from Constantinople, drop bombs and collect information as to the amount and location of shipping.

Again the principal motive was the capture of intelligence on the enemy. The army had to exploit the enemy's vulnerability and apply suitable pressure. Infantry assaults had failed. Sykes expounded his belief in the unique opportunities that the confines of the peninsula offered a bombing campaign. His plan was divided into two elements: strategic reconnaissance and tactical reconnaissance flights. Strategic reconnaissance would cover an area defined as the Gulf of Xeros and enemy ports. Hamilton's General Headquarters was the customer. The belief endured that if they could only squeeze the supply routes sufficiently, they could force the enemy off the peninsula. Harry's old seaplane flight was responsible for the very north and a flight from Charles' No. 3 Wing was tasked with the Gallipoli ports. Tactical reconnaissance involved location of enemy guns and trenches with divisional and corps headquarters as the customers. Responsibility for this was allocated to Arthur's wing. Sykes' support of the army was recognised in official communiqués: '. . . afforded the intelligence Branch of the General Staff M.E.F. great service in giving timely warning of the movement of troops etc.'

Sykes was an organisational wonder. Every day, Summary of Information reports were compiled and printed (usually) on one side of an A4 page. These were typed reports with three headings: area, sources of information and intelligence details. The most common entries under 'area' included: Helles, Anzac, Suvla, Bulair and shipping. Similarly, the 'sources of information' listed the air units engaged: 3 Wing, 2 Wing, *Ark Royal*, *Hector*, *Canning* and *Ben-my-Chree*. The intelligence described was designed for its military readers. An extract for 8 October reads:

ANZAC 2nd Wing Reconnaissance of OLIVE GROVE between 5.30 a.m. and 7 a.m.

SUVLA:

From very low altitude reported:

Large stores and dugouts in 55 P. 9.

Long row of dugouts in 56 G. 4 5 & 6.

Large gun emplacement in 56 I. 3.

Two encampments partly concealed in 55 U. 1–4. Two batteries in 58 Y. 9. Left hand one 4 covered emplacements; right hand one 3 emplacements, 2 occupied.

31 photographs were taken of the Gaba Tepe area.

The location of Turkish works and camps was plotted on the common 1:10,000 map which was overlaid by an artillery grid similar to the 1:40,000 sheet maps. The substance of these reports was also included in a daily 'Intelligence Bulletin' published by the Intelligence Department at General Headquarters. This report fused Egyptian War Office, Naval Intelligence Department and diplomatic cables to provide an overview of enemy activity in the area of operations. The bulletin was an intelligence product of a high standard. It equalled in brevity the Daily Intsum (Intelligence Summary) that a Watchkeeper would deliver during the Iraq War. At a glance a senior officer was given a neat overview of enemy activity.

Sykes also established a comprehensive photographic section along the lines of the RFC's in France. This main photographic section managed smaller sections attached to each wing and the seaplane flight to coordinate the tasking and processing of photographic plates. Six cameras were allocated to each wing, with two for the seaplane flight. The photographic section standardised publication of imagery of immediate relevance to the Survey Office of the General Headquarters' Map and Survey Department. The Air Headquarters staff produced a number of glossy five-by-four-inch black and white photographs. These were sent to the map office and later to the Shore Printing Establishment on HMS *Endeavour*. From here drawings, trench mapping and topographical maps were printed.

Sykes' vision for an active air service was codified in his own Standing Instructions on 1 November. This 20-page set of orders was divided into seven chapters: Intelligence, Photography, Signals, Interior Economy, Pay, Supplies and Medical. It also came with two appendices: response to the Turkish Air Service and lines of inter-communication:

The objective of instituting a definitive system in dealing with photography is firstly to expedite the work of the Survey Office.

The general conditions existing at the Dardanelles. Enemy holds natural positions giving a superiority of fire alone countered by RNAS spotting. Fire from warships is of great value as little siege artillery or batteries in proportion to number of troops. Aerial reconnaissance of more value because of the confined nature of the terrain.

In truth, bombing was subordinate to the capture of intelligence and photography. Air photography evolved from crudely drawn trench maps sketched from photographic plates exposed in handheld cameras to imagery taken by gyroscopic mounted cameras on dedicated aeroplanes. These were then fine-tuned into professional maps on the 1:10,000 mapping scale. Maps were initially published by the Survey Office using captured 1:20,000 scale maps taken from dead enemy soldiers and improved to 1:10,000 maps using controls in Allied-held territory (for triangulation) to build photo compilations of the terrain. These small-scale maps were considered accurate for gunnery and were widely distributed across the Dardanelles Army. The raw data or the photographs themselves were also used as a source for military planning. The Australian War Memorial photography section has copies of many of these original photographs.

The demand for such work was enormous and caused acute supply problems. A sense of the scale of this operation is evident in the actions of the air staff who requested their friends to scour London for orders of 1000 sheets of five-by-four glossy paper. Supplies had to be sourced outside the Admiralty supply office as the demand could not be met by formal procurement. Air staff were sent to Kodak suppliers in Egypt to secure materials to meet demand.

Lieutenant Colonel Aspinall in General Headquarters described the contribution of RNAS photographical work in his British official history of the war. Curiously, Aspinall lamented in his history that no mapping had been available during the Gallipoli campaign. However, his signature on the memorandum below suggests that he not only had access to mapping at the time, but was reviewing aerial photographic product:

> Photographs taken by the Air Service have proved of such value that an increased distribution is desirable in order that subordinate Commanders may be supplied with sets covering their immediate front.

Aspinall demanded that the air service supply a minimum of six copies of each photograph, with larger numbers when points of importance were captured. Recognising the lack of resources, he offered the assistance of the General Headquarters in obtaining materials from Egypt or from home. Sykes replied that the RNAS supplied one print with negatives to the Survey Office of Headquarters and that he did not have the resources to commit to making multiple copies.

The scale of production is staggering. Sykes directed each of his units to report on the effort and scale of photographic missions. Arthur's wing reported in excess of 1500 exposures using the Thornton-Pickard camera from 28 August to 19 November. Inclusive of this number were 160 failures of procedure and two cameras and 120 plates lost through accidents. His wing produced a further 2500 reprints of five-by-four-inch images with 158 enlargements to ten-by-eight-inch images. *Ben-my-Chree* took a total of 30 dozen five-by-four-inch and two gross ten-by-eight-inch plates. Cinematographic film for an 'aeroscope camera' was supplied, with cinematic filming conducted from the air. These cans probably remain in an attic somewhere gathering dust: 'Cinematograph for aeroscope camera supplied and remaining unused 8-250 foot rolls', wrote Sykes in one of his many reports.

Ark Royal took 123 photographs with three handheld cameras. Her list of photographic work includes 55 photographs of the Gaba Tepe area resulting in a new map produced by the printing section of Army Headquarters. Typically, Charles Samson did not provide a written report.

Turkish 1st Aircraft Company raids increased throughout the autumn months. Replacement aeroplanes and seaplanes were sent on rail cars to the Gallipoli front. A new German Commanding Officer, *Kapitan* Korner, and more powerful variants of Albatros C1 biplanes, improved the capability of the 1st Aircraft Company. Also in support, the *Wasserfliegerabteilung* was reinforced with three powerful Gotha WD 1 seaplanes powered by Mercedes 160hp engines which replaced the 100hp earlier variants. They continued to operate from a camouflaged shed near Channakale. The newer seaplane was a potent machine; the observer stood in a cage (on top of the fuselage and just behind the upper wing) gripping a 7.62 machine-gun. Heavier bombs were also carried in under-wing racks. The Gothas conducted almost daily missions, specifically targeting the SSA shed and the aerodrome behind K Beach. Turkish air raids were sporadic in nature but had an immediate effect, partly because most had previously felt safe on an Aegean island. Bombing raids had a disproportionate result on officers used to the creature comforts of rear echelon positions. Harry recorded the effect of Turkish air raids and drew some conclusions as to their value:

> Then during the night the Huns came again. It was curious and eerie having their bombs whistling down and wondering where they would burst. The first raid wounded 5 of our men and we were lucky to get off so cheaply.
>
> 18 October. The German Air Service got a lot of new machines and pilots and became disgustingly active—one morning we had 4 of them over headquarters dropping bombs and spikes. The next day only 3 machines took part in the daily raid on GHQ. By this time we all had dugouts. They killed Samson's servant and wounded one of my messengers. From what I saw in the way of loss of nerve at GHQ and from the tales of prisoners I became a convert to the bomb which previously I had regarded as a useless weapon, but that I saw [it reach] places out of reach of gunfire. There is a larger moral effect and considerable damage if one is lucky. Each day I used to select some target and tell them to attack it.

As a result a bomb shelter was built in front of Hamilton's headquarters—a hut made almost completely of stone— which still stands. Outside the front door, stone stairs lead down to twin chambers beneath the ground. The roof is covered in concrete slabs offering significant overhead protection. Today the chambers are filled with water. Goats wisely hide from the elements in Sir Ian Hamilton's stone hut.

Kapitan Korner's company increased in capability. Sykes, as a veteran of the European theatre, was alarmed by the scale of the developing struggle. He knew that the contest for the air would end in scouting and escort missions. Sykes warned London and the Director of the Air Department that the Turkish Air Service was gaining in experience and potency. He anticipated significant aerial battles over the kite balloon ships.

Hector's diarist recorded a series of raids in autumn with Turkish aeroplanes bombing both day and night, singly and in pairs. Sykes was aware that command of the air was a feature of the battlefield that the Allied army had taken for granted. He foresaw a change for the worse: 'Had good moral effect because RNAS kept command of the air. The converse would be a greater disadvantage.'

Kapitan Korner's mix of German and Turkish pilots frequently bombed K Beach on Imbros with the air service a favoured target. Harry and Bernard recorded a series of raids:

19 September. [Bernard] Enemy's aeroplanes raided Kephalo last night. 3(?) casualties.

28 September. [Bernard] Hostile aeroplane dropped three bombs near airship shed no damage done.

28 September. [Bernard] At about 11.30 bombs crashed into our camp. We had no warning. Poor old Garwood was killed outright, a Turk prisoner was wounded and another man wounded in thigh. Our tent was riddled with shrapnel with one bullet going through William's cigarette box. Erskine St Aubyn [midshipman aged 14 years] had a marvellous escape, a bullet having

passed through his cap and shirt while he was lying flat. We had a greater revenge in afternoon. Commander Samson, Marix, Thomson with Jopp went up to drop bombs. Jopp dropped 20 lbs bombs in hospital by mistake which was a pity and Samson cursed him.

29 September. [Bernard] Taube alarms all night, but no machines come over.

5 October. [Bernard] While walking with Dunn [No. 2 Wing] between here and their camp a German machine passed over and dropped two bombs. We heard it whistling down but had no time for cover, so we lay down flat.

5 October. [Harry] Hostile aeroplane dropped bombs on airship headquarters (damage unknown).

6 October. [Harry] Two hostile aeroplanes bombarded harbour no damage done, see some of our aeroplanes chasing them.

6 October. [Bernard] Slept badly. Taube alarms by telephone but no Taubes.

2 December. [Bernard] At 3 am we are awakened by the alarm. A German machine flies over; our guns didn't fire. It went over No. 2 Wing and dropped two bombs. Haven't heard results. Another alarm sounded at 6 am and yet another 8.30. Our shooting was quite good but machine escaped. Machine was a seaplane. It was same machine on all occasions.

While it is difficult to estimate the number of air raids based on accounts from diaries, *Kapitan* Korner's pilots were certainly busy targeting the blimp and the aerodrome. Harry describes the growing hate between the two air services which would soon tip heavily in the Turks' favour with the introduction of the deadly Fokker Eindecker plane:

> While at Imbros we were treated to our first intensive bombing. Six or seven machines came over from Channakale fairly regularly both by day and night. Their bombs made a loud whistling sound so we had ample time to walk to our funk holes and be safe from anything except a direct hit. I was sitting in my hut writing when a steel dart went bang through the table and buried itself in the ground between my feet.

Harry was replaced by Major Groves as General Staff Officer Grade 3 in October, allowing him to return to flying duties, which he preferred. Groves had served with the RFC in France from April 1915 and was attached at Sykes' request. Like Harry, he was also a qualified pilot and observer. He continued the reporting and intelligence systems that Harry had established. Harry rejoined his friends on *Ark Royal* before the aircraft carrier was sent to the Salonika front in November 1915.

Sir Ian Hamilton and General Walter Braithwaite were recalled to London on 14 October with Hamilton's replacement, the former Third Army Commander in France, General Sir Charles Monro, arriving soon after. Lord Kitchener attempted to soften the blow, but Hamilton saw the telegram for what it was:

The War Council held last night decided that though the Government fully appreciate your work and the gallant manner in which you personally have struggled to make the enterprise a success in the face of the terrible difficulties you have had to contend against, they, all the same, wish to make a change in the command which will give them an opportunity of seeing you.

Hamilton wrote later:

I rode over to the new Headquarters at Kephalo to say good-bye to my own Staff. Although I had meant to live there until we drove the Turks far enough back to let us live on the Peninsula, I had found time to see my little stone hut built by Greek peasants on the side of the hill:— deliciously snug. To-day, this very day, I was to have struck my tent and taken up these cosy winter quarters; now I move, right enough, but on the wrong road.

Lord Kitchener's instructions to Sir Charles Monro were to find a way out or remove the deadlock on the peninsula including the option of evacuation. Monro arrived on the Gallipoli Peninsula on 28 October and conferred with his three corps commanders on the likely options. In his report to Lord Kitchener he recommended a speedy evacuation as terrain and circumstances forbade a renewed push. On receipt of this news, Lord Kitchener visited the peninsula for a week from 9 November and saw the difficulties for himself. Following the return of the Secretary of State for War to London, the corps commanders, lieutenants general de Lisle, Davies and Birdwood, sent Lord Kitchener a further memorandum warning him that the cost of withdrawal could see a casualty toll as high as 40 per cent of the force.

On 8 December the cabinet decided to evacuate Suvla and Anzac despite the cost and loss of prestige and the forecast of heavy casualties.

Private Richard Bulkeley recovered from his wounds in Cairo and returned to Anzac Cove in the second week of November. His diary and letters tell of the effects of the weather; clearly the Dardanelles Army was struggling. It was no longer attacking—it was under siege:

Gallipoli
30 November 1915

My dear all,

We have been having a pretty rough time of it for the last week. Several days rain, & the night before last a decent fall of snow. It is terribly cold & very miserable when there is icy mud & slush in the trenches over your boots. I have to wear a pair of sox over my mitts, to keep my hands warm & pile on all the clothes I had. The water in my bottle is frozen at mid-day. However someone has to do the job & we can pretty nearly stand anything now. We can stand the cold, but just dread the wet.

We should get a mail in soon, the last one was lost. I hope there were no nice things in it for me. Things have been pretty quiet for the last week or so, except for artillery, which was pretty heavy yesterday.

Hope you are all well, am O.K. myself—the cold weather gives me a good appetite.

Love to all
Dick

Withdrawal was a political and army matter and the RNAS had no voice in the decision. Despite this, Sykes expressed a strong view on the role of air support in any potential withdrawal. He wrote a detailed report to the Air Department, also sending it to army and navy headquarters, arguing for an increase in aircraft numbers in preparation for the evacuation:

> The following points are put forward at this time when the general strategic and political situation is at the decisive point. The long distance of operations from home and the increasing danger from submarine attack on the lines of communication render it important in the highest degree that no time should be lost in strengthening the establishment of the Air Service in the Eastern Mediterranean.

Sykes was correct in his assumption that the RNAS would play a key role protecting the army during its withdrawal.

The successful withdrawal of the Dardanelles Army from the Gallipoli Peninsula was the greatest achievement of the campaign and stands as an example of sound military planning. Orderly withdrawal from contact with the enemy is one of the most difficult tasks in the military lexicon. To conduct a withdrawal of over 80,000 troops and equipment from the peninsula without loss was a remarkable feat.

What history has not recorded is the role Sykes' aviators played in this extraordinary achievement.

CHAPTER 9

The escape

Lord Kitchener approved Sir Charles Monro's recommendation that the Mediterranean Expeditionary Force be placed under command of General William Birdwood and retitled the 'Dardanelles Army' with its headquarters at Imbros. Monro had a clear grasp of the difficult situation facing the Dardanelles Army. In his first despatch he summarised the situation:

> The positions occupied by our troops presented a military situation unique in history. The mere fringe of the coast line had been secured. The beaches and piers upon which they depended for all requirements in personnel and material were exposed to registered and observed Artillery fire. Our entrenchments were dominated almost throughout by the Turks. The possible Artillery positions were insufficient and defective. The Force, in short, held a line possessing every possible military defect. The position was without depth,

the communications were insecure and dependent on the weather. No means existed for the concealment and deployment of fresh troops destined for the offensive whilst the Turks enjoyed full powers of observation, abundant Artillery positions, and they had been given the time to supplement the natural advantages which the position presented by all the devices at the disposal of the Field Engineer.

With the reorganisation came the opportunity for the newly promoted Australian Brigadier General Cyril Brudenell White to orchestrate the withdrawal of two army corps from Anzac and Suvla based on a ruse. He was elevated from the 1st Australian Division to become Birdwood's Chief of Staff because of his consummate planning skills. The Allied plan initially retained the Cape Helles lodgement fearing that open terrain precluded any chance of safe withdrawal. Monro wrote:

> I directed Birdwood to prepare a scheme to this end, in order that all details should be ready in case of sanction being given to this operation. On 8 December, I directed the army to proceed with the evacuation of Suvla and Anzac at once. Rapidity of action was imperative, having in view the unsettled weather which might be expected in the Aegean. The success of our operations was entirely dependent on weather conditions. Birdwood proceeded on receipt of his orders with the skill and promptitude which is characteristic of all that he undertakes, and after consultation with Rear-Admiral Wemyss, it was decided, provided the weather was propitious, to complete the evacuation on the night of the 19th/20th December.

Brudenell White's plan was to secretly embark troops and matériel over a number of nights while maintaining an appearance of 'business as usual' during daylight hours. The last few remaining troops would play a part in a dangerous pantomime promoting the illusion that the trenches were still fully manned. From the beginning of the withdrawal phase, Sykes' aviators embarked on aggressive air raids to mask the drawdown in troop numbers. Sykes wrote eagerly to London that, 'The opportunity for aerial attack is unique and I feel sure that, given the personnel and machines, we should be in a position to assist very materially in the operations.'

Sykes' headquarters and the aviators of the RNAS played key roles in the two evacuations. Simply stated, Erich Serno's Turkish Air Service had to be kept from overflying the trenches. If the evacuation was discovered the Turkish 5th Army would attack Anzac and Suvla as they did later at Cape Helles, break through the thinly held lines and inflict severe casualties. The air service surged anti-aircraft patrols to keep enemy aeroplanes from approaching Anzac and Suvla. By January attempts to deny enemy flights over Cape Helles had become costly as the enemy had gained air superiority in the final week before the withdrawal. Turkish observers reported a 'drawdown' in British troops but the strength of the British bombardment during abortive Turkish infantry assaults told another story. Ultimately the Dardanelles Army was evacuated successfully.

Total missions for December amounted to 271 with 78 reconnaissance, 56 spotting, 5 photography, 35 bombing, 15 maritime patrol, 43 anti-aircraft patrols, 37 other plus two transit flights. Training missions for new pilots accounted for the high number of 'other' missions. The total figure for January was 56 with a similar emphasis on anti-aircraft patrolling. Despite its apparent success in keeping the ruse 'alive', Sykes' air service had been enormously challenged.

The winter weather in December and January had a major impact on air operations. The kite balloons were severely restricted. *Canning* and No. 7 Kite Balloon Section could only spot on 10, 11 and 12 December, with gunnery officers complaining of heavy mist and low cloud obscuring targets. On each occasion the kite balloon stayed aloft for over four hours and varied its height trying to slip beneath the cloud layer. Vice Admiral Sir Rosslyn Wemyss, who had replaced John de Robeck, emphasised the importance of warships registering onto targets, aware that inclement weather and competing priorities would restrict air support. Gunnery officers were reminded to maintain range cards using cross bearings and buoys.

Sykes did not accept that military withdrawal from the peninsula should entail a reduction in aircraft. Instead he argued for an increase. He wrote to Wemyss anticipating an expansion in operations, requesting data for new landing grounds, airship bases, and anchorages for seaplane carriers across the Mediterranean from Port Said to Salonika. In support, he argued that the navy must expand to counter the rising threat of the Turkish Air Service. Sykes lamented that in December he had two wings manned by only 17 pilots, 18 observers and 23 'ready' aeroplanes. Against this number he pointed to the RNAS establishment tables of two wings with 72 pilots, 64 observers and 120 aeroplanes. Undaunted by the prospect of refusal, he sought to double his strength by citing a War Office memorandum dated 7 December which stated that the establishment of the RNAS in the Eastern Mediterranean should, in fact, be double the establishment agreed in October. Sykes was relentless in pursuit of his aims.

He asserted that 'from a military point of view an increase of the Aeroplane strength in this theatre to a total of four Wings [is] essential', and queried whether the expansion he sought would be forthcoming.

Sykes also found another unassailable reason to assist in his paper war. He wrote again to the Admiralty in London asking for aircraft, based not on the decisive pressure that could be applied to the beleaguered enemy army, but on the obverse—that the enemy were in the ascendency over the beaches:

> In view of the fact that in the near future a considerable addition to the strength of the enemy aircraft is to be anticipated, both as regards number and power and that the present command of the air should not be allowed to fall in hostile hands. Recently enemy aeroplanes have made several attacks, dropping bombs on the various headquarters of the Mediterranean Expeditionary Force. By a strong counter attack the British aircraft destroyed two enemy aeroplane bases and have caused the enemy to desist from further attacks. It may be considered as certain that the Germans will send many of the most recent type of long distance fighting machines to co-operate in the operations in this theatre.

Charles Samson complained about the standard of pilots arriving as replacements, bemoaning their lack of experience. Most had fewer than 15 hours in the air. Charles also took the opportunity to attack Sykes, complaining that three aeroplanes had been lost because of errors made by barely competent pilots. He also pointed to the poor quality of observers. Charles became political, blaming his boss as he sent a number of pilots home as 'unfit for employment'. He

341

sent a letter directly to Wemyss without Sykes's knowledge: 'I have the honour to report that the following letter may be forwarded to the proper Authorities . . .'

Charles was oblivious to the effect of the 'Fokker scourge' in the skies over France. Since July 1915, the German Air Service had cut deeply into the RFC with the superiority of its two new fighters, the Albatros C1 and the Fokker Eindecker. Casualties were mounting within the RFC, so new pilots with only 15 hours' experience had become the norm in France where demand was high. In Charles' opinion this latest tranche of pilots had proven incapable of flying the new machines, let alone in war service against increasingly hostile enemy aeroplanes. Worse was to come: three new Fokker Eindeckers were on their way to supplement the two Albatros C1 already operating at Galatia.

For Private Richard Bulkeley, life in the trenches went on as usual with one exception—now his experience as a surveyor was proving useful:

1 December: Nice sunny day. Taube (enemy aeroplane) over in the morning.

2 December: Beautiful warm day. Taube over in the morning.

3 December: Light mist all day. On survey work.

4 December: Not a bad day. Surveying tunnel in the afternoon. Very heavy bombardment to north in the afternoon.

5 December: Surveying tunnels all day with [Corporal Joseph] Naylor.

6, 7, 8 December: On survey work all day.

9 December: Got tracing & plans up to date. Transferred into 10 Platoon under Sgt Foley. Six ships bombarded to the south of us, for about 2 hours, a great sight.

'High profile' bombing missions were prosecuted to mask the withdrawal with a concentration of effort against shipping in the straits. Sykes ordered 28 bombing missions on shipping in the final four weeks. Kilid Bahr village was also heavily shelled on 1 December following Wemyss' note to Sykes that 'it is of first importance that the town of Kilid Bahr should be set on fire'. The enemy replied. The 1st Aircraft Company at Galatia was under command of the army and attacks on villages, where ammunition and food was often stored, was clearly a vulnerability.

On 2 December four aeroplanes were ordered to strike a steamer unloading at Kilia Liman. Charles Samson scored the only successful strike, hitting the 300-foot steamer with two 20lb bombs. Port infrastructure was also targeted and Sykes' air service spotted naval gunfire onto villages across the Gallipoli Peninsula where enemy headquarters and Turkish staff officers were known to be housed. On 3 December, the village of Boghali behind Anzac was targeted. Boghali was shelled again on 7 December. Heriot and John Sissmore were ordered 'to spot for M29 onto Boghali and stores at KILIA LIMAN'. Villages were continually shelled up and down the peninsula and flames and smoke could be seen across the Aegean on Imbros. The sustained show of aggression was designed to mask the withdrawal.

Bernard Isaac no longer cared about the handiwork of his squadron; he had finally been recalled, not because of fatigue, but to visit the dentist as there were no surgeries in the Aegean. No doubt excessive grinding of his teeth, a result of the pressures of his appointment as the squadron's Intelligence Officer, had turned a problem into a serious condition requiring surgery:

> Consulted Dr Duncan RN who quite saw the necessity of my going to Malta to have my teeth seen to. He also said it would be a good scheme to get me some leave as I was 'run down'.

Bernard was delighted; it was a chance to visit his loving wife Vi and to see his two children. As he looked for a boat to take him to Mudros, the air war continued behind him:

No. 2 Wing Flying Reports Orders: Spot for M 16 onto port AK BASHI

9 December 1915.

The observer flew over to the peninsula, found a thick bank of clouds, came down to 2000 feet to slip under the clouds, but there was too much haze to allow him to see across the peninsula. So the trip was abandoned.

On 12 December HMS *Canning* with 7 Kite Balloon Section hoisted its balloon at 10.32 am and operated off the coast near Sogun Dere until 5.30 pm when the balloon was retrieved, the 'general idea to crush Turkish operations in these areas'. The balloon corrected the fire of *Cornwallis* and *Prince George* onto gun batteries hidden in a nullah. Three air service aeroplanes were required for this mission which included anti-aircraft patrolling—two flew staggered duty with a third on patrol for hostile submarines. Serno's Turkish Air Service was now affecting Allied air operations.

Spotting missions were expanded with orders to directly support the evacuation of Anzac. On 9 December a heavy bombardment of the olive grove was ordered. Several warships shelled specific grid squares where Turkish gun batteries were known to be dug in. Spotting aircraft circled overhead correcting the accuracy of fire. Considerable effort was spent in silencing these troublesome batteries that had targeted the beaches both day and night. The day-long bombardment was considered successful as enemy guns in the olive grove ceased firing and remained silent.

Sykes also attempted to smash enemy aeroplanes on the ground. He ordered attacks on the Turkish aerodromes at Galatia and the seaplane station at Channakale. But these raids were not as successful as he later described to London. The first two bombing missions of December comprised a raid on the seaplane base at Channakale at a height of 8500 feet and both failed to hit the sheds. In pursuit of an attack on Galatia, one of the Bristol Scouts flown with Keith Jopp as observer was engaged in aerial combat by an enemy 'twin seater biplane', an Albatros C1, its observer armed with a machine-gun. The Albatros had a clear advantage, peppering the Bristol and prompting the pilot to dive and run for home. Keith was armed with a Lewis gun, but it jammed after 20 rounds:

No. 3 Wing Flying Report
2 December 1915.
H7 Cdr Busk and Jopp

Observed the Galatia aerodrome and noted 2 pairs of packing cases. 2 cases on road at end of pier around which there was a certain amount of movement. There were two machines on the Aerodrome in the open. Aggressively engaged by a two seater at 9,000 feet.

Bombing Galatia aerodrome incurred stiff resistance and an Albatros attacked Charles Samson's aeroplane on three out of four attempts. The Albatros was challenging the RNAS Bristol and Henri Farman aeroplanes for control of the air.

On the ground, Cyril Brudenell White's plans for a gradual withdrawal at Anzac and Suvla were approved by Monro. The withdrawal of men and equipment was explained to the troops as meeting the requirement for a reduced garrison during the winter months. This occurred, silently at night, through the first two weeks of December, leaving fewer than 20,000 troops ashore. Detailed orders were published down to section level to ensure that signs denoting a withdrawal were concealed from the enemy. The Brigade Major of the 1st Infantry Brigade told his battalions on 24 November:

> On the approach of hostile aircraft
>
> i. All movement will cease; the men will not look up as upturned faces are easily noticeable to aircraft observers. Field glasses will not be used except from cover, Working parties will sit down and be quiet.
>
> ii. Strict silence will be maintained; the presence of troops has often been detected by noise.

Brudenell White's plan was highly detailed. Ships approached the beaches at night after the moon had set to take off a quota of men and war materials. The men wrapped their boots in sandbags to muffle the sound of their tread. But the threat remained from enemy aeroplanes. Detailed orders were necessary as the enemy conducted an average of one flight per day over the ANZAC lines before the weather grounded the aircraft. On 9 December, during a break in the winter weather, an enemy flight was recorded at 4.45 pm by the 2nd Infantry Brigade and a report sent to headquarters which stated that 'enemy aircraft flew over lines firing machine gun'.

Anti-aircraft machine-guns were ordered in the 1st Australian Division Operation Order No. 43, dated 10 December 1915, which also warned individual Australian units to remain alert during the latter stages of the withdrawal. This was further codified:

> ... immediate and rapid fire will be opened by anti aircraft guns and machine guns on all hostile aircraft passing near or over our lines, in order to compel them to alter their course, and hinder observation.

Brudenell White had no doubt that the ruse would be revealed from the air. The troops were given clear instructions and so was Sykes:

> The Army Commander hopes that the RNAS will do its utmost during the ensuing week to carry out as continuous a series of flights as possible in the neighbourhood of ANZAC and SUVLA in order to minimise the chances of observation by enemy aeroplanes, of unusual activity on and about the beaches.

Sykes replied to Army Headquarters on 14 December reiterating his support and adding his own ideas on how to deal with the growing threat of enemy aerial reconnaissance:

Air Headquarters to Dardanelles Army

So far as weather conditions permit the maximum effort will be made during the ensuing week as requested. Both the balloon ships and aeroplanes have been told to give further assistance. I am of the opinion that the greater part of the flying should be done East and West of our lines in order not to give the enemy the impression that our increased aircraft activity is of a protective nature.

The departure schedules worked like clockwork. During the day, empty boxes were unloaded at the pier and carried up to the front lines. Soldiers were ordered to walk up and down Monash Valley, giving the appearance of normal activity. A cricket match was played as a further demonstration of normality. At night, cooking fires were lit outside empty bivouacs:

1 Australian Division Order No. 4

Orders have been received for the embarkation of the Army Corps and its transfer to MUDROS.

1. . . . The operation will be effected during the hours of darkness of two nights. The principle upon which the withdrawal will be [based is] a gradual reduction from our present fire trenches . . .

The remaining few soldiers were ordered to show themselves at points under observation by the enemy, where troops had been in the habit of congregating. A free issue of cigarettes was made to encourage them to maintain 'normal' conditions.

In case of the appearance of hostile aeroplanes, men were warned to come out of their dugouts and show themselves.

Private Richard Bulkeley learnt of the withdrawal through rumour long before he was officially informed. He had earnt promotion on his return, thanks to his surveying work finding hidden routes to the beach:

14 December: In reserve. Got three stripes today. All kinds of wild rumours going round about us evacuating. All kinds of strange things happening, destroying stores etc.

15 December: Rumours of evacuation gradually confirmed but do not know yet when we leave.

16 December: Expecting to leave tonight. In the afternoon went down to the beach with the other NCOs to learn the track. Find 2am to be one of the last party to leave.

17 December: Picked to stay with the last 12 in C Coy. Went down to the beach before stand to. On duty in the firing line all day. Two men killed with a shell in the afternoon.

18 December: On duty in the firing line all day & at night also. One party left tonight.

19 December: Preparing all day to leave in the evening. At 6am one party left the trenches with muffled feet. Left only 10 men in the firing line. Perfect organisation; taken out to a boat in large barges holding 500. Perfect night, a brilliant moon & the sea quite calm.

20 December: Woke up in Mudros Harbour, went ashore about 9am & got into camp. Fixing up camp all the afternoon.

Wemyss printed a memorandum in the form of a pamphlet on the naval role in the withdrawal:

General Orders for the Final Stage of the Evacuation of the Army from Suvla and ANZAC. 12 December 1915.

The final stage of the evacuation will be completed on two consecutive nights viz-those of the 18 and 19 December . . .

IV GENERAL

AIRCRAFT. Generally during evacuation and especially on the last two days aircraft must endeavour to keep off the enemy who may be reconnoitring. For this reason it is considered that unusual activities on the part of our aircraft which tend to bring out those of the enemy shall be avoided. In the event of a big attack by day or night the Wing Captain will arrange to support with as many aircraft as possible carrying bombs. Etc. One aeroplane is to be prepared to spot for ships at Suvla and one for ships at ANZAC in the event of an attack, senior officers of squadrons signalling direct to Wing Captain when required.

In response to the orders in paragraph IV on aircraft activity, Sykes printed his own orders to the wing captains of No. 2 and 3 Wings:

Preliminary Instructions for units of the RNAS

ARRANGEMENTS TO BE CARRIED OUT IN THE EVENT OF THE EVACUATION OF SUVLA AND ANZAC AND THE STRENGTHENING OF HELLES.

Headquarters RNAS
12 December 1915

All the available strength of the Air Service will be concentrated at Imbros to assist in the above operations. If necessary it will remain concentrated until the strong attacks, which it is anticipated the enemy will make upon Helles will be repulsed. When these operations, the extent and length of which it is not possible at the present time to foresee, are complete, Headquarters RNAS and the No. 3 Wing will move to Mudros, No. 2 Wing will remain at Imbros, and other units will be distributed in accordance with strategic requirements.

There was no guarantee of success. It was highly likely that they would be discovered, so the RNAS aviators were duly warned. During the last two days at Anzac and Suvla—18 and 19 December—only a bare minimum of men remained in the trenches waiting for the final posts to be taken aboard. The RNAS orders describe the risky final period:

Preliminary Instructions to Units of the RNAS with regards to the evacuation of ANZAC and Suvla

If bombing operations should take place great care must be exercised not to drop bombs near any locality which is designated by red crescent flag or other ground signals as a hospital.

It is possible that a number of our wounded may be left behind. No bombing operations will therefore be carried out subsequent to the evacuation without reference to HQ RNAS.

Orders for the embarkation in these Preliminary Instructions were explicit, requiring a protective anti-aircraft patrol over Anzac and Suvla throughout the day:

On the 18 and 19 December a continuous hostile aircraft patrol will be maintained in the ANZAC and Suvla area from dawn to dusk. Machines will relieve each other every two hours; they will be fitted with wireless, and, on sighting a hostile machine will, while moving to attack it, send repeatedly the call 'HN' followed by 'A' or 'S' [meaning Anzac or Suvla] . . . one scout will stand ready to move at short notice and on receipt of the signal will immediately proceed to Anzac or Suvla to assist in drawing off the hostile aircraft and to engage other hostile machines which may be attempting to reconnoitre in the area.

Arthur's No. 2 Wing submitted reports showing compliance with Sykes' orders while the lack of response from No. 3 Squadron indicated the continued rift with Charles. In his memoirs written after the war, Charles describes himself as doing what he enjoyed most:

On the 18th I took up a 500 lb bomb on a Henri Farman; this was by far the biggest bomb that up to date had ever been dropped by an aeroplane in the war. The Henri took it up like a bird, much to my delight. I searched for over half an hour between ANZAC and the port of Kilia Liman looking for a suitable target at which to drop it; but there seemed to be a lack that day of objects worthwhile. Finally I selected a long building from which smoke was appearing, deciding it must be full of Turks. I let go the bomb and decided to see the result. I had scored a direct hit; the building which was about 60 foot long, was absolutely wrecked. Amongst the ruins I saw no fewer than three bayonets sticking up between the bricks.

Sykes' Preliminary Instructions called for continuous overlapping flights from dawn to dusk with special reconnaissance and early warning of enemy activity at the Galatia aerodrome. He divided responsibilities between both wings by giving them either morning or afternoon patrolling; it was up to the commanders to apportion their aircraft. Charles followed orders, but did not file a report. However he did mention his contribution in his memoirs: 'I can safely say that we kept up a continuous patrol during daylight, and no enemy ever came close.'

Winter weather was a significant factor in the air war. Cloud cover, occasionally as low as 600 feet, and ground mist reduced observation from both the dominant ridge-lines and from the air. On 14 December, Commander Busk, one of Arthur's pilots, reported that he had been unable to observe enemy trenches 'despite varying my altitude from 8,000 feet to 1,000 feet, a heavy cloud bank prevented observation of the ground'. Post-mission reports comment on visibility from 4 December to 20 December telling of winter weather patterns with dense cloud from

1800 feet to a ceiling of 8000 feet, while the terrain was continually obscured with a heavy ground mist. Thirteen missions for 18 December describe low cloud at 1500 feet with a heavy haze obscuring observation and note that no enemy aeroplanes were seen on patrol. Flight Lieutenant Buss and Second Lieutenant Bourne of No. 2 Wing conducted an:

Anti-Aircraft guard of SUVLA & ANZAC

18 December 1915
Avro 1043
2 pm until 3.30 pm.

Unable to do reconnaissance, owing to clouds. No hostile aircraft seen.

Low cloud and poor visibility were reported continually throughout the day. Rather than conducting a contest of strength between the two services, it was fortunate for Sykes' aviators that the Turkish Air Service was busy assembling airframes unpacked from cases. The Turks were reluctant to risk these new machines in poor weather conditions—coincidentally, just as the withdrawal from Suvla and Anzac was in progress. The last flight for the day was:

No. 3 Wing Flying Report

Flight Commander Smyth-Pigott
H5
18 December 1915

Orders: Search for hostile submarine off SUVLA POINT. Reconnaissance at dusk and after dark of SUVLA area.

No sign of the submarine, saw a school of porpoises. I was fired at by our own troops sustaining one hit to my machine.

No night patrols were conducted as both the enemy and the air service rarely flew at night without lunar illumination and in poor visibility.

On the last day the RNAS flew 19 missions. Flying reports describe poor visibility and no enemy aeroplanes were seen aloft. In the morning constant anti-aircraft patrols kept watch for enemy aeroplanes. None was seen. In the afternoon, missions were skewed towards scouting the Turkish reserve areas in order to identify movement of enemy troops towards Anzac and Suvla. Pilots and observers told of nil sightings of Turkish troops along the roads and approaches. These reports provided some relief to the Dardanelles Army:

No. 2 Wing Flying Report

Flight Sub Lieutenant Munday
3.25 p.m. to 4.30 p.m. 19 December 1915

Orders: Search for troops reported moving from Kilid Bahr to ANZAC. Four 16 lb bombs taken.

Patrolled from ANZAC to KILID BAHR for 30 mins. Saw no troops, either on roads or adjacent country.

Flight Commander Smyth-Pigott of No. 2 Wing conducted an evening mission from 6 pm to 8.30 pm. It was the final flight of the day. He flew over the olive grove and its hidden artillery batteries:

> Orders: Fly over SUVLA and ANZAC to keep down gunfire.

> Muzzle flashes from enemy batteries reduced when my aeroplane was over the enemy lines. Many more flashes in the Helles sector than at ANZAC.

The withdrawal from the ANZAC sector was a complete success with the Turkish 5th Army surprised by the enemy's departure. Liman von Sanders was woken on the morning of 20 December by his Chief of Staff and told the news. Sir Charles Monro was delighted with the (unattributed) Australian plan:

> The night was perfectly calm with a slight haze over the moon, an additional stroke of good luck, as there was a full moon on that night. Soon after dark the covering ships were all in position, and the final withdrawal began. At 1.30 a.m. the withdrawal of the rear parties commenced from the front trenches at Suvla and the left of Anzac. Those on the right of Anzac who were nearer the Beach remained in position until 2 a.m. By 5.30 a.m. the last man had quitted the trenches . . . At Suvla every gun, vehicle and animal was embarked, and all that remained was a small stock of supplies which were burnt.

Sergeant Robert Hunter, 6th Light Horse Regiment, described his experience of the evacuation to his parents:

THE ESCAPE

Cairo
9 January 1916

My dear Mother and Father

. . . things seemed to get a bit unsettled and we noticed units being shifted about, and all men at all sick being taken away; . . . later on we noticed men being taken away in fairly large numbers, and heavy guns being taken to the beach. Of course we all had theories of our own . . . but it was not till we saw men's clothing, equipment, guns and all sorts of things going, that we realised something was really being done, and we were being taken off the peninsula and then towards the last, ammunition of all sorts, shells and rifle cartridges, bombs and all kinds of explosions were to be seen, or being thrown into the sea, it seemed an awful shame and waste to see thousands of pounds of stuff thrown into the sea, but of course it was better there than in the Turk's hands.

. . . there we were, 10 out of each squadron, and an officer, left to hold probably thousands of Turks, only fifty yards, and in some places only about 14 yards from us.

It was a glorious night, bright moonlight, and we looked down on the sea as calm as Sydney Harbour, like glass almost . . . everything seemed so peaceful and clear that it showed up the ridiculous position we seemed in by contrast. And so we manned our firing line about one man per 20 yards or more and kept up a desultory fire, and a keen lookout. Every now and then old Beachy Bill, a Turkish gun, boomed out and sent a shell along the beach, as if to let us know they were awake. We all had to wear socks over our boots as mufflers when marching out. Abdul must either have had no knowledge of what was going on, or else was misguided, because at 2:15 we got ready and soon after fired our final shots and left, wearing socks, moccasins, bits of underpants, sleeves of shirts and all manner of things round our feet, we had several pieces of halting and got safely to the boats at 3:10, all were on board ready to move out, and then the fireworks started. The fuses for blowing up various mines and guns, were timed for then or after that time, and first there was an explosion and then one of our artillery pieces was made useless, and then another, then a terrific explosion blew the whole of a neck of land out which had connected part of our position with the Turks, the mines here were about 50 feet deep and about 2 and a half tons of gun-cotton was used, goodness knows how many Turks went up, as our mines and tunnels went right under their trenches, then after other explosions, a pier up at Suvla Bay lit up and was apparently stacked up with shells and when they started to go off, there was a display, and all the time our little destroyer kept such a strong light between us and the Turks that they could not see us, though embarking almost under their noses. For a long time we could hear Abdul still firing away; apparently not then knowing we were all gone. Rifles were left set in all the firing lines, timed to go off at intervals after we left and no doubt this puzzled him a little . . .

From your very loving boy
Robert.

Sykes ordered missions over the deserted beaches of Suvla and Anzac on 20 December to report the Turkish response.

The weather now cleared for a few days. Aerial reports told of the movement of troops and guns southwards towards the front line at Helles.

The success of Cyril Brudenell White's ruse encouraged a decision to evacuate IX Corps from Cape Helles on 6 January 1916 and Sykes was tasked with providing air support. The RNAS had significantly more difficulty supporting the British IX Corps' silent withdrawal. Sir Charles Monro was aware of the growing threat Turkish aeroplanes posed to the withdrawal at Helles:

> The situation on the Peninsula had not materially changed owing to our withdrawal from Suvla and Anzac, except that there was a marked increased activity in aerial reconnaissance over our positions, and the islands of Mudros and Imbros, and that hostile patrolling of our trenches was more frequent and daring.

The enemy finally won air superiority in the first week of January as the RNAS suffered in unequal aerial combats against superior airframes. Aviators contested the airspace over 'the vineyard' and V Beach. Casualties mounted:

2 Wing RNAS
3168 Nieuport 10

20 December

Aircraft shot down over Suvla

Sub Lieutenant Beeson Killed in Action; Petty Officer O Auger Wounded in Action

Erich Serno's Turkish Air Service entered an aggressive phase from 20 December, peaking just at the point of the withdrawal from Helles on 9 January. Up until December the Turkish Air Service had flown 150 missions dropping over 200 bombs. The 1st Aircraft Company at Galatia had eight operational airframes following the arrival of two Albatros C1 *Kampfflugzuege* (fighter aircraft). The addition of Fokker Eindeckers significantly changed the balance of air power. The newly formed unit Jasta 6 was now fully operational: three Fokker Eindeckers were ready for flight as soon as there was a break in the cloud cover. British Flying Reports up until the New Year make no mention of a monoplane, probably because no pilot survived the engagement. A variant of biplane was, however, described in reports. Sykes' aviators found themselves in an unequal contest once again with the Albatros C1 and had to exert significant effort to meet this new threat. On Christmas day a Voisin 8502 was spotting when it 'was attacked by a hostile machine. Before I could get into position he had dived underneath me where it was impossible to fire at him.' A Bristol scout went to his aid:

No. 2 Wing Flying Reports
Bristol 1262

25 December 1915

Sighted hostile machine attacking 8502 Voisin. Dove towards the machine which had left Voisin and was coming towards me . . . Hostile machine was a tractor biplane, grey in colour with top plane larger than bottom and swept back towards trailing edge. Pilot appeared to be seated in front and passenger, with machine gun behind.

On 27 December Sykes reported the troubling news: aircraft were not returning to the Cape Kephalo aerodromes.

The Turkish Air Service had recently received major reinforcements consisting of large numbers of German fighting machines manned by pilots who, judging from their methods of manoeuvre, had gained experience of aerial warfare in other theatres. Missions were flown to protect the slower and more vulnerable Henri Farman pushers from this new threat. A representative flight occurred on 29 December:

> No. 3 Wing Flying Report
> Bristol 1262
>
> 29 December 1915
>
> Orders: protect spotting machine against attack and patrol Helles.

Despite these efforts, four air service aeroplanes were shot down in the first two weeks of January, effectively placing air superiority in the hands of the Turkish Air Service at the point of departure, just as Sykes had foreseen. Turkish records show a total of 17 reconnaissance flights over December and January.

To make matters more acute Charles Samson, Richard Davies VC, Reginald Marix, Gordon Thomson and three other experienced pilots were ordered home in January before the withdrawal of IX Corps. Captain Keith Jopp was returned, without ceremony, to Egypt and his artillery battery. Prior to his departure, Charles recommended that No. 2 and 3 Wings be amalgamated because of the lack of experienced aircrew. A junior officer aged 21 was left in command of No. 3 Wing during the withdrawal at Cape

Helles. After ten months' continuous flying, Charles was finally forced to rest:

> I said farewell to Imbros, I can safely say, with regret, although I had had enough. I felt by no means well, and hadn't been right for some time. I was immediately prostrate with jaundice, and had a beastly journey home, lying in my cabin praying for a submarine to end my distressing condition. Davies and Thomson between them got me home. I came suddenly to life in the Pullman car immediately we left Folkestone, and shouted for eggs and bacon.

The RNAS was in sharp decline in the first week of January and could not prevent the enemy overflying Cape Helles. Despite this, the early stages of the evacuation proceeded smoothly, as Sir Charles Monro wrote in his post-evacuation report:

> The evacuation, following the same system as was practised at Suvla and Anzac, proceeded without delay. The French Infantry remaining on the Peninsula were relieved on the night of the 1st-2nd January, and were embarked by the French Navy on the following nights. Progress, however, was slower than had been hoped, owing to delays caused by accident and the weather . . . the same time strong winds sprang up which interfered materially with work on the beaches. The character of the weather now setting in offered so little hope of a calm period of any duration, that General Sir W. Birdwood arranged with Admiral Sir J. de Robeck for the assistance of some Destroyers in order to accelerate the progress of re-embarkation. They then determined to fix the final stage

of the evacuation for 8 January, or for the first fine night after that date.

Reconnaissance remained a priority despite the dangers of unequal combat. Most of these were short-range flights to assess the movement of Turkish troops as an indicator that a sustained attack on the Helles sector was imminent. Aircraft spotting continued to mask the Helles withdrawal prior to 9 January 1916, despite winter weather forcing more than half of these flights to be abandoned. Naval shelling played an important role in covering the British front lines.

The Turkish 5th Army responded to the evacuation of the northern sector by re-orientating its divisions south-wards. General Liman von Sanders ordered his staff to plan an assault in the south with four divisions. The Turkish 5th Army anticipated that the British were withdrawing and attacked the depleted lines. On 7 January the Southern Group launched its assault but its infantry was repulsed following heavy naval gunfire support, which convinced Liman von Sanders that the British were not in the process of with-drawing. Reports from his own pilots and observers told him otherwise as Turkish aeroplanes were able to overfly the Cape Helles trenches. Looking down, the ruse was exposed; the trenches appeared to have emptied. But the ground attack was strongly repulsed by heavy artillery and naval bombardment using large stockpiles of remaining shells and, in the face of this level of resistance, the Turkish assault was abandoned in the belief that the British were staying. Monro reported the Turkish attack, noting that it was a half-hearted affair:

> On 7 January the enemy developed heavy artillery fire on the trenches held by the 13th Division, while the Asiatic guns shelled those occupied by the Royal Naval

Division. The bombardment, which was reported to be the heaviest experienced since we landed in April, lasted from noon until 5 p.m., and was intensive between 3 p.m. and 3.30. Considerable damage was done to our parapets and communication trenches, and telephone communications were interrupted. At 3.30 p.m. two Turkish mines were sprung near Fusilier Bluff, and the Turkish trenches were seen to be full of men whom their officers appeared to be urging to the assault. No attack, however, was developed except against Fusilier Bluff, where a half-hearted assault was quickly repulsed. Our shortage of artillery at this time was amply compensated for by the support received from the fire of the supporting naval squadron.

Turkish 5th Army command was again taken by surprise, only reacting on the morning as the last British troops withdrew. Without doubt, had they known the British were escaping, the Turkish guns would have targeted the beaches. Stores were detonated just as dawn's early light broke over the peninsula. The last man to step off the peninsula was Lieutenant General Sir Frederick Stanley Maude, commander of the 13th Division. He had decided that he and his headquarters staff would be the last to leave. To the exasperation of all waiting in the last boat at W Beach, Maude was over two hours late. He caught his bags in barbed wire and was delayed extricating himself and his baggage in the darkness. He reached the lighter just as dawn was breaking. Ribald verse was written in his honour:

Come into the lighter, Maude,
For the fuse has long been lit,
Come into the lighter, Maude,

And never mind your kit,
I've waited here an hour or more,
The news that your march is over.
The sea runs high, but what care I,
It's better to be sick than blown sky high,
So jump into the lighter, Maude,
The allotted time is flown,
Come into the lighter, Maude,
I'm off in the launch alone,
I'm off in the lighter a-lone.

Now that the Dardanelles Army had left the peninsula, Sykes' hopes of maintaining a strong RNAS presence were dashed. His Air Headquarters was disestablished and the two wings amalgamated on 27 January 1916. Sykes wrote to the Chief of the General Staff at General Headquarters, Dardanelles Army, now evacuated to Mudros, with the news:

> I have the honour to report that the Admiralty has decided that the headquarters RNAS will now, in view of the army's withdrawal from the peninsula, no longer be required.

Arthur Longmore's No. 2 Wing was left in place and absorbed aeroplanes and supplies from Charles' No. 3 Wing whose members returned to England. Arthur's wing remained to contribute to the Salonika campaign and to patrol the straits watching for the emergence of *Goeben* into the Mediterranean. Arthur's wing remained in theatre throughout the war and became No. 62 Wing on the formation of the RAF. Istanbul was eventually bombed although, happily, no damage was done to the mosques and beautiful architecture of the city. Air stations were maintained at Imbros and Mudros to continue supporting the fleet.

The last man to die on the Gallipoli Peninsula was an Australian pilot. He was killed at 4000 feet by a young German air ace, *Hauptmann* Hans Joachim Buddecke. Hans was a famous pilot, gaining his first victories with Max Immelmann in France flying the Fokker Eindecker. He was an adventurer, commissioning in his father's 115 Lifeguard Infantry Regiment in 1904, where he stayed only six years. He left, against his parents' wishes, on a steamship for the United States. There he worked in an automobile factory, saving to pay for his flying lessons. At the outbreak of war, Buddecke returned home and was commissioned as a pilot in the German Air Service flying in combat over France. In October 1915 he volunteered to head a new unit, Jasta 6, comprising three Fokker Eindeckers, which was to be sent to Gallipoli. The aeroplanes arrived in crates at Galatia aerodrome in early December, but poor weather grounded the machines; they were too precious to be wrecked in an accident.

Buddecke was 25 when he flew his Fokker E3 over Gallipoli. In the small cockpit of his monoplane he sat upright, the single wing below the main fuselage providing him excellent vision above and to each side. After Buddecke completed his simple pre-flight checks, the wooden propeller was swung by the engineer. The rotary engine coughed into life. Buddecke could feel the torque as the engine—attached to the propeller—revolved in increasing revolutions. The fabric of the monoplane trembled; the machine wanted to madly pull to the right. Buddecke, his left foot compensating on the rudder bar, shot across the grass strip and into the grey skies above. Word had reached him that the British had pulled out of the peninsula. He went hunting for enemy machines to exact his revenge. Turning south and climbing, he could feel the uneasiness of his aeroplane; it was essentially unstable. Turning was difficult. Max Immelmann had discovered the rising turn—the pilot shot upwards, standing on the tail, then fell in the new direction, left or right. This 'Immelmann turn' allowed the machine to pounce on the enemy from above like a hawk.

Over Cape Helles, Buddecke saw a Henri Farman pusher. Its pilot, Sydney-born Horace Brimsmead, was one of the pilots of whom Charles Samson had despaired. He was new to the Dardanelles and had fewer than 20 hours of flying experience. Brimsmead had been ordered to report on the Turkish reaction to the evacuation. This was his first flight over the peninsula. He looked down at the spider web of trenches. The *River Clyde* remained marooned off V Beach. Shell holes dotted the barren waste at the toe which had been stripped of vegetation.

Brimsmead's observer was also looking over the side as tiny brown figures swarmed towards the coast looking for booty. Royal Navy warships were waiting off the coast to launch their shells, particularly as so many of the enemy were thoughtlessly walking in the open. The hate was continuing. The observer had belayed 150 feet of aerial behind the aeroplane. Targeting was about to be tapped on the Morse key. Brimsmead was too inexperienced to look over his shoulder, or to look above. A 22-year-old sub-lieutenant, he had only commissioned in the RNAS on 11 June 1915.

Buddecke swooped from above. His Fokker had twin 7.62mm machine-guns mounted on the nose of his aeroplane, which fired directly through the propeller arc. An interrupter gear ensured he did not break the wooden shaft as it spun at enormous speeds. Pressing the button on his control column, he was momentarily deafened as the twin machine-guns spat directly at the two men sitting in the front of the enemy pusher. The observer slumped forward. In panic Brimsmead attempted a steep turn; the aeroplane banked left, slowing.

Buddecke continued his dive behind the enemy machine. He pulled up and shot into the air behind his target. At the apex of his climb he gently pushed the right rudder pedal with his foot and the machine dropped. He now faced his enemy from the other side and fired heavily into the engine and airframe. The wings simply folded. To his surprise, the machine twisted and Brimsmead fell over the side. The figure fell to earth. The crumpling machine followed. Buddecke was awarded the *Pour Le Merite* or 'Blue Max' for his efforts.

Colonel Kannengiesser was now free to stand and move about in daylight. The British had withdrawn in the night. Whooping Turkish soldiers rushed forward, desperate to claim the incredible wealth rumoured to have been left behind at Ari Burnu and eager to see what they could find. Then the German colonel looked into the sky:

> In the air, a battle between aeroplanes which ended in the destruction of the English. We saw the body of the aviator fall like a doll, with outstretched arms and legs, into the sea, the aeroplane fluttering behind. Torpedo boats hastened up, sought vainly for the aviator and took the aeroplane in tow. That was my final picture of Gallipoli.
>
> I feel that the reader must agree with me that never in the course of the world's previous history has a campaign been fought so rich in dramatic pictures of such differing types of warfare which, in spite of its wealth of incidents, has been compressed into such narrow limits

of time, and space. It is in itself a real treasure trove of experience in the numerous branches of military science, because every conceivable class of weapons was used here, including floating, flying, and those below water.

CHAPTER 10

A hot wash-up

Almost since General Maude finally stepped into the last boat to leave the shores of the Gallipoli Peninsula, debate has raged over the execution of this failed campaign. Among the plethora of published material that has sought to provide answers, little has been written on the air war and the role of the RNAS. This book is an attempt to kick-start further debate.

It is difficult to find any phase of the Gallipoli campaign in which aeroplanes or balloons were not intimately involved. In balance, the most significant contribution by aviators of all descriptions lay in providing intelligence on the enemy. Thanks to Harry Strain and Bernard Isaac, reporting was timely and used in the planning of each stage of operations—from the two amphibious assaults to denouement and withdrawal. This alone was decisive in the Allied defence of its tenuous holdings, allowing the army to choose its own time and means of departure.

The total mission count for the RNAS from 17 February

1915 to 9 January 1916 was 2314 missions. The greatest effort was devoted to 726 reconnaissance missions which comprised 31 per cent, followed in descending order by 644 spotting missions at 28 per cent, 242 bombing missions at 11 per cent, 228 other or experimental missions at 10 per cent, 146 photography missions at 6 per cent, 118 anti-aircraft patrols or 5 per cent, 115 transit missions at 5 per cent, and finally 95 anti-submarine missions at 4 per cent of the mission total. Reconnaissance easily accounted for the majority of effort with reporting on the enemy a secondary duty of all missions flown, as flying reports attest. The air campaign was not independent of the surface battles. The contribution of the aviators was thus measured against the achievements and failures of Allied naval and military forces.

The failure of the campaign led to the Dardanelles Commission in 1916 which investigated the cause of such enormous losses of men and matériel. Its report to Parliament in 1917 concluded, quite blandly, that insufficient planning had been undertaken with too few resources for such a campaign and that it should not have proceeded. Over 30 witnesses were examined from September to December 1916, ranging from Winston Churchill to Sir Ian Hamilton. However, no representatives of the RNAS were called. In his deliberations Hamilton blamed the lack of intelligence for the casualties on 25 April. A failure of intelligence on the enemy was an acceptable cause of campaign failure. But Hamilton was unable to use this excuse for the Suvla landing; the report concluded that the intelligence gathered was timely and, ultimately, proved accurate. This report comprised the first official British reaction.

Bernard made a written submission to the Dardanelles Commission. He did so from a sense of outrage, rather than as a response to a formal request:

NOTES ON DARDANELLES EXPEDITION

From 28th March, 1915, till about the end of August, the No. 3 Wing of the Royal Naval Air Service, which consisted of twenty officers and 200 men, did all the flying that was demanded by the naval and military forces. There were too few efficient machines and too few pilots, but during this time 100,000 miles were flown over and all reconnaissances of all roads, camps and gun emplacements were made from Helles to Bulair. In addition spotting for Naval and field guns, patrol for submarines and enemy aircraft, and to photograph the trenches roads and etc over the whole of the peninsula.

Hamilton complained in his earlier despatches that with the exception of what he could see from the top of a mast, he had no reconnaissance!

Following the Dardanelles Commission a further investigation, the 'Mitchell Report', was commissioned in 1919 to examine lessons learnt in preparation for future amphibious operations. Its formal title was: *Report of the Committee Appointed to Investigate the Attacks delivered on the Enemy Defences of the Dardanelles Straits, 1919.* As a tribute to its timelessness, its findings were re-examined in 1943 during the planning for D Day. On the investigative committee were six serving members including Group Captain Charles Samson of the RAF, representing the role of the RNAS. Charles emphasised the importance of bombing by his squadron, and the pressure it exerted on enemy supplies. He did so at the expense of the role of aerial intelligence. Typically, Charles completely ignored Frederick Sykes' role in establishing the Air Headquarters. Charles finally had his revenge.

Both General Sir Ian Hamilton and General Otto Liman von Sanders published their memoirs, and both minimised the effects of the air war, although for different reasons. During the campaign Hamilton deliberately excluded aerial intelligence from his despatches. It was an easy explanation for failure. Several years after the end of the war and in the safety of his retirement, Hamilton published *Gallipoli Diary* which included details of the roles of aircraft and even described his examination of aerial photography of the landing beaches on 14 April, but couched this apparent contradiction in terms of an interesting sideshow. On the opposing side, Liman von Sanders, as the victor, in *Five Years in Turkey*, ignored the air war and focused on the great land battles which he insisted he orchestrated. Another member of the German Military Mission, Hans Kannengiesser Pasha, catalogued the effects of the RNAS including the many 'near misses' he experienced on the receiving end of air activity.

An influential description of the air war over the Dardanelles was included in a chapter of British official air historian H. A. Jones' *The War in the Air: Being the story of the part played in the Great War by the Royal Air Force*. His study included the RNAS and the RFC prior to the formation of the RAF in April 1918. As an Oxford academic and a civilian, he corresponded with aviators and conducted face-to-face interviews. Jones owed much to the Mitchell Report, as his description of the air campaign reflected Charles Samson's personal narrative. He too focused on the air service's potentially strategic effect in its disruption of the Turkish supply lines. Jones was considerably influenced by Charles who was given the opportunity to correct the early script prior to its publication. In many ways, Jones' official history stood as a sentinel for some 80 years, containing the only complete and detailed narrative of the air war. Buried within his narrative was a startling proposition:

> Had these two weapons [Allied submarines and air-craft] been on the spot, in sufficient numbers to attack decisively the precarious Turkish communications to the peninsula, the enemy could not have stood his ground. Inadequate as they were, they nearly did prove decisive . . .

This sentiment is, however, off target. Jones was overly influenced by Charles and his homage to the power of the bomb—not the desk-bound work of typed intelligence reporting. Charles was consistent. His opinion is well known, retold by Hamilton in his *Gallipoli Diary* during his account of a visit to the Tenedos aerodrome on 14 April:

> If, requirement had been met, we had only a bomb-ing force at our disposal, the Gallipoli Peninsula, being a very limited space with only one road and two or three harbours on it, could probably be made unten-able. Commander Samson's estimate of a minimum force for this 'stunt', as he calls our great enterprise, is 30 good two-seater machines; 24 fighters; 40 pilots and 400 men. So equipped he reckons he could take the Peninsula by himself and save us all a vast lot of trouble.

Charles also compiled a personal memoir, *Fights and Flights*, a breathless firsthand description of the events of the cam-paign from his perspective. His memoir focused on the colourful personal drama of bombing missions and the occasional duel with the Turkish Air Service. As expected, Charles remained consistent in his minimising of the 'bookish' role of Bernard Isaac while ignoring his political enemy, Frederick Sykes.

Following the evacuation of Gallipoli, Sykes returned to the air battles of the RFC in France. When the RAF was established, Charles was once again outranked by his rival. Sykes rose to become the RAF's Chief of Air Staff and made an equally significant claim in his memoir, *Aviation in Peace and War*, published in 1922:

> When in future years the story of Helles and ANZAC and Suvla is weighed, it will, I think, appear that had the necessary air service been built up from the beginning and sustained, the Army and the Navy could have forced the Straits and taken Constantinople.

Given that such claims come from the official air historian and both Charles and Sykes, they should, perhaps, be accorded some examination.

The bombing campaign was the central pillar in the story of the air war at Gallipoli for over 90 years—Charles and Sykes eventually agreed on something. However, the bombing campaign was, in fact, spasmodic and ill defined until raids on the railways in November and shipping in December. Only one mission in ten was a specific bombing mission. The air service never had sufficient airframes or pilots to place significant pressure on the Turkish 5th Army's fighting potential or logistic supply. At no point were Turkish supplies in jeopardy from either aircraft bombing or the torpedoes of submarines. The Turkish 5th Army used an overland route and shipping continued to transit the Marmara. Daily Air Intelligence reports indicate that vessels were constantly observed at Maidos, Ak Bashi Liman, Gallipoli and Channakale.

Although it is perilous to question an eyewitness and a practitioner of Sykes' ability, his own reports remark on the importance of the Turkish overland route. This was enhanced with the opening of the railway and, although targeted by aeroplanes, was not interrupted. Supply columns were reported on the railways and roads servicing the peninsula and they proceeded largely without significant interference. Further, the Turks had the option of sea lines of communication, and Sykes' own reporting indicates that, on average, five or six vessels were observed unloading each day throughout the campaign.

Bombing attacks on Turkish logistics were ad hoc in nature and not systematically applied. Harry's and Bernard's diaries point to the varied nature of flying operations rather than a systematic targeting of ports. Bombing attacks, when they did occur, were mostly a by-product of the daily reconnaissance patrols to report enemy activity. Attacks on roads and bridges that provided the safest means of supply to the Turkish 5th Army proved pointless. In his memoirs, Charles describes in glowing terms the bombing and scattering of mule and camel columns. This was nothing more than delay and harassment. The official historian concluded that the bombing of roads was of little consequence as Turks used pack animals which nimbly sidestepped the craters. Similarly, the rather spectacular bombing attacks on the railway at Ferejik, which were raids of some daring and skill, produced nil results despite the effort involved. Bombing required an accuracy that was not possible with the technology available at that time. Turkish anti-aircraft fire kept aeroplanes at 7000 to 8000 feet, significantly reducing the probability of a strike without the use of aiming sights. Indeed, the air service dropped a relatively insignificant payload:

Number of Bombs	Weight
5	500lb
362	100 or 112lb
66	65lb
722	20lb

This amounted to more than 1150 bombs with a total weight of over 59,150 lb or almost 27 tons. It is clearly insufficient to halt supplies to an army the size of the Turkish 5th Army and force its withdrawal.

Such figures undermine both Sykes' and Charles' arguments. A (generous) successful strike rate of 5 per cent would suggest that as few as 50 or so targets were damaged or destroyed. Charles' own evidence in the Mitchell Report and his memoirs tell of only ten steamers and various smaller craft actually hit. While HMS *Ben-my-Chree*'s role in three successful strikes using the aerial delivered torpedo was a significant event and harbinger of the potential of air power, the three ships hit represented an insignificant dent in capability.

Contrary to Western expectations, the Turkish 5th Army was supplied by an efficient Lines of Communication Inspectorate that had access to supplies through large garrison cities. The Inspectorate moved its supply depot from the peninsula to Lapsaki (on the Asian shore, out of range of all guns) and used smaller coastal vessels or disembarked supplies during the day or at night, depending on the risk. Even coupled with a disruptive submarine campaign, effects on the flow of Turkish supplies were moderated with use of the railway and road systems. The Turkish soldier always had abundant ammunition and access to fresh water. Although the villages of Krithia, Kojadere, Boghali and Anafarta were destroyed by naval gunfire, the simple wellhead survived amid the rubble. Similarly, boxed ammunition, carried by dhows and small steamers and also by rail from the small arms factory at Istanbul, survived the many plans to strike it from the air.

Allied prisoner-of-war reports recorded the steady supply of simple foodstuffs to the front line. Even in the winter month of December, Turkish food was equal to, if not better than, Allied fare. Captured soldiers told of their victualling with a simple diet of beans, lentils, olives, currants, Levantine flat bread, Brazil nuts, raisins and, on every second day, a ration of meat, tea and sugar. Similarly, the Turkish soldier was issued with a winter uniform including a coat, new boots and woollen gloves before the onset of winter. Charles and Sykes may have based their belief in the fragility of Turkish supply on their own difficulties, coupled with their prejudices towards the orient.

Discussions of the effectiveness of aerial and submarine attacks on Turkish logistics are myopic unless they include examination of the Allied distribution system. From countless diary entries it is clear that the victualling of Allied troops on the peninsula, and even aviators in the safety of the Aegean islands, was in a permanent state of crisis. Diaries and letters home describe a supply situation characterised by monotony, deprivation and sickness. The simple fact remains that the antagonists did not fight on equal terms: the Allies fought a sustained campaign at the edge of empire, while the Turkish 5th Army fought much closer to its metropolis and supply bases. In fact the obverse was true: the Dardanelles Army was under constant pressure with its exposed beaches and the threat of U boats.

The bombing campaign did not come close to forcing the Turkish infantry from their trenches. The inaccuracy of bombing and the low tonnage was never likely to be more effective than artillery in maiming or killing infantry soldiers. Both sides dug deep trenches and revetments which offered very effective protection. However, bombing had a considerable psychological impact on exhausted Turkish units once recalled to camps behind the firing line. There is ample evidence of these rest camps being targeted as troops were camped in the open and more vulnerable to shrapnel. Colonel Kannengiesser recalled the psychological effect of the kite balloons with their ability to direct artillery fire—the mere sight of these balloons produced feelings of dread among his troops.

Apart from this, for the rank and file who fought the land battle, the air war was either an irrelevancy or a curiosity. Diary entries mentioning aeroplanes blossomed during periods of relative quiet in the trenches, but were absent during times of intense conflict. Aeroplanes were not directly involved in the infantry battle as close air support was not possible because of the level of inaccuracy. This explains why the air narrative is often absent from the latest genre of military histories based on soldiers' accounts. Missions were flown at high altitude to report on the movement of enemy reserves while targets were bombed some distance behind the front lines.

The effectiveness of long-range bombing was certainly recognised, however, and plans were discussed for the strategic bombing of Istanbul and its ammunition factory. At several points through the life of the campaign the bombing of the cartridge factory was considered but failed to mature because the means to conduct such a raid were not yet at hand. The Breguet was considered a possibility for such a raid, but its engine proved unreliable; irrespective of this, such a machine carrying 300lb of ordnance was a mere 'pipe dream'. Similarly, the concept of marrying seaplanes with submarines in the Sea of Marmara to extend their effective range was abandoned because of the high risk involved. The SSA Squadron was more likely to conduct a raid of psychological value but was never pressed into such service. Istanbul was eventually bombed in April 1916 by aeroplanes operating from Imbros, escalating to a series of raids throughout 1917.

Spotting correction, however, enjoyed more success in interrupting Turkish supplies. The shelling of docksides by warships corrected by the kite balloons resulted in the destruction of port installations and the surrounding houses in various port towns. But once the town was burnt and abandoned, the use of the dockside continued as the piers themselves had not been destroyed. Reports from the three kite balloon sections told of Turkish transports weighing anchor and steaming out of range when ships' captains were warned of the approaching balloon. This caused some disruption to daylight transhipment of goods, considering a balloon was aloft on average every second day of the campaign. However, such interruption was merely temporary as the transhipment could then occur at night without pause.

Aeroplane and balloon spotting as a means to direct naval gunnery and artillery onto military targets was certainly tactically significant. Spotting effectively began with the shelling of Turkish 3 Corps camps in an attempt to destroy the Turkish defences behind Z Beach on 19 April. Later in the campaign the critical shortage of artillery rounds made the accurate registration of artillery onto targets an important enabler. This role was clearly defined in Standing Orders at that time. Advances towards Krithia from late June onwards were made with the aid of range cards and data provided by the air service. Artillery correction based on photo-mosaics also improved accuracy. Such methodology was important given the extremely limited supply of ammunition, with shells often rationed to as few as two rounds per gun per day. The restrictions on expenditure of artillery and the close cooperation of the aeroplanes were features noted in aviators' accounts of the campaign. Nevertheless the artillery effort on the peninsula was never sufficient to allow domination of the ground war and played a diminutive role compared with the expenditure of ammunition on the Western Front. The several infantry assaults that defined the land campaign on the peninsula proceeded with a minimum of artillery registered by experienced air observers employing an increasingly effective system.

The three kite balloons featured significantly in naval gunfire support. The 120 missions flown by kite balloons, although only 5 per cent of total RNAS missions, under-represent their importance as a single day's flight lasted up to eight hours. Multiple ships made use of the balloon and its presence out to sea had a curtailing impact on Turkish activity for half the days the army was fighting on the peninsula. The use of the kite balloons in the direction of shelling enabled warships and artillery to strike targets outside visual range of land-based observers.

However, the true value of the air war lies in the realm of intelligence. All missions over disputed territory had an intelligence function, either as the primary or secondary objective. Following each mission, regardless of type, aircrew were questioned by the unit Intelligence Officer and this information was collated, assessed and distributed as intelligence reporting to army and naval units. This process was significant in the planning phase for the amphibious assaults of 25 April with the information graphically displayed on mapping. Similarly, intelligence on the opportunities presented at Suvla Bay was confirmed by reconnaissance missions and proved also to be correct. RNAS intelligence reports came in many forms, with the simplest and most direct form of information dissemination the typed post-mission report. By such a method, grid references supplied for Turkish gun batteries, trenches, redoubts, barbed-wire entanglements, troop movements, shipping movements, sea mines and the Nagara net were all reported in a timely fashion. There is no greater accolade to the effectiveness of the RNAS reconnaissance than its warning to ANZAC of the Turkish infantry assault of 19 May. This date was the high point of the RNAS contribution as it clearly demonstrated its role and importance on the battlefield. The RNAS robbed the Turkish 5th Army's Northern Group of the element of surprise and the attack was halted with punishing casualties. The Turkish 5th Army abandoned plans to push the invaders back into the sea until the infantry assault on a presumed lightly defended Cape Helles in January 1916. This fact alone should win the RNAS a place in the debate on the campaign.

The RNAS also conducted surveillance of particular areas of interest to the army and navy. Surveillance of the maritime approaches was of immediate interest to the navy which was supporting submarine operations in the Sea of Marmara and conducting anti-submarine patrols against German U boats. The seaplane flight was initially tasked with this duty until the arrival of the SSA Squadron which then assumed responsibility. The blimp conducted 46 missions from 12 September while SS7 prosecuted broad-ranging surveillance from Imbros westwards to protect Allied shipping transiting the Aegean. The SSA Squadron was undoubtedly viewed as a threat as it was targeted by the Turkish Air Service well out of proportion to its capability to affect the campaign.

The Turkish 1st Aircraft Company also benefitted from intelligence-gathering. Frequent flights to Imbros and

Mudros told of Allied build-up and preparations for offensive operations. From as early as 18 March to the overflying of British trenches at Cape Helles in January 1916, the Turkish Air Service provided warnings of impending movement. Until Turkish reports are translated, one of the better sources on the Turkish Air Service is included in Charles Samson's submission to the Mitchell Report. In March 1919 he visited Istanbul and toured Gallipoli interviewing Turkish staff officers, the gaps and assumptions in his reporting perhaps reflecting his departure in December before the Turkish Air Service won air superiority. In précis:

> During the early months enemy aircraft were inactive principally due to there being only three aeroplanes and one seaplane available. The average number in action during the last half of 1915 was 8 aeroplanes and one seaplane. Turkish aviators interviewed spoke very highly of the German pilots, and seemed impressed by their skill. There is no doubt from a combat point of view the German aeroplane was a better fighting machine than the majority of Allied aeroplanes except for the Nieuport and Bristol Scouts. No German aeroplane courted combat with an Allied aeroplane. In fact their one idea seemed to be to avoid aerial fighting. At aerial photography they were in 1915 certainly ahead of the British. Photographs seen at Constantinople were much better than ours. They paid a great deal of attention to bomb dropping especially in September when they kept up an attack on Kephalo both by day and night. The bombs were small of 20 lbs and at least 25 per cent dropped failed to explode. The enemy dropped 186 bombs resulting in the deaths of 5 officers and men, wounding 8, and killing 9 horses. There

is no doubt that a certain amount of moral effect was produced from these attacks.

The development of aerial photography was another important enabler in the stalled and failing campaign. Experimentation with aerial photography developed to a point in June whereby headquarters staff had an aid to understanding the complexity of terrain and defences arrayed against them. The photograph depicted the work and activity of the enemy to a certain date, time and place and was distributed to headquarters and the unit ordered to seize an objective, allowing certainty in operational planning. Without access to photography and its products, the Allied staff officer was effectively blind. The magnitude of this benefit is clear to those who visit the ANZAC Headquarters position at the entrance to Monash Valley. Even from the edge of Lone Pine, the view is blocked by the high ground once dominated by Turkish trenches. When a photograph taken in July is held in one hand, and the 1:10,000 scale trench map in the other, the value of aerial intelligence becomes immediate. There was no greater potential in payload than photographic plates.

The importance of the aerial perspective was seized on by a number of officers. The flight of Major Charles Villiers-Stuart on 14 April was an example of ANZAC recognition and was emblematic of the importance of the aerial perspective to its two divisional headquarters. Later Sir Ian Hamilton, William Birdwood, John de Robeck, Hugh Simpson Baikie and several submarine captains also recognised its value. More than this, aerial photography spread the aerial perspective to a wider audience. Crucially, the photograph allowed detailed study, under a magnifying glass, of points of significance and changes over time.

Much has been written about mapping since the publication of the British official history. Most opinions and
comments have rested with the description of the early
1:40,000 scaled maps printed by the Egyptian War Office
in March 1915. But this was not the sole map-producing
facility; the Mediterranean Expeditionary Force's Map
Department produced accurate mapping on the 1:20,000
scale from captured Turkish maps. This was initially cor-
roborated with aerial photography depicting defensive
works. These maps were further improved by complex and
deliberate aerial mapping missions to produce a 1:10,000
scale map of a high degree of integrity.

Apart from the final withdrawal phases, infrequent anti-
aircraft patrols were evidence that the Turkish Air Service
was considered a nuisance rather than a direct threat to
operations. From the beginning of the naval attempt on
17 February until late December, the RNAS enjoyed control
of the air, a feature recognised by Frederick Sykes. Anti-
aircraft patrols accounted for 5 per cent of total flights, with
the majority of these flights conducted to deny the enemy
reconnaissance of the beachheads during the withdrawal of
the Dardanelles Army. Up to this point the greatest threat
to the RNAS came from local conditions including weather,
dust and exhaustion of aircrew. Even the SSA Squadron on
Cape Kephalo, which was subjected to approximately eight
air raids, was removed not because of the threat of bombing, but because of a rent in the canvas hangar caused by
persistent strong winds. Both air services engaged in tit-
for-tat bombing of each other's aerodromes, but because of
inaccuracies characteristic of such missions, little damage
was actually caused.

Clearly the RNAS was not alone. A French escadrille
operated from Tenedos from late May, although it provided

only a small addition to air capability. Focus on the RNAS is valid as it provided the greater air capability, prosecuting 80 per cent of all missions flown. It had significantly more aeroplanes than the French escadrille, with a ratio greater than 12:1. Analysis of the Turkish Air Service and the French escadrille is beyond the scope of this work and I leave it to others who have the linguistic ability to research foreign language archival material.

Jones, as the official air historian, makes other claims that appear to be more bravado than fact. He writes, for example, that 'The air service, as the year wore on, became so strong that it was able to deny to the enemy any sight of an intention to withdraw from the peninsula.' However, by December 1915, Sykes' air service was in serious decline. At the same time the Turkish Air Service's fighting ability had improved significantly with the arrival of new aeroplanes following the opening of the rail route from Germany. The Dardanelles Army was fortunate that winter weather affected flight operations in mid-December, or the Turkish Air Service would have won air superiority far earlier. Sykes contradicted Jones' claims (based on Jones' reliance on Charles' bombast) in his final report in January 1916:

> If the process of evacuation at Suvla, ANZAC, and Helles had resulted as was expected, in heavy fighting, the Royal Naval Air Service could not have met the additional requirements for spotting machines etc and disastrous results might have ensued.

The RNAS experience in the Dardanelles was characterised by experimentation. The deployment of *Ark Royal* and *Manica* in the naval phase was on the cusp of emerging technologies. *Ark Royal* conducted its first flight evolutions at Malta en route, while 1 Experimental Kite Section inflated *Manica*'s balloon for the first time following its arrival in theatre. Consequently, this emerging technology did not meet early expectations as there was no previous experience of correcting gunfire from warships onto land-based targets. Experimentation flourished in the Dardanelles as distance from supply depots in England encouraged the 'make and mend' mentality of the navy. Even the projection of air power at such distance from supporting bases was considered unique and favourably endorsed in the April Air Department conference.

The development of ordnance in theatre was not unique to Gallipoli. Even so, the design of an incendiary device to destroy 'Beachy Bill' and parachute mines to sink the Nagara net demonstrate RNAS interest in creating weapons. In the same vein the development of an aerial torpedo was also entirely experimental and was a brilliant but fleeting achievement as it could not be replicated. By far the most profound achievement, however, was the slow but efficient development of spotting warships onto targets beyond visual range, particularly with the use of aerial photography to produce accurate corrections.

But the colourful panoply of the air service and its order of battle also had its disappointments. The failure of the RNAS to contribute more effectively during the August offensive was its greatest disappointment. The arrival of IX Corps was not matched with a commensurate number of aeroplanes. At this critical point there was also a crisis of command with both Charles Samson and Frederick Sykes absent. The air service could do little but exist on the periphery as the ANZAC assault on Sari Bair ground to a halt short of the objective. More effective intelligence reporting could have been achieved with an efficient command structure in place.

Charles and Sykes were looking in the wrong place to construct an argument for inclusion of the air war in the Gallipoli narrative. The RNAS was at the very centre of the fight for information. From the very beginning of the naval campaign, seaplanes were seen as a new mechanical means to fix the locations of Turkish defences on charts and mapping. Nor does the inclusion of the air services in the Gallipoli narrative detract from the central role of the army in its struggle for the high ground, although its exclusion leaves the narrative much poorer. It had 'no portentous ifs' but created for the military the conditions to remain by denying the enemy the element of surprise. This neutralised at least one of the advantages of terrain. Likewise, the RNAS was ordered to deny the Turkish 5th Army indicators of the withdrawal and succeeded admirably. Indeed it is difficult to find any point in the campaign where it did not contribute. It is tragically fitting that the last man to die in the campaign was an Australian aviator.

Ninety-eight years have passed since Horace Brimsmead fell to his death. War is still a terrifying business. The Gallipoli campaign left behind tranquil cemeteries surrounded by brambles and wild thyme which belie the agony of their origins. From the trenches behind Anzac Cove rose Mustafa Kemal who became the first president of a powerful modern Turkey. With the benefit of wartime experience, Mustafa masterfully kept his country from the furnace of the Second World War. Today Istanbul stands, a peaceful and enchanting city.

It is ten years since the Iraq War erupted with shellfire that blew apart the heart of Baghdad. On Anzac Day 2013 I attended a reunion with my squadron and mulled over triumphs and tragedies past, just as the surviving ANZACs did at the first Anzac Day commemorations following the end of the Great War. In the aftermath of the Iraq War the stoic Iraqi people have embraced democracy with over 100 political parties vying for representation in the Iraqi parliament. There is hope. There is hope also that the terrible face of world war is one that will not reappear. From the devastation of mass conflict come the sweet fruits of peace.

APPENDIX A

Turkish artillery batteries identified by the RNAS up to 18 April in the vicinity of Gaba Tepe

Grid Reference	Size	Comments
224 Q	Gun emplacement with 1 gun position; many guns?	ANZAC Cove
224 O 8	Field work 1 gun emplacement	
224 S	7 gun battery	ANZAC Cove
224 O	1 gun	Inland ANZAC Cove
225 M	2 guns	South Kojadere
226 N	Field Artillery Brigade	Ivo Boghali
211 P	7 gun emplacements with 3 guns	Gaba Tepe point
212 L 2	4 guns	Gaba Tepe
212 I 9 to M 7	1 gun battery and 4 empty emplacements (empty?)	Gaba Tepe
212 C	4 gun pits	Inland Gaba Tepe
212 D	6 gun pits	Inland Gaba Tepe

Grid Reference	Size	Comments
213 F	4 gun battery facing west	Off Boghali–Maidos road
202 K	4 empty gun emplacements	South Asmak Dere coast
202 P 1 and O 9	2 four-gun batteries	South Asmak Dere coast
202 S	4 gun battery & 4 empty emplacements	Overlooking coast south Gaba Tepe & Asmak Dere
203 A 7	4 emplacements occupied	As above
203 M	2 gun battery	Off Gaba Tepe road
203 X	4 occupied emplacements	Kilid Bahr Plateau
203 X 8	8 gun battery in emplacements (now complete)	Kilid Bahr Plateau
203 G 2	1 four-gun battery	Kilid Bahr Plateau
204 R 5 and R 8	1 four-gun battery & infantry redoubt	Kilid Bahr Plateau
205 A	1 four-gun battery	Maidos & East coast
205 M	2 gun batteries & redoubt	South Maidos
193 O 5	2 four-gun batteries	W coast & Gaba Tepe road
193 Z	1 four-gun battery	W coast & Gaba Tepe road
194 C	4 gun pits	Kilid Bahr Plateau
194 W	4 gun pits	Kilid Bahr Plateau
195 K	8 gun battery with arrow pointing SE	Kilid Bahr Plateau
196 G	4 gun battery facing west	Kilid Bahr Plateau
196 J	Concealed guns	Kilid Bahr Plateau
196 J	4 gun battery	Kilid Bahr Plateau
196 J	6 guns	Kilid Bahr Plateau
196 O	Concealed battery	Kilid Bahr Plateau
196 O	2 gun battery	Kilid Bahr Plateau
196 O	Concealed battery	Kilid Bahr Plateau

APPENDIX B

Turkish military camps identified by the RNAS up to 18 April in the vicinity of Gaba Tepe

Grid reference	Size	Comments
224 N	20 tents	Second Ridge
225 M	Camp (no numbers)	Village of Kojadere
226 B	100 tents	North Boghali side of road
226 O	Hutments covering ¼ mile	West Boghali village by road
226 R	200 tents (6 battalions)	South Boghali village by road
226 T	50 tents	Boghali side of road
212 L 5	20 tents	Gaba Tepe
214 B	20 tents	Kilia Liman Bay
205 T	Camp of 32 tents	
202 T	Camp 15 tents	Peren Ovasi
203 R	32 tents	Peren Ovasi

Grid reference	Size	Comments
203 T	Large Camp 700 tents—not seen 21 April.	Kilid Bahr Plateau
204 D	50 tents	Akmaz Dagh ivo Maidos
203 F	200 to 300 tents	Akmaz Dagh ivo Maidos
203 O	80 tents (HQ)	Fruit Orchards ivo Maidos
193 R	New camp of 400 tents	Chana Ovasi
193 W 6	New camp of 400 tents	Chana Ovasi
195 S 6	Camp of 450 tents	Jisoi

APPENDIX C

Aircraft numbers – 25 April 1915

Ark Royal's seaplane flight

Number	Aircraft	Engine
136	Short Folder Seaplane	200hp Canton Unne
161	Short Folder Seaplane	200hp Canton Unne
172	Wight Pusher Seaplane	200hp Canton Unne
173	Wight Pusher Seaplane	200hp Canton Unne
176	Wight Pusher Seaplane	200hp Canton Unne
807	Sopwith 807 Folder Seaplane	100hp Gnome
808	Sopwith 807 Folder Seaplane	100hp Gnome
922	Sopwith 807 Folder Seaplane	100hp Gnome
1201	Sopwith Tabloid	80hp Gnome
1202	Sopwith Tabloid	80hp Gnome
1203	Sopwith Tabloid	80hp Gnome

Number	Aircraft	Engine
1204	Sopwith Tabloid	80hp Gnome
1437	Sopwith Schneider	100hp Gnome
1438	Sopwith Schneider	100hp Gnome
860	Sopwith Type 860 Seaplane	225hp Sunbeam
857	Sopwith Type 860 Seaplane	225hp Sunbeam

1 Experimental Kite Balloon Section aboard SS *Manica*

	Manica
Kite Balloon	1
Spherical Balloon	1

No. 3 Squadron

Number	Aeroplane	Engine
1370	H. Farman pusher	100hp Renault
1371	H. Farman	100hp Renault
1391	Breguet	200hp Canton Unne
1518	H. Farman	80hp Gnome
1519	H. Farman	80hp Gnome
1520	H. Farman	80hp Gnome
1521	H. Farman	80hp Gnome
1522	H. Farman	80hp Gnome
1523	H. Farman	80hp Gnome
1524	H. Farman	80hp Gnome
1525	H. Farman	80hp Gnome

Number	Aeroplane	Engine
50	BE2	70hp Renault
964	BE2C	70hp Renault
965	BE2C	70hp Renault
1205	Sopwith Tabloid	80hp Gnome
1206	Sopwith Tabloid	80hp Gnome
1241	M. Farman	135hp Canton Unne
1369	M. Farman	100hp Renault

APPENDIX D

Aircraft numbers – 20 October 1915

Ark Royal's seaplane flight

Number	Seaplane	Engine
?	Short Folder Seaplane	200hp CU
?	Short Folder Seaplane	200hp CU
?	Short Folder Seaplane	200hp CU
161	Short Folder Seaplane	200hp CU
163	Short Folder Seaplane	200hp CU
165	Short Folder Seaplane	200hp CU
?	Sopwith Schneider	100 MG
1577	Sopwith Schneider	100 MG

	Reserve	
166	Short	200hp CU
1578	Sopwith Schneider	100hp CU
1579	Sopwith Schneider	100hp CU
2713	Sopwith Schneider	100hp CU

Ben-my-Chree's seaplane flight

Number	Seaplane	Engine
?	Short	225hp Sunbeam
?	Short	225hp Sunbeam
845	Short	225hp Sunbeam
850	Short	225hp Sunbeam
?	Sopwith Schneider	100hp MG
3722	Sopwith Schneider	100hp MG

	Reserve	
?	Short	225hp Sunbeam
?	Sopwith Schneider	100hp MG

No. 2 Wing

Number	Aeroplane	Engine
?	BE2C	75hp Renault
?	BE2C	75hp Renault
?	BE2C	75hp Renault
?	BE2C	75hp Renault
1110	BE2C	75hp Renault
1125	BE2C	75hp Renault
1129	BE2C	75hp Renault
979	BE2C	75hp Renault
?	Bristol Scout	80hp Gnome
?	Bristol Scout	80hp Gnome
?	Bristol Scout	80hp Gnome
1261	Bristol Scout	80hp Gnome

No. 2 Wing continued

Number	Aeroplane	Engine
1263	Bristol Scout	80hp Gnome
?	Morane mono	80hp Le Rhone
?	Morane mono	80hp Le Rhone
?	Morane mono	80hp Le Rhone
3259	Morane mono	80hp Le Rhone
3261	Morane mono	80hp Le Rhone
?	Avro	80hp Gnome
?	Avro	80hp Gnome
1041	Avro	80hp Gnome
1043	Avro	80hp Gnome

No. 3 Wing

Number	Aeroplane	Engine
?	M. Farman	100hp Renault
?	M. Farman	110hp Renault
?	M. Farman	110hp Renault
?	M. Farman	110hp Renault
1380	M. Farman	110hp Renault
1382	M. Farman	110hp Renault
1384	M. Farman	110hp Renault
1386	M. Farman	110hp Renault
?	H. Farman	140hp Canton
?	H. Farman	140hp Canton
?	H. Farman	140hp Canton

Number	Aeroplane	Engine
?	H. Farman	140hp Canton
3628	H. Farman	140hp Canton
3631	H. Farman	140hp Canton
3633	H. Farman	140hp Canton
82??	H. Farman	140hp Canton
?	Nieuport Scout	80hp Le Rhone
?	Nieuport Scout	80hp Le Rhone
?	Nieuport Scout	80hp Le Rhone
3172	Nieuport Scout	80hp Le Rhone
3174	Nieuport Scout	80hp Le Rhone
3179	Nieuport Scout	80hp Le Rhone

Airship flight

Number	Airship	Engine
?	S.S. Type	70hp Renault
7	S.S. Type	70hp Renault

No. 3 Kite Balloon Section, *Hector*

	Hector
Kite Balloon	1
Kite Balloon	1

No. 7 Kite Balloon Section, *Canning*

	Canning
Kite Balloon	1
Kite Balloon	1

Repair and Erection Section (Air Headquarters)

Number	Aeroplane	Engine
?	Voisin	140hp Canton
?	Voisin	140hp Canton
?	Voisin	140hp Canton
8501	Voisin	140hp Canton
8503	Voisin	140hp Canton
?	Caudron	80hp Gnome
?	Caudron	80hp Gnome
3876	Caudron	80hp Gnome
3878	Caudron	80hp Gnome
?	H. Farman	80hp Gnome
1527	H. Farman	80hp Gnome
?	Breguet	200hp Canton

Note: all 80hp Henri Farman and Caudron aeroplanes were being sent back to England, as they were too slow to be flown over Gallipoli but were serviceable as school machines.

APPENDIX E

Aircraft numbers – 30 December 1915

No. 2 Wing

Number	Aeroplane	Engine	Status
1041	Avro	80hp Gnome	Under repairs
1043	Avro	80hp Gnome	Under repairs
981	BE2C	70hp Renault	Ready
1111	BE2C	70hp Renault	Under repairs
1125	BE2C	70hp Renault	Ready
1129	BE2C	70hp Renault	Under repairs
1130	BE2C	70hp Renault	Ready
1259	Bristol	80hp Gnome	Ready
1261	Bristol	80hp Gnome	Under repairs
1262	Bristol	80hp Gnome	Ready
1264	Bristol	80hp Gnome	Ready
3168	Nieuport	80hp LeRhone	Ready

No. 2 Wing continued

Number	Aeroplane	Engine	Status
3258	Morane	80hp Rhone	Ready
3260	Morane	80hp Rhone	Under repairs
3262	Morane	80hp Rhone	Under repairs
8501	Voisin	140hp CU	Ready
8502	Voisin	140hp CU	Under Repairs
8503	Voisin	140hp CU	Ready
1202	Sopwith	80hp Gnome	Not erected

No. 3 Wing

Number	Aeroplane	Engine	Status
3630	H. Farman	140hp CU	Ready
3633	H. Farman	140hp CU	Ready
3634	H. Farman	140hp CU	Ready
3635	H. Farman	130hp CU	Not erected
1370	M. Farman	100hp Renault	Ready
1381	M. Farman	110hp Renault	Under repairs
1383	M. Farman	110hp Renault	Ready
1385	M. Farman	110hp Renault	Not erected
1386	M. Farman	110hp Renault	Not erected
3149	Nieuport	100hp Gnome	Under repairs
3170	Nieuport	80hp Gnome	Under repairs
3171	Nieuport	80hp Gnome	Ready
3174	Nieuport	80hp Gnome	Ready
3175	Nieuport	80hp Gnome	Not erected
3179	Nieuport	80hp Gnome	Not erected

For return to England

Number	Aeroplane	Engine
1391	Breguet	200hp CU
3875	Caudron	80hp Gnome
3876	Caudron	80hp Gnome
3877	Caudron	80hp Gnome
3878	Caudron	80hp Gnome
3874	Caudron	80hp Gnome
1527	H. Farman	80hp Gnome
10	Short	140hp CU
3628	H. Farman	140hp CU
3244	H. Farman	140hp CU

Ark Royal's seaplane flight

Tail No.	Seaplane	Engine	Status
161	Short	200hp CU	Ready
162	Short	200hp CU	Ready
163	Short	200hp CU	Ready
164	Short	200hp CU	Ready
165	Short	200hp CU	Ready
166	Short	200hp CU	Ready
136	Short	200hp CU	Ready
1577	Sopwith Schneider	100hp mono	Ready
1587	Sopwith Schneider	100hp mono	Not erected
1579	Sopwith Schneider	100hp mono	Ready
1566	Sopwith Schneider	100hp mono	Ready
3713	Sopwith Schneider	100hp mono	Ready

Ben-my-Chree's seaplane flight

Tail No.	Seaplane	Engine	Status
846	Short	225hp Sunbeam	Ready
849	Short	225hp Sunbeam	Ready
850	Short	225hp Sunbeam	Ready
3721	Sopwith Schneider	100hp Mono	Ready
3722	Sopwith Schneider	100hp Mono	Ready
3727	Sopwith Schneider	100hp Mono	Not erected

BIBLIOGRAPHY

Primary Sources

Australian War Memorial Collections
11 Infantry Battalion: AWM4 23/28/1, August 1914–April 1915.
12 Infantry Battalion: AWM4 23/29/2, Appendix No 1, Copy No. 8, April 1915.
3 Brigade: 3 Brigade War Diary, AWM4 23/3/2, Part 1.
Administrative Staff, Headquarters 1 Australian Division: AWM4 1/43/5.
Aker, Lieutenant Colonel S.: AWM MSS 1886, 'The Dardanelles: the Ari Burnu Battles and 27 Regiment'.
AWM PR89/85.
Bean: March and April diaries, AWM 38 3DRL 606/3/1 and 4/1.
General Staff General Headquarters Mediterranean Expeditionary Force: AWM4 1/4/1 Part 1, March 1915.
General Staff, Headquarters 1 Australian Division: AWM4 1/42/3, Part 1, April 1915.
——AWM4 1/42/3, Part 2.
General Staff, Headquarters ANZAC: AWM4 1/25/1, Parts 1, 2, 3, 4 and 5, April 1915.
General Staff, Mediterranean Expeditionary Force: AWM4 1/4/1, Part 2, General Staff.
Hillier, H.: diary, AWM1 DRL/0352.
Intelligence Headquarters ANZAC: AWM4 1/27/1, March 1915.
——AWM4 1/27/2, April 1915.
Intelligence, General Staff Headquarters, Mediterranean Expeditionary Force: AWM4 1/5/4, Appendix No. 1, March–April 1915.

Intelligence, Headquarters New Zealand and Australian Division (NZ&A Div): AWM4 1/54/1, April 1915.

McLennan, J.H.: AWM1 DRL 454.

Naval Air Service Training Manual: AWM Library 8622 with quotation from preface, Nov 1914.

Report of the Committee Appointed to Investigate the Attacks delivered on the Enemy Defences of the Dardanelles Straits, AWM 124, 1919.

White, Colonel B.: Colonel Brudenell White diary, entry 18 March 1915, AWM MS 7824 877/2.

Map Collection
ANZAC staff: planning map, AWM G7432 RC03178.

Leane: AWM G7432 G1565J2.

Ross, Colonel A.: AWM G74321 G1S65.

Victorian State Library
Austin: family files, MS10705, Victorian State Library.

Private Holdings
Bulkeley, R.F.: Diary of Richard Farley Bulkeley, Private Collection.

Fisher, J.M.: Diary of Private John Martin Fisher, No. 439, D Coy, 7 Battalion, 2 Infantry Brigade, Private Collection.

The National Archives (UK)
'2 and 3 Wing Reports Nov–Dec 1915', TNA Air 1/2284/209/75/12.

'Aircraft in Dardanelles 25/2/15 to 28/7/15', TNA Air 1/6619/17/122/788.

'Appreciation of the British Naval Effort', TNA ADM 1/8549.

'HMS *Ark Royal* Monthly Returns of Flights 1 April to 22 May 1915', TNA Air 1/479/15/312/239.

'Interview with Lt Col Strain reference Dardanelles', TNA Air 1/137/1.

'Kite Balloons History etc. dated 14 October 1915', TNA Air 1/2013/207/31.

'Report of No.1 Kite Balloon Section, HMS *Manica*, May 1915', TNA Air 1/11/15/1/44.

'Report on Aeronautical Matters in Foreign Countries for 1913', TNA Air 1/7/6/77/3.

'Reports from HMS *Ark Royal* February–May 1915', TNA Air 1/2099/207/20/7.

——TNA Air 1/AH207/20/7.

'RNAS Reports January–December 1915', TNA Air 1/361/15/228/50.

29 Division Intelligence, TNA WO 95/4304.

BIBLIOGRAPHY

Birdwood, General: General Birdwood's Reports, TNA WO 158/574.

Conference Minutes, TNA ADM 1/8497, 3 April 1915.

Douglas, W.S.: 'Notes on First Steps in Air Photography on the Western Front—January to March 1915', TNA Air 1/240/3 No. 1.

HMS *Ark Royal* Flying Log 31 January 1915 to 30 January 1916, TNA Air 137/2.

HMS *Ark Royal* Ship's Log, TNA ADM 1753/340 98.

Hogg, Major: Major Hogg's Report dated 11/5/1915, TNA Air 1/2119/207/72/2.

Introduction and chapter on *Ark Royal* in 'Aircraft carriers, Part 1, 1914–1918', TNA Air 1/47/137/2.

Kitchener: Kitchener's reply, 8 March 1915, TNA 3443 MO192.

Mediterranean War Records, TNA ADM 137/2165.

——TNA ADM 137/787.

Royal Naval Air Service—Organisation, TNA Air/1/361/15/228/51 (C.W. 13964/14 1/7/14).

Royal Navy Air Service Reports, Jan–Dec 1915, TNA Air 1/361/15/228/50.

Standing Orders No. 3 Wing, RNAS from Wing Commander Charles Samson, TNA Air/1/7.

Strain, Colonel H.: diary extract, TNA Air 137/1.

——Letter sent to Air Department 11 June 1923, TNA Air 1/137/1.

TNA ADM 137/1089.

——137/2166.

——137/881.

Imperial War Museum

Ataturk, K.: 'Memoirs of the Anafarta Battles', IWM 76/75/1.

——Memoir, IWM 314/16 K354B.

Gibson: diary, IWM 87/32/2.

Isaac, Lieutenant B.A.: diary, IWM 99/75/1.

Samson, C.R.: Flying Log, Air Commodore C.R. Samson Collection vol. 33, IWM 72/113/1, Part 33.

——Samson Collection 'Report to Committee' dated 10 July 1919, IWM 72/113/3/41.

——The papers of Air Commodore C.R. Samson, 'Night Flights in the Dardanelles', IWM DS/MISC/100.

RAF Museum

Strain, Lieutenant H. RNAS: typed reminiscence of Dardanelles, RAF Museum AC 75/33/3/2.

——typed reminiscence of Dardanelles, RAF Museum AC 75/33/3/3.

Chartwell Trust
Correspondence Churchill and EMS, CHAR 13/48.
——CHAR 13/51.
——CHAR 13/65.

Other
Dardanelles Commission, The Final Report, HMSO, London, 1917.
US Naval Observatory Astronomical Applications Department.
van Engert C.H.: papers, Box 1, folder 23, Georgetown University Library,
    Special Collections Division, Washington, D.C.

Books and Articles
Adam Smith, P., *The ANZACS*, Thomas Nelson Australia Pty Ltd, Syd-
    ney, 1978.
Aspinall-Oglander, Brigadier General C.F., *History of the Great War,
    Military Operations, Gallipoli*, vols. 1 and 2, Heinemann, London, 1929.
Avci, C., *The Skies Of Gallipoli*, Nart Yayinclink, Istanbul, 2003.
Bean, C.E.W., *Gallipoli Mission*, ABC Books, Melbourne, 1990.
——*The Official History of Australia in the War of 1914–1918*, Vol. I, *The
    Story of ANZAC from the outbreak of the war to the end of the first phase of
    the Gallipoli Campaign, 4 May, 1915*, Angus & Robertson, Sydney, 1921.
——*The Official History of Australia in the War of 1914–1918*, Vol. II, *The
    Story of ANZAC from 4 May, 1915, to the evacuation of the peninsula*, Angus
    & Robertson, Sydney, 1924.
——*Two Men I Knew: William Bridges and Brudenell White, Founders of the
    AIF*, Angus & Robertson, Sydney, 1957.
Birdwood, W., *Khaki and Gown*, Ward Lock Press, London, 1941.
Burns, I., *Ben-My Chree, Isle of Wight Packet Steamer and Seaplane Carrier*,
    Colin Huston, Leicester, 2008.
Cameron, D., *25 April 1915*, Allen & Unwin, Sydney, 2007.
Carlyon, L., *Gallipoli*, Pan Macmillan, Sydney, 2001.
Chasseaud, P. and Doyle, P., *Grasping Gallipoli, Terrain, Maps and Failure
    of the Dardanelles, 1915*, Spellmount, London, 2005.
Clark, C., 'Air War over Gallipoli', *Wartime*, issue 30.
——'Naval Aviation at Gallipoli', in Stevens, D. and Reeve, J. (eds), *Sea
    Power Ashore and in the Air*, Halstead Press, Canberra, 2007.
Coulthard-Clark, C.D., *A Heritage of Spirit, A Biography of Major-General
    Sir William Throsby Bridges K.C.B. C.M.G.*, Melbourne University Press,
    Melbourne, 1979.
Erickson, E.J., *Ordered to Die: A History of the Ottoman Army in the First
    Wold War*, Greenwood Press, London, 1950.
——'Strength against Weakness: Ottoman Military Effectiveness at Gal-
    lipoli, 1915', *The Journal of Military History*, vol. 65, no. 4, October 2001.

BIBLIOGRAPHY

Erkal, S. (ed.), *A Brief history of the Channakale Campaign in the First Word War (June 1914–January 1916)*, The Turkish General Staff Printing House, 2004.

Flannagan, B.P., 'The History of the Ottoman Air Service in the Great War. The Reports of Major Eric Serno', *Cross and Cockade*, nos. 2–4, 1970.

Gibson, C., *Airmen Died in the Great War 1914–1918*, Hayward & Son, Suffolk, 1995.

Gillam, J., *Gallipoli Diary*, Strong Oak Press, Stevenage, 1989.

Hamilton, J., 'The King Saw the First Aerial Bomb Dropped', *The West Australian*, Saturday 9 May 1959.

Henshaw, T., *The Sky their Battlefield*, Grub Street, London, 1995.

Isaacs, Group Captain K., 'Wings over Gallipoli', *The Defence Force Journal*, no. 81, March/April 1990.

James, R.R., *Gallipoli*, Batsford Press, London, 1965.

Jones, H.A., *The War in the Air: Being the story of the part played in the Great War by the Royal Air Force*, vols. 1 and 2, Oxford University Press, Oxford, 1928.

Kannengiesser, H., *Gallipoli Bedeutung und Verlauf der Kampfe*, Oldenburg, Berlin, 1927.

——*The Campaign in Gallipoli*, Hutchinson & Co., London, 1923.

Keegan, J., *A History of Warfare*, Cox & Wyman, Reading, 1993.

Keyes, R., *The Fight for Gallipoli: Naval Memoirs of Admiral of the Fleet Sir Roger Keyes*, Eyre and Spottiswoode, London, 1941.

King, B., *Royal Naval Air Service*, Hikoki Publications, Aldershot Hants, 1997.

Layman, R., *Naval Aviation in the First World War: Its Impact and Influence*, Chatham Publishing House, London, 1996.

Liddle, P., *Men of Gallipoli*, Battle Standard, London, 1976.

Liman von Sanders, O., *Five Years in Turkey*, United States Naval Institute, Annapolis, 1927.

Moorehead, A., *Gallipoli*, Ebenezer Baylis & Son, Worcester, 1956.

Nokolajsen, O., *Ottoman Aviation 1911–1919* at website http://www.ole-nikolajsen.co

Price, W.H., *With the Fleet in the Dardanelles*, Andrew Melrose Ltd, London, 1915.

Prior, R., *Gallipoli the End of the Myth*, University of New South Wales Press, Sydney, 2009.

Reduendo, V., *Gallipoli: Attack from the Sea*, University of New South Wales Press, Sydney, 2008.

Roskill, S.W., *Documents Relating to the Naval Air Service*, vol. 1, 1908–1918, Naval Records Society, 1969.

Ryan, L., *Holbrook The Submarine Town*, Greater Hume Shire Council, Holbrook, Victoria, 2008.

Samson, C. R., *Fights and Flights*, Battery Press, Nashville, 1990.

Saunders, H., *Per Ardua, The Rise of British Air Power 1911–1939*, Oxford University Press, Oxon, 1944.

Steel, N. and Hart, P., *Defeat at Gallipoli*, Macmillan, London, 1994.

Stegemanns, H., *Geschichtedes Krieges*, vol. 3, Deutsche Verlags Unstalt, Stuttgart und Berlin, 1919.

Stoker, D., *Straws in the Wind*, Herbert and Jenkins, London, 1925.

Sturtivant, R. and Page, G., *Royal Navy Aircraft Serials and units 1911 to 1919*, Air Britain Publication, The Gresham Press, 1992.

Sueter, M., *Airmen or Noahs Fair Play for Our Airmen*, Pitman & Sons, London, 1928.

Sykes, F., *Aviation in Peace and War*, Edward Arnold, London, 1922.

Travers, T., *Gallipoli 1915*, Tempus Publishing, Gloucestershire, 2002.

——'Liman von Sanders, the Capture of Lieutenant Palmer, and Otto-man Anticipation of the Allied Landings at Gallipoli on 25 April 1915', *Journal of Military History*, vol. 65, issue 4, October 2001.

Tuncoku, M., *Canakkale 1915, Buzdaginin Alti*, Basimevi, Ankara, 2005.

——*Mehmetcik*, Basimevi Ankara, 2005.

——*Canakkale Arastirmalari Turk Yilligi, Canakkale*, Onsekiz Mart Univer-sitesi, 2000.

Wester-Wemyss R., *The Navy in the Dardanelles Campaign*, Hodder and Stoughton, London, 1920.

Whitely, C., 'Ottoman Aviation 1911 to 1916', *The 1914 to 1918 Journal*, 1996.

Willans, Wing Commander G., 'Aircraft over Gallipoli' at www. defence. gov.au/news/raafnews

Williams, P., *The Battle of ANZAC Ridge*, Australian Military History Pub-lications, Sydney, 2006.

Winter, D., *25 April 1915, The Inevitable Tragedy*, University of Queens-land Press, St. Lucia, 1994.

ACKNOWLEDGEMENTS

It is now over a year since I discharged from the Royal Australian Air Force after an interesting and memorable career. I miss my colleagues; I miss their commitment and professionalism. Joining the Australian Defence Force was the best decision I ever made. If I had my time again I would join straight from school and take up an apprenticeship. Now I am over 50 and it is too late to start. So instead I have turned to writing on the evolution of air power. Once again, Gallipoli remains an enticing campaign to begin this story; it remains misunderstood. The role of aircraft has been kept from the fabric of the legend—but no longer.

I remain indebted to the archivists, particularly those of the Australian War Memorial, the Imperial War Museum, the Royal Air Force archive, the Royal Naval Air Service archive at Yeovilton, and also to private collectors. The work of archivists is far less celebrated than it deserves; these are the people who have kept alive the voices of our airmen.

Cathy McCullagh as copy editor has turned my manuscript into a book. Again, this story would have remained scattered in sheets of paper on my desk if not for the support of Jo Lyons as editor and Tom Gilliatt, Non-Fiction Director, at Pan Macmillan.

It remains now for me to apologise to my three sons, Thomas (9), Charlie (5) and Rupert (12 weeks). I have remained ensconced in my study far too long. I hope they will one day read *Gallipoli Air War* and *36 Days* and forgive me my long absences. I hope that one day they will also show an interest in that barren peninsula which holds so much in store for them. One day they will read about their great-grandfather, Temporary Lieutenant Charlie White, who was Mentioned in Despatches for a desperate action at Anzac Cove on 27 April 1915. He was killed in May. He lived longer than many of his friends.

Many Australians are bitten by the 'Gallipoli bug'. My aim is to bring the role of the air war to their attention, to show them that the ill-fated campaign was fought not only on land and at sea, and to tell the stories of the brave men who took to the skies to help win the Dardanelles for the allies. You can best judge whether I have achieved my aim.

INDEX

INDEX